Revival and Change

T0351319

TURNING POINT
ELECTIONS

General Editors: Gerald Baier and R. Kenneth Carty

Since Confederation, Canadians have gone to the polls over forty times in general elections. Sometimes the ruling party was re-elected, other times the government changed hands, but, more often than not, the country would carry on as if little had happened. However, some elections were different. They stirred up underlying divisions, generated debates, gave rise to influential personalities, and energized and reshaped the electorate – ultimately changing the direction the country would follow. Those elections were "turning points." The volumes in this series tell the stories of these turning point elections, focusing on the players, the issues at stake, the campaigns, and the often surprising outcomes that would fundamentally reshape Canadian politics and society. For a list of other titles in the series, see the UBC Press website, ubcpress.ca/turning-point-elections.

Revival and Change

The 1957 and 1958 Diefenbaker Elections

JOHN C. COURTNEY

UBCPress · Vancouver · Toronto

31 30 29 28 27 26 25 24 23 22   5 4 3 2 1

Printed in Canada on FSC-certified ancient-forest-free paper
(100% post-consumer recycled) that is processed chlorine- and acid-free.

Library and Archives Canada Cataloguing in Publication

Title: Revival and change : the 1957 and 1958 Diefenbaker elections /
John C. Courtney.

Names: Courtney, John C. (John Childs), author.

Description: Series statement: Turning point elections |
Includes bibliographical references and index.

Identifiers: Canadiana (print) 20220281017 | Canadiana (ebook) 20220281076 |
ISBN 9780774866644 (softcover) | ISBN 9780774866699 (PDF) |
ISBN 9780774866743 (EPUB)

Subjects: LCSH: Diefenbaker, John G., 1895–1979. | LCSH: Progressive
Conservative Party of Canada. | LCSH: Canada. Parliament – Elections, 1957. |
LCSH: Canada. Parliament – Elections, 1958. | CSH: Canada – Politics
and government – 1957–1963.

Classification: LCC FC615 .C68 2022 | DDC 971.064/2—dc23

Canadä

UBC Press gratefully acknowledges the financial support for our publishing
program of the Government of Canada (through the Canada Book Fund),
the Canada Council for the Arts, and the British Columbia Arts Council.

UBC Press
The University of British Columbia
2029 West Mall
Vancouver, BC V6T 1Z2
www.ubcpress.ca

Contents

Foreword
Turning Point Elections ...
and the Case of the 1957 and 1958 Elections

Gerald Baier and R. Kenneth Carty

FREE, COMPETITIVE ELECTIONS are the lifeblood of modern democracies. And nowhere has this been more apparent than in Canada, a country cobbled together by bargaining politicians who then continually remade it over a century and a half by their electoral ambitions, victories, and losses. In a continually changing country, the political parties that emerged to manage this electoral competition also found themselves continually changing as they sought to reflect and shape the country they sought to govern. The stories of these politicians, these parties, and these elections are a critical part of the twists and turns that have produced Canada.

Canadians have now gone to the polls in forty-four national general elections. The rules, participants, personalities, and issues have varied over time, but the central quest has always been the same – the chance to win the right to govern a complex and dynamic country. About twice as often as not, the electorate has stuck with who they know and returned incumbents to the governing mantle. Only about a third of the time have the government's opponents, promising something new or different, been elevated to power. But whatever the outcome over all forty-four elections, the contest has ultimately been between the Liberal and Conservative parties for the top prize. While other challengers have come and gone, and some have even endured, the persistence of the Liberal/Conservative dichotomy has defined the effective bounds of Canada's democratic politics.

More than one hundred years ago, a visiting French observer, André Siegfried, argued that Canadian elections were essentially meaningless because the core two parties were little more than unprincipled reflections of one another, preoccupied only with their continued existence. To the extent this was true, it reflected Canadian politicians' determination to build "big tent" political parties able to appeal to the wide range of discordant regions and interests, religious and language groups, and parochial claims that dominated the country's political life and public conversations. If the Liberal Party dominated national electoral politics over the twentieth century, to become labelled as the country's "natural governing party," it was because its tent was larger and rooted in an overwhelming mastery of Quebec constituencies. And so, a long list of Liberal leaders – Wilfrid Laurier, Mackenzie King, Louis St. Laurent, Pierre Trudeau, Jean Chrétien – kept leading their party back to office election after election. In a country being continually transformed on almost every conceivable dimension, electoral outcomes were remarkably stoic in comparison.

Occasionally, though, conditions allowed for rather abrupt shocks to this seeming political tranquility. There were exceptions to the familiar story of incumbents cruising to victory. In part, those occasions reflected the workings of a first-past-the-post electoral system that was capable of generating both stability and volatility. The difference between hanging on to power or being roundly booted from grace could be just a few percentage points' change in a party's support, or a strong showing by one or more third parties bleeding off a portion of one of the big tent party's vote. So some elections were different, thrusting new and exciting personalities to the fore, generating principled debates on fundamental issues, electrifying and engaging the electorate, and reshaping the parties and the dynamics of party competition, all with lasting consequences for the direction of the country to follow. These elections stand out as turning points.

The stories of the turning point elections are more than accounts of compelling figures, dramatic campaigns, and new political alignments. They also reveal how the pressures of demographic, socioeconomic, and regional change were challenging the status quo; how they broke the political moulds of previous election contests; and how the turn played out in the politics, policies, and governments of succeeding decades. In each of the turning point elections, we see how the evolving political landscape allowed politicians to crystallize, and often personify, the issues of a distinctive agenda and create a campaign that would mobilize and reshape the complex coalitions of supporters that constituted the nation's political parties. These turning points constituted the starting point for a new and different cycle in the contest between the two great big tent parties that have dominated the struggle for power and office and defined the nature and evolution of Canadian democracy.

THE 1957 AND 1958 ELECTIONS, despite taking place more than sixty years ago, bear striking similarities to contemporary Canadian elections. One finds multiple parties outside of the two primary combatants; uneasy regional coalitions within those parties; the enduring grip of the Liberal Party on government; Conservative Party infighting and leadership struggles; and new forms of mass communication reshaping campaigning and becoming critical to electoral success.

Those uncannily enduring traits aside, the elections of 1957 and 1958 were also remarkable for upending what to that point was the twentieth-century script for most Canadian elections. The 1958 result would be unrecognizable to contemporary eyes; the eventual

Progressive Conservative majority still stands as the largest share of the House of Commons ever achieved.

The Liberal Party dominance of Parliament in the twentieth century was well established before these elections, and every expectation in the months that preceded the 1957 election was that things would stay that way. All seemed to assume that the Liberal machine would continue to roll to easy, if perhaps uninspired, victory under the steady hand of "Uncle" Louis St. Laurent. The Progressive Conservatives had only just emerged from a testy leadership contest that shook party unity, and conditions seemed safe for the extension of a Liberal dynasty.

As John Courtney ably describes it, there was a degree of smugness in the Liberal camp that blinded them to regional disgruntlement and a general receptivity to the messages of a charismatic prairie populist in the form of Progressive Conservative leader John Diefenbaker. That combination allowed the party to expand beyond its traditional base of Toronto elites and create an (eventually) uneasy coalition of regions and interests that truly upended Liberal dominance for the first time in the century.

Courtney highlights a number of important features of the two elections throughout. A key factor in Diefenbaker's astounding success was his relative advantage in exploiting the medium of television, which was both new and fit with the personal style and careful messages that the Progressive Conservatives concocted for their leader and party notables to deliver. While television has now been surpassed as an all-powerful medium for political communication, Diefenbaker truly caught a wave with the technology that gave the Progressive Conservatives a considerable advantage over the less adventurous Liberals.

As Courtney demonstrates, Diefenbaker's appeal to "One Canada," a slogan both vague and filled with meaning by a variety of audiences, allowed the Progressive Conservatives to cobble together an unlikely coalition across the country. Diefenbaker's message and leadership, Courtney reveals, were essential to upending the electoral formula his party had tried and failed with many times before. His was not a singular appeal; a cast of characters across the country helped to sell that message to disparate audiences. Progressive Conservative success obliged the Liberal Party to rethink its message and policies. This turning point was not just about unprecedented turnover in the House of Commons, but it also set a new course for the remainder of the twentieth century, including significant pieces of the Canadian welfare state and rights regime.

Preface

THIS BOOK DRAWS ON a variety of sources: scholarly works on parties and leaders of the 1950s and 1960s by historians and fellow political scientists; memoirs and biographies of the leading politicians of the time; archival material at both the University of Saskatchewan and the University of Toronto; newspaper reports and opinion pieces; government documents, largely from Elections Canada and Statistics Canada; CBC and Radio-Canada sound recordings; and special collections, mainly the Diefenbaker papers held at the Diefenbaker Canada Centre, University of Saskatchewan.

Revival and Change deals with elections, campaigns, leaders, issues, public policies, and international affairs relevant to Canada midway through the twentieth century. It does not delve into the personal side of politicians' lives, notably marriages, families, and the like. For that the reader should consult the biographies referred to in the "Suggestions for Further Reading" section of the book.

I am grateful for the comments on separate sections of the book from two of my colleagues at the Johnson Shoyama Graduate School of Public Policy at the University of Saskatchewan: Murray Fulton on Canadian agriculture in the 1950s, and Michael Atkinson on Social Credit in Alberta. Madeleine Green of Ottawa and Liam

Courtney of Saskatoon helped with several of the book's tables, and Joanne Green was a huge help in finding the "right" photo for the occasion. Three anonymous readers made a variety of constructive suggestions. My Toronto "techie," Murray Green, was invaluable in resolving the occasional challenge presented by the Internet or my laptop computer. My namesake son in Saskatoon helped with the graphs and provided print copies of this book's various iterations without billing me for all the paper they consumed.

UBC Press has lived up to its reputation as one of Canada's pre-eminent scholarly presses. The idea for a series of seven or eight books on "Turning Point" elections in Canadian history came from Randy Schmidt and Ken Carty. Their long involvement with UBC Press has helped cement its reputation as a "turn to" source for professors, students, and the general public who share an interest in Canada. I was delighted when Ken, a long-time professional colleague and friend, called to ask if I would agree to write the book on the 1957 and 1958 federal elections. I hesitated for perhaps five seconds before responding in the affirmative.

Randy Schmidt, UBC Press senior editor, is well known in university circles for his skill in guiding authors through the usual publication hurdles, from pre-publication outlines and drafts to the release of the final printed version. Once again, he lived up to his reputation with this work, for which I am grateful. Katrina Petrik and Carmen Tiampo of UBC Press's production department have provided invaluable advice as they guided this book through its final stages. My thanks to them and to their colleagues.

This book would have been markedly more difficult to complete had it not been for the invaluable archival collections relating to the period under consideration. In particular, I am indebted to Patrick Hayes, Tim Hutchison, and Lindsay Stokalko and their colleagues at the University of Saskatchewan Archives and Special Collections, and to Ken Dahl of the City of Saskatoon Archives. They were invariably able to not only locate the right document for the topic at hand but also produce it expeditiously. Writing a book over the course of the COVID-19 pandemic presented a unique set of challenges that Patrick, Tim, Lindsay, and Ken, as well as others at various archives, helped me overcome.

A common refrain around Ottawa in the 1950s and 1960s was that a disproportionately large number of senior public servants and active politicians hailed from Saskatchewan. Whether this is entirely accurate I cannot say, but to a casual observer it certainly seemed so. I was struck as I wrote this book how the "Saskatchewan connection" was present throughout the period it covers. In addition to the prime minister himself, many Saskatchewanians contributed in some capacity to government, parties, or public policy at the federal level, including Jimmy Gardiner, Alvin Hamilton, Tommy Douglas, M.J. Coldwell, Emmett Hall, Merrill Menzies, Hazen Argue, M.A. Macpherson, and Dr. David Baltzan. There were others, I have no doubt.

I came away from writing this book convinced that Canadian politics in the 1950s was a gentler, simpler, and more civilized activity than it has since become. Attack ads aimed at political opponents; the widespread use of social media with all the attendant risks for misrepresentation and misunderstanding of public policies and party platforms; televised "debates" that not infrequently devolve into little more than poorly controlled shouting matches; the growth in the level of distrust of government and politicians – all of these lay beyond the 1957 and 1958 elections. Politics in Canada in the 1950s was, for the most part, a "gentlemanly" affair (both literally and figuratively), conducted, again for the most part, in a civil manner. Pointed and forceful criticisms of party leaders, cabinet ministers, and opposition frontbenchers were, of course, part of the political give-and-take. But the period covered by this book was not marked by the bitterness and divisiveness that has come to characterize contemporary party politics and competitive elections.

At some point during the writing of this book, I came across a photo of three leading politicians of the mid-1950s having dinner together at a Chinese restaurant in Ottawa: M.J. Coldwell, leader of the CCF; John Diefenbaker, soon to become leader of the Progressive Conservative Party; and Stuart Garson, Liberal minister of Justice, were being instructed by the bemused staff on the proper use of chopsticks. It is hard to imagine by today's standards of politics the equivalent of these three leading figures from different parties dining together in such a situation.

Finally, my heartfelt thanks to my favourite critic and sounding board, Helen. Little did we think when we married in 1959 that I would be writing a book sixty-odd years later about the very period in which we met and dated while students at the University of Manitoba. The names and events of those years brought back a host of memories for both of us. They reminded us of how much simpler politics and life were in the 1950s in Canada. This book is dedicated to Helen and our family.

Revival and Change

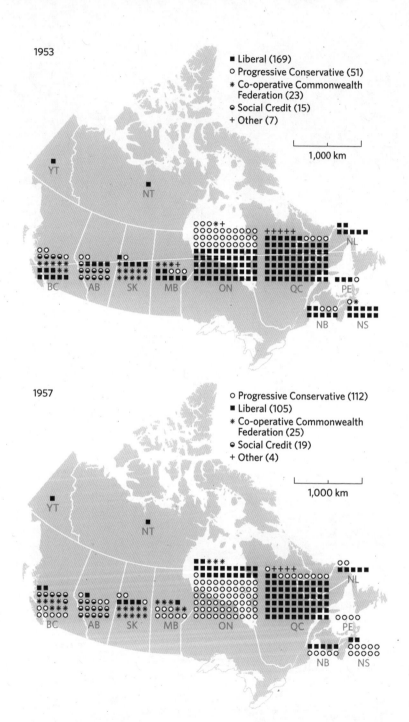

1953

- Liberal (169)
- Progressive Conservative (51)
- Co-operative Commonwealth Federation (23)
- Social Credit (15)
- Other (7)

1,000 km

YT
NT
BC
AB
SK
MB
ON
QC
NL
PE
NB
NS

1957

- Progressive Conservative (112)
- Liberal (105)
- Co-operative Commonwealth Federation (25)
- Social Credit (19)
- Other (4)

1,000 km

YT
NT
BC
AB
SK
MB
ON
QC
NL
PE
NB
NS

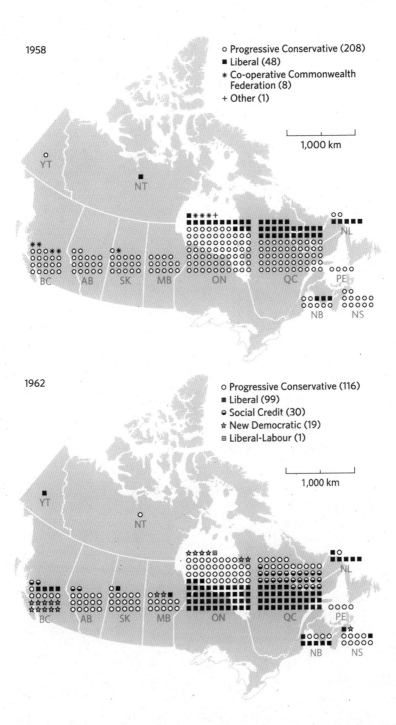

1958

o Progressive Conservative (208)
■ Liberal (48)
∗ Co-operative Commonwealth
  Federation (8)
+ Other (1)

1,000 km

1962

o Progressive Conservative (116)
■ Liberal (99)
◕ Social Credit (30)
☆ New Democratic (19)
⊞ Liberal-Labour (1)

1,000 km

1

On the Cusp of Change

THE 1957 AND 1958 Canadian general elections were unlike any that had gone before. They were fought between a prairie populist recently chosen to lead a party whose relatively small electoral base owed more to the city of Toronto and parts of rural Ontario than to any other region in the country; a governing party with close links to corporate Canada whose skillful accommodation of regional and sectional interests had enabled it to retain power for an unprecedented twenty-two years; and two small but persistent regional parties whose impact on federal public policy was in one case spotty, in the other non-existent.

When the 1957 election was called, the governing Liberals had been in office for over two decades. They were widely expected to be returned with their sixth straight majority win. The fragmented opposition was divided among three parties – the Progressive Conservatives, the Co-operative Commonwealth Federation (CCF), and Social Credit – each dependent on a different regional support base. None was considered likely to mount a successful challenge to the Liberals.

But as the two campaigns progressed, it became clear that these elections would be remembered as "Diefenbaker elections," for John

Diefenbaker, the new Conservative leader, overshadowed his opponents. Since John A. Macdonald's time, party leaders have invariably been the central focus of a party's election campaign. Diefenbaker, however, stood in a class of his own. He seized the opportunity offered by the new communications technology – television – and used it to great effect. As he criss-crossed the country in 1957 and 1958, his campaign gained momentum and his rallies attracted ever larger and more supportive audiences. They were roughly akin to secular versions of evangelical revival meetings, with boisterous and enthusiastic crowds. His speeches, well reported by the press, captured the mood of the country. He painted a picture of Liberal arrogance and, by contrast, of hope for Canada if he and the Progressive Conservatives gained office.

By the end of the second election, the Liberals had been reduced to their smallest number of seats in Parliament since Confederation, the CCF had lost both its leader and all but eight Members of Parliament, and Social Credit was wiped out completely. It was a rout unmatched in Canadian history to that point. This is the story of those elections, the government and opposition they produced, the issues that defined the six-year period of the government's life, and the eventual contribution of the Diefenbaker government to Canadian politics and society. Diefenbaker's government changed the country – for better or worse – in several respects, perhaps in no way more than in the configuration of its party system. Ultimately, the story of those elections serves as an object lesson of what lay ahead for all parties, specifically the inherent difficulty of building and maintaining a coalition of prairie voters predisposed to populist conservativism, Central Canadian and West Coast metropolitan electors, and Quebec nationalists.

Diefenbaker revitalized his largely dormant party; dominated the campaigns by focusing relentlessly on the Liberals' arrogance and alleged abuse of power; used television to reach a vastly larger audience of potential voters than ever before; captured the support of Canadians who in the past would never have considered voting for the Conservatives, let alone a prairie populist, but who bought into his "visions" of northern development and of "One Canada"; and engaged the electorate to such an extent that, in tandem with the unprecedented shifts in voting behaviour, the levels of voter turnout reached record highs that remain unmatched to this day. Later Conservative prime ministers regarded him as a hero. Stephen Harper, for example, named an icebreaker and a government building after Diefenbaker and believed "no other prime minister of any stripe did more for the cause of fairness and equality and inclusion than John Diefenbaker."[1]

Diefenbaker's One Canada refrain appears throughout this book, for good reason. It was central to his belief system. At its core, it unabashedly endorsed "an egalitarian and individualistic ethos," for individual equality was the "bedrock" of his political philosophy.[2] It introduced a new way for Canadians to view society and their place in it. Accordingly, it found favour with many who became "followers" of John Diefenbaker, some of them short-term followers, others lasting. Nowhere did the One Canada message resonate more than on the prairies, and its lasting effect has been the existence of a distinctive political constituency for the Progressive Conservatives and their heirs in that region. The downside of the One Canada principle became painfully obvious, however, over the course of Diefenbaker's six years in office, for it all but ensured that the prime minister was incapable of accommodating Quebec in the early years of the Quiet Revolution.

Unlike the single-election studies in this series, this book considers the two consecutive elections of 1957 and 1958, and the extent to which they constitute turning points in Canadian political history. The elections have been lumped together as two parts of the same whole, as it were, for in the short run they not only were held within months of each another but also amounted to two stages of a single process of removing the Liberals from office. The following eight chapters explore the Conservative victories, the party's six years in office, and its fall from grace in 1962 and 1963. Chapter 2 describes the party system heading into 1957, and Chapters 3, 4, and 5 examine the major players, the issues, and the outcome of the 1957 election. Chapter 6 looks at the principal players and the campaign in 1958, and Chapter 7 explores the challenges faced by the government, its failures and defeat, and the post-1958 reorganization of the three opposition parties. Chapter 8 reviews the Diefenbaker government's legacies, and the final chapter summarizes the changes that the parties and the party system underwent as a result of the "Diefenbaker Revolution."

To understand what shaped the party system before the 1957 and 1958 elections, we need to go back a few years and briefly describe the economy, changes on the international and domestic fronts, demographic shifts, and the party system. Coming out of the Second World War in 1945, Canada was on the cusp of a major social and economic revolution. Within a decade, it would add a political revolution to that list.

The Economy

Canada had emerged from the war as an industrial powerhouse. Industries of all sorts, ranging from chemical and automotive assembly plants to garment factories and agricultural commodities, had been converted to the production of military equipment, armaments, and food supplies needed by Canada and its allies for the war effort. To help manage and direct the economy, Prime Minister William Lyon Mackenzie King's government created twenty-eight federal Crown corporations and established strict wage and price controls.

The overall direction of the war economy was entrusted to C.D. Howe (1886–1960), minister of the newly created Department of Munitions and Supply. A professional engineer by training, Howe had emigrated to Canada from the United States in 1908. Following a short stint as a professor of engineering at Dalhousie University, he succeeded as a businessman whose company built several large grain elevators, the majority in Western Canada. He entered Parliament in 1935 and became one of the most powerful ministers in Canadian history. Over the course of his twenty-two uninterrupted years in the cabinets of Mackenzie King and Louis St. Laurent, he served as minister of numerous departments and as the chief of several Crown corporations founded during the war.[3]

Over the course of the Second World War (1939–45), Canadian firms produced "more than 800,000 military transport vehicles, 50,000 tanks, 40,000 field, naval, and anti-aircraft guns, and 1,700,000 small arms."[4] Canadian factories assembled 16,000 training and combat aircraft, and, through the British Commonwealth Air Training Plan, 131,000 pilots, flight engineers, and other air crew members were trained for the Royal Canadian Air Force (RCAF) and allied air forces. Between 1939 and 1945, more than a million Canadian men and women served full time in the armed services.

These were notable achievements for a country of roughly 11.5 million people. Understandably, they led to substantial changes in the economic and social fabric of the country that, in the immediate aftermath of the war, brought Canada to a new and in many ways unfamiliar point, both internationally and domestically. Canada in the second half of the twentieth century never returned to what it had been in the first half.

International and Domestic Changes

On the international front, Canada played an important part in establishing several multilateral organizations, notably the United Nations (UN) in 1945 and, as the Cold War began to heat up, the North Atlantic Treaty Organization (NATO) in 1949. The country's influence abroad can be judged by the fact that Canada became a signatory party to the Universal Declaration of Human Rights (a document drafted in large part by Canadian legal scholar John Humphrey) in 1948 and played an instrumental role in the transformation of the British Commonwealth to the Commonwealth of Nations in 1949. Less than five years after the end of the Second World War, Canada entered the Korean War (1950–53) along with other UN member countries. The Canadian ambassador to the United Nations, Lester Pearson (who would soon become leader of the Liberal Party of Canada), was elected president of the seventh session of the UN General Assembly in 1952. It can safely be said that in the first decade following the war, Canada "pulled its weight" internationally.

Canada's foreign relations have not always played much role, if any, at election time. Such was not the case, however, in late 1956 and in the run-up to the June 1957 election, when the strength of the Western alliance was tested for first time since the Second World War by the Suez Crisis. As we shall see in Chapter 4, how the Liberal government and the Conservatives in opposition reacted to that clash played an important part in the election campaign.

On the domestic postwar front, party politics at the federal level continued much as they had over the previous decade. The Liberals, no longer led by Mackenzie King, won a sizable majority in 1949 with Louis St. Laurent as leader. The three parties on the opposition benches were all returned to the Commons in 1949, but with fewer seats than they had won in the previous election. Nothing much had changed from the 1945 election, apart from the parties' relative strength in Parliament. Perhaps most important was the fact that the Liberals guided a booming economy and retained the close links with corporate Canada that had been established during the war. This made fundraising relatively easy (and lucrative) for the party at election time.

The federal election of 1953 produced results similar to those of 1949. The Liberals retained office, though with a smaller majority; the Progressive Conservatives once again became the official opposition with a slightly larger number of seats; and the CCF and Social Credit remained on the opposition benches with a modest increase in the number of districts each won. Much of the media shared the view commonly held by the Liberals that they would be returned to office in the 1957 election.

Demographic Shifts

The party system may not have changed materially in the decade following the Second World War, but the size, location, and demographic composition of the Canadian population had. In the early years of the twentieth century, 63 percent of Canada's population of 5.4 million were classified as rural and 37 percent as urban. By the time of the 1957 election, these percentages had been reversed. The 1956 census determined that two-thirds of the country's population of 16 million resided in urban communities, and one-third in rural Canada.[5]

The out-migration from prairie farms during the Depression and drought of the 1930s accounts for part of the population shift, as does the postwar return of military personnel (many originally from farms and small towns) to the major cities, but a substantial portion of the jump in population resulted from the country's postwar immigration policies. They were driven both by labour shortages in the larger provinces and by programs aimed at resettling displaced persons and refugees from war-torn Europe. In the decade following the war, Canada admitted a total of 1.39 million immigrants, refugees, and displaced persons, almost all of them from the United Kingdom and continental Europe. Added to that were an estimated 35,000 Hungarians in the aftermath of the 1956 uprising in that country. An often-unstated premise underlying Canada's immigration programs at the time was a preference for a "white-only" policy. In the somewhat oblique language of the time, Mackenzie King acknowledged as much in a 1947 speech in the Commons. He pointedly ruled out anything but a "European only" immigration policy so as to preclude "large-scale immigration from the Orient [as it] would change the fundamental composition of the Canadian population."[6] As we shall see, one of the successes of the Diefenbaker government was its changes to the country's immigration regulations that effectively ended the white-only policy.

Norms and Values

Canada's "European only" immigration policy pretty well said it all. It went a long way in defining what postwar Canada was like. There was an enduring attachment to Britain and the monarchy in most parts of the Dominion, save for francophone Quebec, although by the mid-1950s an attachment to the United States had started to become more pronounced, both in government policies and public preferences. Reflecting the puritanical attitudes of the day in much of the country, strict Sabbatarian laws applied to work, shopping, professional sports, entertainment, and the like. Men dominated politics, commerce, and the professions, whereas women, if they worked outside the home at all, typically found employment as nurses, teachers, and office secretaries or clerks. Scant attention was paid to Indigenous people, as their appalling socio-economic conditions sadly confirmed. And on the political front, preferences often mirrored those of one's parents and one's religious affiliation. As Richard Johnston has determined, "for much of the twentieth century, the best single predictor of major-party support in Canadian elections was religious denomination, with Catholics much more likely than non-Catholics to support the Liberals and shun the Conservatives."[7] Many of these aspects of Canadian society underwent a slow process of change during the Diefenbaker years.

The Upset

In all, things looked propitious for the Liberals in advance of the 1957 election. They had benefited from a strong postwar economy, a sizable jump in European immigration, generous and consistent electoral support in Quebec, and a cozy relationship with corporate Canada. But they faced an obstacle of their own making as the election approached: hubris. That character flaw, widespread among the Liberals, provided a valuable entry point for the three parties challenging them. Of the three, none was better at seizing the opportunity than the Conservatives under Diefenbaker.

First elected to Parliament in 1940, John Diefenbaker (1895–1979) was known for his oratorical skills, having practised law in Saskatchewan for many years, arguing persuasively on behalf of defendants in criminal cases. Working out of his one-man law office in the town of Wakaw and, later, in partnership in a small firm in the city of Prince Albert, he had gained a reputation as an articulate and convincing advocate for "the little guy," or, as he liked to say, "the average Canadian." Described as a "rogue" and "renegade" within his own party, Diefenbaker nonetheless easily won the Progressive Conservative leadership in December 1956, capturing the votes of the rank-and-file convention delegates, who ignored the advice of senior party members.

Even more than the opposition benches in Parliament, the 1957 and 1958 general election campaigns were ideal for Diefenbaker's silver-tongued and theatrical speech making. His style of campaigning was a clear break from the recent past. It came as a refreshing contrast to the dour and wearisome style of long-time Liberal prime minister Mackenzie King, who had retired from public life barely nine years earlier, and even to King's successor, Louis St. Laurent, whose folksy and engaging style of campaigning in his first two elections as Liberal prime minister (1949 and 1953) lost some of its edge as he became uncharacteristically defensive and combative as the 1957 campaign wore on.

The simple, direct themes and slogans that the Conservatives presented in both elections matched the kind of campaign that Diefenbaker's closest advisers felt were suited to his oratorical skills. In 1957, it was "Time for a Change," with the two smaller parties adding their voices to the same refrain, making it something of a chorus on the campaign trail. By contrast, Conservative strategy and advertising in 1958 focused almost entirely on the new prime minister, whose populist approach to politics complemented his charismatic appeal on the hustings. The party's 1958 campaign amounted to little more than a John Diefenbaker campaign, captured best by its messianic message to voters to "Follow John." And follow John they did, handing the Conservatives a massive victory.

As noted, television was the "new kid on the media block" in the early to mid-1950s. Diefenbaker saw its potential to reach countless voters who would never attend a partisan rally or pay much attention to campaign coverage in their daily newspaper. As a bonus for the Conservatives, television was a medium suited to Diefenbaker's flamboyant, colourful, accusatory style of speech making. The Tory leader's success in using the new medium to his and his party's advantage, together with the almost simultaneous rise of public relations professionals and advertising specialists in the political arena, meant that politicians of the future could speak directly to vastly larger, and in many cases more dispersed and isolated, audiences. From Diefenbaker's time onward, strategists have crafted campaigns with sound bites and commercials targeting specific groups of voters. Parties have also structured their daily press releases, media interviews, and photo-ops around making the evening television news. Diefenbaker led the way on this too.

Except for Newfoundland and Labrador, where they won only two of the province's seven seats, the Conservatives in 1958 won every parliamentary seat in some provinces or a decisive majority of seats in all others. There was no better demonstration of how the party system had been turned upside down in 1958 than the Conservative success in Quebec. Diefenbaker accomplished in that election what no Tory leader had to that point in the twentieth century, leading his party to victory in two-thirds of Quebec's seventy-five ridings.

The 1957 and 1958 elections proved to be watershed moments for the Liberals and the two smaller parties. The Liberals, now led by Lester Pearson, reinvented themselves in their period out of office. By convening a policy conference and attracting new blood to the party, Pearson oversaw a fundamental rebranding of Liberalism by making the party more reformist and slightly left-of-centre than during the time of Mackenzie King and Louis St. Laurent. The Liberals were about to begin another largely uninterrupted twenty-year stint in office.[8]

The two minor parties followed different paths after their dismal showing in 1958. The CCF joined forces with organized labour and re-created itself in 1961 as the New Democratic Party. It has had a continuous presence on both the federal and provincial scene and has enjoyed a measure of success in parts of Canada that had rebuffed the old agrarian protest party. Those new centres of support have more than compensated for the loss of its former power base, Saskatchewan. Social Credit, on the other hand, had a short-lived resurgence from 1962 to 1979 (albeit in a different guise), thanks to a shift in support from its long-term base of Alberta to rural Quebec. Eventually reduced to garnering less than 2 percent of the popular vote and electing no Social Credit candidates, the party disappeared from the federal scene.

What Came of It?

The Diefenbaker government held office for six years, and by the sixth year it was in considerable disarray. Following the Conservatives' defeat both in the Commons and at the polls in 1963, judgments of all sorts poured in. To some, the Tory leader was a hero who stood up to vested interests, who looked out for the "average Canadian" as he said he would, and whose commitment to equality for all Canadians challenged the idea of special status or treatment for any province, group, or individual. To others, Diefenbaker's overarching commitment to individual equality denied the reality of Canada and impaired relations between Quebec and the rest of Canada, and between Central Canada and the West. The controversy over Diefenbaker's leadership lives on.[9]

In the political sphere, three changes that took place during the Diefenbaker years had a lasting impact on parties and the party system. First, Canadian politics up to 1957–58 was as close as possible to being the exclusive preserve of white, middle-aged men. Diefenbaker took the first small steps to change that by bringing into his caucus and cabinet a more diverse social mix. This set a precedent for later parties, leaders, and prime ministers. "Diversity" and "inclusion" are now very much a part not only of the language of politics but also of the institutional structures of parties and governments.

Second, the fallout from the intra-party disputes over Diefenbaker's leadership in the 1960s led to an adjustment of some significance in the internal structure of the two major parties. Both Conservatives and Liberals amended their constitutions to allow for periodic reviews of the leader's performance. For the Liberals, the move was prompted by the younger, more activist members of the party who wanted a say over party leadership. The top-down control of the Liberal apparatus of the Mackenzie King–St. Laurent era ended. For the Conservatives, the change was prompted by unrest over Diefenbaker's continued leadership after the party's defeat in 1963. A successful rebellion was launched by the extra-parliamentary party, a national leadership convention was convened, and Diefenbaker was replaced after eleven years at the helm. As with the Liberals, the step signalled a shift in internal party centres of power, from the caucus, party leadership, and executive officers, to rank-and-file constituency activists.[10]

Third, the most significant of the turning points of the Diefenbaker period arose from the shift in the parties' respective bases of electoral support. In the case of the Conservatives, it amounted to a dwindling of support in their long-time bastions of the city of

Toronto ("Tory Toronto") and parts of rural southern Ontario; a shift westward in support; the development of a more distinctly conservative, but nonetheless populist, prairie political culture; and a return to something approaching the status quo ante for Progressive Conservatives in Quebec. It also spelled the beginning of what has amounted to a substantial cleavage between urban and rural Canada. For the Liberals, the metropolitan Toronto region (later dubbed "905" after its telephone area code) has, with the occasional interlude, become largely theirs since the end of the Diefenbaker government. By regaining their dominant position in Quebec and making major inroads in Ontario, the Liberals were once again the party to beat during the Lester Pearson/Pierre Trudeau years and beyond.

The Diefenbaker government undertook several initiatives that have had a lasting impact on Canada. To meet the objections of several provinces, programs such as federal-provincial financial transfer arrangements and the nascent hospitalization insurance plan were altered. The prime minister's "average Canadian" and "One Canada" appeals proved to be attractive to "individuals and regions aggrieved that they had not participated in the prosperity of the postwar boom" and to those "who felt marginalized by the central provinces' domination of the corridors of political and economic power."[11] Accordingly, policies designed to promote regional economic development were well received. Regulatory agencies to oversee the broadcasting and energy sectors of the economy were established. The reports of two Royal Commissions appointed by the Diefenbaker government, whose principal recommendations were later implemented by the Liberals, led in one case to a much-needed restructuring of the rail and airline transportation regime and in another to the adoption of Canada's universal, publicly funded medical care plan. Enhanced agricultural support programs and sales of Canadian grain to new and untapped markets, notably China, were begun. Significant immigration policy changes signalled the end of the white-only practices of the past. Diefenbaker was determined to grant the vote to Status Indians and delivered on this in 1960. Major infrastructure projects were launched, in part to fulfill campaign promises, in part to encourage the future development of Canada's largely untapped natural resources of the North, and in part to try to offset in some measure the effects of the ongoing economic recession. Canada played an important role in establishing the multinational World Food Bank and in bringing about South Africa's withdrawal from the Commonwealth over the issue of apartheid. The Canadian Bill of Rights adopted by Parliament in 1960 helped in its own, limited way to inform Canadians about rights and freedoms.

As notable as some of these changes were, criticisms were nonetheless levelled at the government from many quarters. The Tories were faulted for their ham-fisted attempt to fire the governor of the Bank of Canada in 1961 over the bank's tight monetary policy. The cancellation in 1959 of the Avro Arrow supersonic jet interceptor airplane – a cancellation the previous Liberal government would likely have carried out had it remained in office – was considered a fatal blow to Canada's aerospace industry. It led to sizable job losses, largely in the Toronto area, where the jets were to have been manufactured, that made it impossible for the Conservatives to hold on to the seats they won in 1958 in much of southern Ontario. The government's delay in meeting its obligations under the joint Canadian-American NORAD defence agreement in the early stages of the Cuban Missile Crisis enraged President John F. Kennedy, fed into Diefenbaker's latent anti-Americanism, and contributed to considerable cabinet unrest over Diefenbaker's handling of the issue. This was soon followed by the deeply divisive question of arming the Bomarc missiles on Canadian soil with nuclear warheads. Diefenbaker appeared increasingly distrustful of some cabinet colleagues, senior members of the public service, the Kennedy administration, and reporters of long standing in the Ottawa press gallery. After a year-long recession in 1960–61, followed by a run on the Canadian dollar, the government was in a free fall. Three cabinet ministers, all of whom had supported Diefenbaker in his successful run for the Tory leadership in 1956, resigned in advance of the 1963 election, which saw the Liberals under Lester Pearson voted back into office.

Quebec represented Diefenbaker's greatest challenge – and lost opportunity – on the political front. Although they had won two-thirds of the province's seats and nearly one-half of its popular vote in 1958, the Conservative Party failed to establish any semblance of a permanent presence there. Diefenbaker had little apparent interest in, or knowledge of, the province, and with an activist, reform-minded Liberal government elected in Quebec in 1960, it was clear that the prime minister's message of "One Canada" would fall on largely deaf ears as the province embarked on its Quiet Revolution.

By 1962–63 it had become obvious that Diefenbaker understood the Prairies better than any other part of the country, a fact reflected in his well-honed knack of speaking to "prairie folk" as one of their own. He had a familiarity with the social mix of prairie society and the hardship many – Indigenous and newcomers – had endured. Small towns, different languages, and varying ancestral roots defined the region, and he played to these successfully. But his strength in that region proved to be his weakness elsewhere, as attested by his failure to maintain a strong presence in Quebec and in metropolitan Toronto in the 1962 and 1963 general elections. His prairie populism did not serve him well outside his own environs.

The 1962 and 1963 elections serve as opposite bookends, as it were, to the 1957 and 1958 elections, encapsulating the Diefenbaker era. What follows is an account of the changes that brought the later bookends about, as well as an exploration of this book's principal themes: the challenges that "One Canada" presents in a country as varied as Canada, and the fact that the turning point in Canada's electoral history resulted from two elections that were uniquely "Diefenbaker elections." What happened over the period between 1957–58 and 1962–63 and, more important, what was notably different about that six-year period from what had come before?

2

The Parties Heading into
the 1957 Election

THREE DISTINCT PERIODS OF party system development marked the period between Confederation and the Conservative victory in 1957: 1867–1917, 1921–30, and 1935–53. What becomes apparent from the following account is how the two post-1921 periods heralded a fundamental transformation from a two-party to a multiparty system in Canada.

In the first period, from 1867 to 1917, Canadian elections were the exclusive preserve of two parties competing against each other across the expanding country. Each party had areas of regional strength and weakness, of course, and the period was marked by stretches of one-party dominance – notably the Conservatives under John A. Macdonald and the Liberals under Wilfrid Laurier. The early post-Confederation era was unmistakably Canada's age of classic "two-partyism," with close to 98 percent of the total votes cast over that fifty-year period going to the two older parties. Moreover, the two parties split the vote almost evenly over the thirteen elections in that period: 49.5 percent for the Conservatives and 48.2 percent for the Liberals (see Table 2.1).

R.K. Carty has characterized this first phase of party system development as having a distinctively decentralized character.

TABLE 2.1

Total two-party share of vote, 1867–1953

	1867–1917 (*N* = 13)	1921–30 (*N* = 4)	1935–53 (*N* = 5)
Conservative[a]	49.6	42.7	29.6
Liberal[b]	48.2	42.9	47.1
Progressive	–	9.9	–
CCF	–	–	11.6
Social Credit	–	–	3.7
Other[c]	2.2	4.4	8.0
Total two-party share	97.8	85.6	76.7

Source: Raw data for the table as well as party labels are adapted from the twenty-two federal election tables, 1867–1953, in J. Murray Beck, *Pendulum of Power: Canada's Federal Elections* (Scarborough, ON: Prentice-Hall of Canada, 1968).

Note: The parties' shares of the vote are given as percentages. Figures may not add up to 100% due to rounding.

a "Liberal-Conservative Party" in 1867 and 1872; "Unionist Party" in 1917; "National Liberal and Conservative Party" in 1921; "Liberal and Conservative Party" in 1925–35; "National Government Party" in 1940; "Progressive Conservative Party" in 1945, 1949, and 1953.

b "Opposition" in 1867 and "Opposition Liberals" in 1917.

c Includes the Reconstruction Party in 1935.

Patronage at the constituency level "was the life-blood of the parties," and "national parties were little more than coteries of [local] political notables."[1] But the election of 1921 brought this to an abrupt end by introducing a new element into Canada's developing party system: a party with a strong regional base of support whose electoral success would profoundly affect the claim of either or both of the older parties to be a pan-Canadian party.

The overnight success of the Progressive Party in 1921 rocked the traditional party system. An insurgent agrarian party whose support came almost totally from the Prairies and southwestern rural Ontario, the Progressives did not have staying power. They won almost one-quarter of the vote in 1921 and elected more MPs (sixty-five) than the Conservatives, but by the end of the decade they had all but disappeared from the federal scene. Their experience, however, pointed to the possibility that other start-up parties could challenge the two older parties and succeed in targeted regions. Over the short life of the Progressives, the combined share of the two older parties' popular vote dropped by 12 percentage points, from 97.8 percent in the first period to 85.6 percent. Only the disappearance of the Progressives in the 1930 election brought the two-party combined vote to approximately what it had been in the first period. Ninety-four percent of those voting in 1930 supported either the Conservatives under R.B. Bennett (48.8 percent) or William Lyon Mackenzie King's Liberals (45.2 percent). But this was a one-off, for once the Co-operative Commonwealth Federation (CCF) and Social Credit came on the scene in 1935, the combined Liberal and Conservative vote never returned in the second phase of party system development to its previous level.

Taken collectively, the two periods – from the elections of 1921 to 1930 and 1935 to 1953 – saw the party system undergo profound changes. More correctly, it was the Liberal Party that underwent the greatest change, controlling office for more than three decades (except for one five-year stretch in the first half of the 1930s and a brief interlude in 1926) and transforming its organizational mechanisms. During that long period of the King and St. Laurent governments, the party's focus shifted from constituency-based, patronage operations to powerful regional ministers who dominated or controlled the party in their respective region or province. Those ministers, in turn, perfected the management style of "brokerage" politics around the cabinet table. Intra-state federalism, whereby regional or provincial interests are represented within an institution of the central government, such as the cabinet, succeeded the localism and decentralization of the earlier period.

The brokerage practices that characterized the King and St. Laurent period came to an end with the victories of John Diefenbaker in the 1950s and Lester Pearson in the 1960s. These prime ministers were never able to emulate (had they even chosen to) the intra-cabinet negotiating practices of powerful regional ministers that characterized the years of Liberal hegemony. Additionally, the growing power and influence of the Prime Minister's Office and the Privy Council Office that began modestly with Diefenbaker and Pearson reached an unprecedented level under Pierre Trudeau. By that point, the ministerialist government of the King–St. Laurent years had become but a memory.

Table 2.1 shows that at the aggregate level, the total vote cast for the two major parties slipped by more than 20 percentage points over the course of the three stages of party system development from 1867 to 1953: from 97.7 percent to 76.7 percent. But the aggregate figure is misleading, for it was the Tories who took the hit, not the Liberals. The Conservative share of the vote fell by an average of 20 percentage points, from nearly one-half (49.5 percent) during Canada's first fifty years to less than one-third (29.6 percent) in the five elections leading up to the 1957 election. On the other hand, the Liberal share of the vote barely moved – from 48.2 percent between 1867–1917 in the first period to 47.1 percent in the third. In fact, it actually increased in the 1935–53 period from what it had been in the 1920s by a little over 4 points: from 42.9 to 47.1 percent.

Clearly the combination of the Liberals' near-monopoly of Quebec and their sizable support in the Maritimes, parts of Ontario, and the West, together with the regional strength of the two new "protest" parties in Western Canada, meant that the squeeze was on the Tories. They had little chance of gaining national support, election after election. They had been reduced to relatively small pockets of support in the city of Toronto and parts of rural Ontario, and at best they were able to win a handful of seats in other parts of the country in the elections prior to 1957.

Weak organization and disagreements over policy and leadership, combined with an inability to make inroads in Quebec (the Tories fielded candidates in only twenty-nine of Quebec's sixty-five federal

FIGURE 2.1

Canadian general election results: Parties' share of popular vote, 1935–53

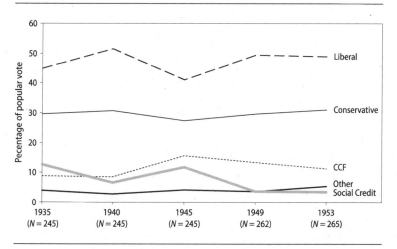

Source: Data from Tables 2-4 to 2-16 in Frank Feigert, *Canada Votes: 1935–1988* (Durham, NC: Duke University Press, 1989).

districts in the 1945 election, its worst electoral presence in the province's history), contributed to the fact that by the early 1950s, the Conservatives had become a "sorely tried party."[2] During the decades of Liberal ascendancy, a string of Tory leaders who were saddled with a feeble and underfunded organization were unable to mount an election campaign equal to the task of defeating the Liberals.

The share of the popular vote of the four parties competing in the five federal elections heading into 1957 showed comparatively little change from one election to the next (see Figure 2.1). The Liberals held on to office (once, in 1945, by the skin of their teeth, at other times comfortably); the Conservatives, unable to gain even one-third of the vote over the course of the five elections, nonetheless retained official opposition status; and the two smaller parties were largely dependent on their regional support in the Prairies, although the CCF had modest success in electing members from a few provinces other than Saskatchewan.

In the months leading up to the 1957 election, few changes in the party system and in the parties' standing in the House of Commons were expected. The Liberals were "certain" to maintain control of Quebec, much of Ontario, Atlantic Canada (where they had won twenty-seven of the region's thirty-two seats in 1953), and parts of Western Canada. The Tories would retain their dominant position in Toronto. But the conventional wisdom was that with Diefenbaker as leader, the Conservatives would never make serious inroads in Quebec or much of Ontario outside of Toronto and a few steadfastly Conservative rural areas. With the party's weakness in both Eastern and Western Canada unlikely to change, the Conservatives would, once again, be returned to the opposition benches. The CCF and Social Credit might make small gains, but they would still be dependent on their relatively small regional bases, from which they would elect the core of their parliamentary representation. (See map on page 2 for 1953 election results.)

The Third Parties

The toll taken by the Depression, particularly on Western Canadian farmers, where it coincided with a decade-long drought, helped initiate the third stage of party development, 1935–53. Two new, self-proclaimed "protest" parties were created: the CCF in 1932–33 and Social Credit in 1935. Both won power at the provincial level for extended periods, the CCF in Saskatchewan for two decades (1944–64) and Social Credit in Alberta for thirty-six years (1935–71), but they did not fare well federally. In none of the elections between 1935 and 1953 did they hold the balance of power in a minority Parliament. In fact, as a sign of Liberal dominance of the period, there *were no* minority parliaments. Their regional bases were pretty well all that the two smaller parties had to go on federally. Of the seventy-nine CCF members elected in the federal elections from 1935 to 1953, slightly more than one-half (forty-one) were from Saskatchewan. Social Credit was even more heavily dependent on Alberta: of the sixty-five MPs the party elected between 1935 and 1953, all but six were from Alberta.

It is true that the two smaller parties competing in the 1957 and 1958 elections shared "protest" in common that was "fueled by policy grievances and a sense of regional alienation."[3] Once in office in their respective provinces, however, the CCF and Social Credit moved in increasingly divergent ways. Armed with its avowedly socialist platform, the CCF came to power in Saskatchewan in 1944 and began a series of state-sponsored social and economic initiatives unlike any seen to that point in Canada. For its part, the Social Credit government of Alberta attempted in its early years to apply some of its radical monetary theories, but after failing to implement its ideas, it moved in an increasingly conservative, pro-business direction. The discovery of oil in the province in 1947 and the subsequent development of the oil industry played a large part in leading the Social Credit government in Alberta and the party at the federal level to espouse free enterprise policies in the postwar period.

The CCF

The Co-operative Commonwealth Federation began as a political movement in the early years of the Depression. It was an amalgam of various left-of-centre groups and individuals from across Canada: trade unionists, Social Gospel adherents, radical farm movement supporters on the prairies, assorted academics, and leaders and members of several cooperative organizations. (A number of those from Eastern Canada were humorously referred to by constitutional law expert Eugene Forsey, one of the founders of the CCF, as the "Brahmin priests" of the party.) Many of the founders and organizations had previously backed one or the other of the two older parties, and a sizable number from Western Canada had been Progressive Party supporters. The dire economic conditions of the early

1930s led these disparate groups to search for new, radical alternatives to the established parties.

The CCF's statement of aims was adopted as the "Regina Manifesto" in 1933, when the movement's membership voted to become a political party under the leadership of J.S. Woodsworth.[4] Before entering politics, Woodsworth (1874–1942) had served as a Methodist clergyman and social worker in North End Winnipeg. He is often credited with leading Mackenzie King's government to introduce an old-age pension program in 1927. A pacifist, he was the only Member of Parliament to oppose Canada's entry into the Second World War. First elected to Parliament in 1921 as one of two Independent Labour Party MPs, Woodsworth was known as an "inspirational" and "charismatic" leader who preached the message of the Social Gospel.[5] A substantial part of the CCF's support base from the 1930s up to the elections of 1957 and 1958 shared his commitment to the Social Gospel, described by one expert as "an attempt to apply Christianity to the collective ills of an industrializing society."[6]

Although an able parliamentarian with a devoted group of followers in farm, cooperative, and labour circles, Woodsworth lacked the skills of an accomplished politician and was resolute about advancing the socialist cause without compromise. Such was not the case with his much more pragmatic successor, M.J. Coldwell, whose early years in politics, as will be seen in the next chapter, bore similarities to Diefenbaker's. Once in the Commons, Coldwell demonstrated an ability to use parliamentary rules to his party's advantage.

From 1933 to 1957, the CCF had a mixed election record. In the two years prior to the 1945 federal election, the party's prospects had never been better. It grew in popularity during the war years, so much so that by September 1943, the Gallup Poll found that the CCF enjoyed a one-point lead nationally over both the Liberals and Conservatives. CCF membership had grown, the party could count on strong support from much of the leadership of Canada's labour movement, and its organizational and fundraising capacities were the best since the party's creation.

Provincially, the British Columbia party won enough seats to form the official opposition in 1941, the Ontario party came close to winning office in 1943, and in Saskatchewan the party was elected to power with a massive victory under T.C. (Tommy) Douglas in 1944. In all, these signs constituted "a happy augur" for the federal election to come at the end of the Second World War.[7] The CCF's impressive gains in the early 1940s prompted Prime Minister King to read the tea leaves. Accordingly, he "moved [his government] leftward" to head off any chance of the CCF's winning office in the 1945 federal election.[8] The Liberals' more socially progressive agenda towards the end and in the immediate aftermath of the war can best be seen as a direct response to the CCF threat.

The results of the 1945 federal election came as a great disappointment to the CCF. More than that, they were also a watershed. Although the party's share of the popular vote doubled to nearly 16 percent in 1945 and a record twenty-eight MPs were elected, the results fell "far short of the expectations" created by its favourable showing in the 1943 Gallup Poll and its recent provincial electoral successes.[9] The party saw its level of popular support slip steadily from one federal election to another over the next decade (see Figure 2.1).

Even though the party remained an important presence in a few provinces (and held office in Saskatchewan until 1964), its decline in support at the federal level combined with King's replacement as prime minister by the popular Louis St. Laurent in 1948 ended the CCF's hopes of winning office in Ottawa. By the early 1950s, the Regina Manifesto had become an albatross to the party. The statement of principles had been regularly seized upon by Liberals and Tories alike at election time to paint a bleak future for the country if the socialists were elected. They reminded voters that the Regina

Manifesto promised to nationalize banks, transportation, and communication companies, and to establish state-run public utilities. All of these would be operated in the public interest by planning commissions and control boards. The final paragraph of the manifesto contained a bold statement that came back to haunt the party at election time. Other parties were only too ready to seize upon it as a reason *not* to vote CCF:

> No C.C.F. Government will rest content until it has eradicated capitalism and put into operation the full programme of socialized planning which will lead to the full establishment in Canada of the Co-operative Commonwealth.[10]

By the early 1950s, various socialist groups and individuals that had been instrumental in creating the CCF were debating the future of the party. Especially problematic was its stated intention to eradicate capitalism. Among the most influential intellectuals in the party, F.R. Scott, constitutional law professor at McGill University, argued upon stepping down as party chairman in 1950 that "a re-interpretation of [the party's] principles is overdue."[11] After considerable internal debate over the years leading up to the 1957 election, the CCF accepted a reformulated statement of its democratic socialist goals. During a 1956 national convention, the membership voted – not without strong opposition from the party's more fervent socialists – to replace the Regina Manifesto with the Winnipeg Declaration.

Political scientist Murray Beck was not alone in concluding that the Winnipeg Declaration "constituted a significant shift to the right," most notably in its attitude towards private enterprise.[12] It read in part that the CCF "recognizes that in many fields there will be need for private enterprise which can make a useful contribution to the development of our economy."[13] In this respect, it attempted to move the party away from the socialist doctrinairism of its founders, but in other respects, notably in its call for social justice and increased welfare services, the party's goals remained the same. All in all, the platform presented by the party in the 1957 election reflected the more moderate and centrist theories of social democracy advanced in the 1956 Winnipeg Declaration rather than those found in the Regina Manifesto of twenty-three years earlier. Armed with its revamped statement of goals, a respected leader, and ardent supporters, the CCF readied itself for the 1957 election.

Social Credit

In his magisterial study of the 1957 election, John Meisel observed that "if the C.C.F. was the main party of the Left, the Social Credit party must be placed on the extreme right of the traditional political spectrum."[14] The parties had in common a sense of being "oppressed by the operation of the eastern Canadian financial system,"[15] but their proposals to correct such oppression were wildly different. The radical socialism of the CCF was anathema to adherents of Social Credit, who gave no support to the CCF's anti-capitalist approach to solving the economic hardships resulting from the Depression.

At its creation, the Social Credit movement combined "evangelical religion and populist politics" with a "base antisemitism."[16] Its central economic principles, grounded in the teachings of Major C.H. Douglas of England, were clearly outside the norms of Canadian politics. To correct for the "chronic under consumption" produced by capitalism, Douglas proposed that state-generated monetary payments (or "social credit") be made directly to all citizens. To Albertans suffering through the Depression and the coincident drought, this simplistic solution to their predicament (dubbed "funny money" by its critics) proved to be immensely attractive.[17] By 1956, Social Credit had abandoned Douglas's unconventional economic theories and moved well to the right on the Canadian political spectrum. In the elections of the 1950s, it often described itself as the only *genuine* conservative party in Canada.

In the lead-up to the 1957 election, however, the party took stock of the fact that it, much like the CCF, had made no progress over its twenty years of competing in federal elections. It had failed to make any significant electoral advances federally outside Alberta. Over the course of five federal elections, it had won an average of only thirteen seats per election. It remained popular in Alberta but was unable to connect with the wider Canadian electorate. Reflecting his party's standing in the House of Commons, Social Credit's Solon Low was invariably the fourth, and last, party leader to speak on motions or debates on bills. Accordingly, he and his party received at best only modest coverage in the national media.

Social Credit remained an enigma to most Canadians. Its economic doctrine made little sense, in part because it was ridiculed by those who paid any attention to it, and in part because the party's base of support remained distant from Central Canada. Most Liberal and Conservative candidates in Ontario, Quebec, and Atlantic Canada ignored Social Credit and its right-wing proposals completely as the party and its local candidates posed no threat to them.

The Two Older Parties

Although the two smaller parties were players in the 1957 election, the real story of that election was the battle between Canada's oldest parties. It was not a battle of equals, however, but more of a David-and-Goliath contest. As noted previously, the Liberals went into the 1957 election as the widely accepted front-runner likely to be returned to office, whereas the Conservatives under the leadership of an acknowledged outsider, even in his own party, were considered unlikely to make any serious inroads against the government. The Liberals enjoyed a clear edge in financing their campaign, a popular leader, and an experienced group of organizers. As well, the public opinion polls in the months leading up to the June election consistently showed them with a comfortable lead.

On one facet of the campaign, the two parties were more or less evenly matched, and this in itself was important for it ensured widespread local and national media coverage: the number of candidates nominated. The Liberals fielded a full slate of 265 candidates and the Conservatives 257, whereas the two smaller parties fell well short of those numbers. The CCF nominated 162 and Social Credit 115.

The Liberals

First, a word about William Lyon Mackenzie King, for without King there might well have been no Prime Minister Louis St. Laurent or Lester Pearson. King (1874–1950) devoted almost his entire adult life to public service of some sort, beginning in 1900 as deputy minister, followed by a stint as minister, of the fledgling Department of Labour, and ending in 1948 after a total of twenty-two years as prime minister. He was known as a cautious, pragmatic social reformer intent on wedding the allegiance of Catholic Quebec to a more modern and urban Liberal party of English Canada.[18] His political craftsmanship became the stuff of legend, prompting some of his compatriots to dub him "Wily Willie."

The Liberals dominated the federal electoral scene for over two decades before the 1957 election, forming five consecutive majority governments between 1935 and 1953, a record unequalled in Canada before or since. They held office through the last half of the Great Depression, the six years of the Second World War, and the decade of postwar recovery, with just two leaders: Mackenzie King from 1935 to 1948 and Louis St. Laurent from 1948 to 1957. It was a notable achievement for the party, its leaders, and its supporters.

Ironically, however, therein lies part of the explanation for the Liberals' loss to the Progressive Conservatives in 1957. Under the

Liberals, Canada had become a one-party-dominated political system at the federal level, in part through the government's relatively adept management of international and domestic economic and political matters, and in part through the persistent electoral ineptitude of the principal opposition party. The Progressive Conservatives were the only opposition party that stood a chance of defeating the Liberals, but they had a history of fumbling the ball at critical points. The Liberals seemed destined to win again in 1957.

King's operating style of government was carried on by his successor, St. Laurent. It was defined by close linkages to the federal bureaucracy, ties to the country's business and financial elites, and, in John Meisel's words, an outlook on their own governing abilities "based on a haughty, arrogant self-confidence."[19] To most observers, the Liberals believed that they were destined to govern Canada, an attitude that pervaded their 1957 campaign.

Over their twenty-two years in office, the Liberals had assembled a strong team of cabinet members, perhaps unmatched since the first years in office of John A. Macdonald and Wilfrid Laurier. As prime minister in the 1920s and again from 1935 to 1948, King co-opted many members of his cabinet directly into his inner circle without their having been elected to Parliament. More than 25 percent of his ministers (nineteen of sixty-nine) had no seat in the House of Commons at the time of their appointment. King's approach to political leadership favoured those with a proven record of success in their fields – whether in politics or not.

King's ministers were drawn directly into cabinet from business, academia, the military, public service, and provincial politics. No fewer than eight cabinet ministers were former provincial premiers. No other party has come close to matching that feat. Among the notables co-opted directly into the cabinet without first having run for Parliament were the distinguished Quebec lawyer and future prime minister Louis St. Laurent; provincial premiers Jimmy Gardiner of Saskatchewan and Angus L. MacDonald of Nova Scotia, both with renowned political machines in their respective provinces; businessman and engineer C.D. Howe, who became unquestionably the most powerful minister during the years the Liberals held office; and Lester Pearson, public servant and senior diplomat and another future prime minister.

King had little apparent interest in promoting backbenchers when he could go outside the Commons to find just the right man. His guarded and calculating style of leadership found expression in countless meetings with his staff and his cabinet. A diary entry describing his reaction to Liberal by-election victories captures his measured approach to political leadership: "The results of the by-elections justified [the] party's attitude and mine in not being too specific in platform declarations, not speaking too often – or being too radical & above all in not adopting 'plans.'"[20]

Louis St. Laurent took a similarly cautious approach to public policy announcements and election promises, but his managerial style was different from King's. Rather than exerting great control over cabinet and individual ministers, he clearly preferred to devolve considerable authority onto regionally powerful cabinet ministers. As the 1957 election campaign got underway, he chose what might best be described as a "steady as she goes" approach to the campaign: moderate, uncontroversial, and without promises of bold new initiatives. It had worked well for him in 1949 and 1953, and there was no reason to think it would not work well this time. Meisel described the Liberal strategy in the following terms:

> To the extent that any overall plan of the [Liberal] campaign was formulated at all, it seemed to consist of the notion that nothing dramatic was to be attempted, that a quiet campaign was desirable, and that the most effective thing the party could do was to discredit the opposition.[21]

Mackenzie King would have approved.

St. Laurent's biographer notes that when the 1957 election was called, "most Liberals [in Parliament] assumed that the government would be returned with between 150 and 160 seats" out of 265, a comfortable majority.[22] It was a reasonable assumption to make, for with a 14-point lead over the Progressive Conservatives (46.8 percent to 32.9 percent) in the Gallup Poll barely a month before the June 10 election, the smart money was on the Liberals' once again winning a majority. As it turned out, the election's outcome proved to be "the most surprising" to that point in Canadian history.[23] The period of Liberal hegemony was about to end.

The Progressive Conservatives

After losing to Mackenzie King's Liberals in the 1935 federal election, the Conservatives were reduced to what was essentially a southern Ontario base. Of the forty seats the party won nationally that year, twenty-five were in Ontario, and of those over one-half were in and around its mainstay – the city of Toronto. In Quebec, where the Tories continued to pay a heavy price for introducing conscription in the First World War, the party could do no better than to elect four MPs, all from predominantly anglophone districts in Montreal. In two provinces – Nova Scotia and Prince Edward Island – not a single Conservative candidate was elected in 1935. In the country as a whole, the party's share of the vote fell dramatically, from 48.7 percent in 1930 to 29.6 percent in 1935.[24]

The Conservative defeat in 1935 marked the beginning of over twenty years in the political wilderness. In not one of the federal elections from 1935 to 1957 did the party win more than one-third of the vote (range: 27.4–31 percent). According to George Perlin's excellent analysis of the Conservatives in the twentieth century, the "party was so badly shaken by its defeat [in 1935] that it seemed unable to respond." In the lead-up to that election, party organization was "neglected" and "policy was allowed to drift."[25] Those were to become hallmarks of the party over the next twenty years. Conservative Party organization, finance, and electoral prospects were found to be no different at the time of the 1953 election than they had been in 1935. Conservative speechwriter, strategist, and organizer Dalton Camp pointedly observed of his party in the 1953 election: "We were dead." The party was "in a state of ruin [lacking] coherent purpose, organizational thrust, poise and self-confidence."[26]

A large part of the explanation for the Liberal dominance from 1935 to 1957 can be found in the persistent internal squabbling and organizational ineffectiveness that marked the Conservative Party. In the eighteen years between R.B. Bennett's resignation as Conservative leader (1938) and John Diefenbaker's selection as party leader (1956), the Tories were led by five different men, scarcely a formula for building a stable and effective organization and developing a set of coherent policies.[27] None of the five was able to close the gap with the Liberals in terms of party organization and finance or popular vote in elections and seats in Parliament.

The two longest serving of the five leaders, John Bracken of Manitoba and George Drew of Ontario, had been premiers of their provinces when they were chosen. Neither succeeded in transferring his popularity from provincial to federal politics. In Bracken's case, the Conservatives attempted to make their party less dependent on its urban base in Toronto and more in tune with the interests of rural Ontario, the Maritimes, and Western Canada. Delegates at the 1942 convention agreed to a condition Bracken laid out in advance of becoming leader: the party would be renamed the "Progressive Conservative Party of Canada." By that time, Bracken himself had served as premier of Manitoba for twenty years, leading first a United Farmers and then a Liberal-Progressive government. The hope was that with such a base on which the party might grow, broader electoral support would ensue federally for the Tories.

The change in party leadership and name worked to the extent that in the 1945 election the Progressive Conservatives picked up a slightly larger share of the popular vote and elected members in every province and the Yukon. But with forty-eight of the party's sixty-seven MPs coming from Ontario (a fifth of them from the city of Toronto), the Tory old guard was still ascendant. Bracken's days as leader were numbered, especially in light of the almost certain retirement of Mackenzie King with the popular Louis St. Laurent as his likely successor. But the party's new name stuck – until 2003, when the Progressive Conservative Party merged with the Canadian Alliance to form the new Conservative Party of Canada.

The term "Progressive Conservative" strikes some observers as an oxymoron. Although there are various nuances to both "progressive" and "conservative" in Canada,[28] "progressive" generally implies moving ahead, blazing new trails, and leaving the past behind, whereas "conservative" suggests cautious acceptance of change and a preference for maintaining something akin to the status quo. Yet odd as it may seem, the name "Progressive Conservative" captured two different threads of Canadian political history. It is no surprise that the term should have originated with a Western Canadian premier, specifically one from the prairies who "combine[d] libertarian individualism with progressive societal values of community."[29] For much of the next five decades, this defined the Progressive Conservatism of such prairie provincial premiers as Duff Roblin of Manitoba and Peter Lougheed of Alberta and of federal party leaders and prime ministers John Diefenbaker and Joe Clark.

As we have seen, the electoral success of the Progressive Party in 1921 effectively ended the two-party system that had dominated federal politics from the time of Confederation. By winning, the Progressives demonstrated that a protest movement could be organized on relatively short notice by electors who felt aggrieved by "big economic interests" over which they had no control. Banks and railways (centred, as Progressive leaders liked to remind their audiences, on Montreal and Toronto) were seen to be exploitive. The result was that farmers' cooperatives, credit unions, and wheat pools sprang up across the prairies. With a new-found sense of co-operation and defiance among the region's relatively recent settlers and the emergence of a movement opposed to "the old ways of doing things," the older established parties were relegated to, at best, second place and, certainly in the case of the Conservatives, third place. These were the economic, social, and political features of the Western Canada in which John Diefenbaker was educated and practised law, and where his world view was shaped.

As far as the "Conservative" part of the Progressive Conservative label was concerned, it carried with it a strong attachment to the past and a fondness for tradition. Conservativism in Canada had been a part of the politics of Ontario, Quebec, and the Maritimes dating back to the formation of the Château Clique and the Family Compact of the early nineteenth century and the arrival of the United Empire Loyalists in the wake of the American Revolution. Substantial elements of the Conservative Party, particularly among Tories in Toronto, rural Ontario, and the Maritimes, continued to share a strong affection for the monarchy and attachment to the British connection well into the mid-twentieth century. That was obvious in the lead-up to the 1957 election when the Conservative opposition launched a major offensive in the Commons against the St. Laurent government's response to the 1956 Suez Crisis.

Ontario's Conservative premier, George Drew, succeeded John Bracken. A distinguished veteran of the First World War, Drew was chosen in a national leadership convention in 1948. He appeared to offer considerable promise for the party in the next election, widely expected in 1949. He was seen by many party stalwarts as bringing several attractive features to the national party. Among them was the fact that he had led his party in Ontario to victory, first with a minority government in 1943 and then with two con-secutive majority governments in 1945 and 1948. Several Con-servatives also thought Drew offered the party some hope of making inroads in Quebec.[30] Realistically, however, the odds of this happening could at best be described as slim. St. Laurent remained immensely popular in his home province and, outside of pockets of support in anglophone Montreal and the occasional riding outside the major cities, the Conservative organization was largely non-existent in the province and its brand was anathema to most Quebecers.

Drew led the party through two federal elections, in 1949 and 1953, but whatever promise his selection as leader had held out came to naught. He was forced by ill health to step down in 1956 even though he, along with many close to him, sensed that victory was within their grasp. The fierce debates over the Liberal government's plan to build the TransCanada pipeline, over its response to the Suez Crisis, and over its tight-fisted handling of Canada's old-age pension scheme contributed to Drew's declining health, raising the possibility that he lacked the stamina to lead the party in the 1957 campaign.

It is quite likely that John Diefenbaker would never have been chosen as George Drew's successor had the party not selected its leader in a national convention with 1,300 voting delegates from across the country in December 1956. Had the party replaced Drew by way of the "old boys' network" that both the Conservatives and Liberals had used for the first half-century of Canadian history – with the leadership being determined by a small coterie of party notables in Parliament – Diefenbaker would not have made it. He acknowledged as much in his *Memoirs,* where he argued that the 1956 convention was "the first since 1927 that saw a real and effective determination on the part of the rank and file of the Party to be represented, rather than to have the leadership clique [control] the Party machinery."[31]

Although a Member of Parliament for sixteen years by the time he became the party leader, Diefenbaker was seen by the Tory establishment as a maverick who was said to have difficulty cooperating with his fellow caucus members. He certainly had never

been part of the old guard of the party, of the Conservative establishment that was mostly from Toronto and anglophone Montreal.
It was reported that "with two or three exceptions, every member
of the Conservative front bench was opposed" to Diefenbaker.[32] The
overwhelming majority of frontbench Tories favoured either
MPs Donald Fleming of Toronto or Davie Fulton of British Columbia, or, if he could be drafted (which he could not), University
of Toronto president Sidney Smith.

At fifty-one, Donald Fleming (1905–86) was the older of the
two candidates running against Diefenbaker. First elected to Parliament in 1945 for Toronto's Eglington constituency, he was, like
both Diefenbaker and Fulton, a lawyer by profession. A lifelong
Tory, he first campaigned for the party in 1926. Known for his
attention to detail, he was said by some to "take himself too seriously," but he was trusted and liked by his colleagues.[33] Like
Diefenbaker, he had sought the Conservative leadership in 1948,
but both men lost to George Drew on the first ballot.

David ("Davie") Fulton (1916–2000), MP for Kamloops, British
Columbia, was one of several Second World War veterans in the
Conservative caucus. Along with Fleming, he was first elected to
Parliament in 1945. One of the youngest MPs when he ran for his
party's leadership at age forty, Fulton had gained a reputation as a
moderate Tory and a capable parliamentarian. A Rhodes Scholar,
he appealed to the "more intellectually inclined Conservatives,"[34]
who felt that the Liberals were destined to be returned to office in
1957 and that what the Tories needed most was a young leader
who could rebuild the party and win power down the line. Both
Fleming and Fulton ran against Diefenbaker in 1956, and both lost
decisively, with Diefenbaker capturing 60 percent of the first ballot
votes: 774 votes to 393 for Fleming and 117 for Fulton.

The principal criticism of Diefenbaker (among many) was that
he would be utterly unacceptable to Quebec. His French was barely
tolerable, and at no point in his career had he indicated any

understanding of Quebec's uniqueness. Diefenbaker's oft-repeated mantra of "One Canada" was interpreted by many in the province as dismissive of Quebec's distinctive culture. His critics thought that his selection as leader would prove the death knell for a party already weak in Quebec. Drew had at least attempted to improve the Conservatives' position in Quebec by having the party spend a considerable portion of its relatively small war chest on the 1949 and 1953 campaigns in the province, but that had met with practically no success. Drew was among the notables opposed to Diefenbaker's selection. So was the most influential Tory in Quebec, Léon Balcer, who, in addition to being the MP for Trois-Rivières and head of the Quebec delegation to the 1956 convention, served as president of the Progressive Conservative Association of Canada at the time of the convention. Balcer also co-chaired the convention and openly attacked Diefenbaker from the podium.

Léon Balcer (1917–90) had seen active service with the Royal Canadian Navy during the Second World War. A lawyer from Trois-Rivières, he was that rarity in Quebec politics: a French Canadian Progressive Conservative Member of Parliament. First elected to the Commons in 1949 and re-elected four years later, he considered himself, in his own words, an "anti-establishment" politician who "wanted things to change."[35] When it was announced that Diefenbaker had won the leadership, a number of Quebec delegates walked out.[36] Diefenbaker had added to the ill will felt by Quebec delegates by having his nomination moved by an Atlantic Canada premier (Hugh John Flemming of New Brunswick) and a British Columbia MP (George Pearkes), thus breaking with the practice of one of the two nominators being from Quebec and the other from a different province.

Diefenbaker's early electoral history had been far from stellar. In two previous attempts to win the national leadership (1942 and 1948), he fell far short of his goal. Apart from serving one three-year term as an elected alderman in the town of Wakaw, Saskatchewan (where he had established his first law office in July 1919), he failed to win a single election, federally or provincially, until 1940. He was defeated twice in federal elections (once losing to Prime Minister King in the Prince Albert constituency) and twice in provincial elections (1929 and 1938). Under his leadership, the Conservative Party of Saskatchewan failed to elect a single member to the provincial legislature in 1938. Diefenbaker was not wide of the mark when he frequently quipped that the only protection Conservatives had in the province of Saskatchewan came from the game laws.

There can be little surprise that a "Stop Diefenbaker" movement formed in the early stages of the 1956 leadership campaign. So, the obvious question is this: with the federal party establishment against Diefenbaker, the Quebec Conservatives openly hostile to him, and a series of electoral defeats that constituted a record of his first forty years in politics, how is it that Diefenbaker won the Tory leadership so handily in 1956?

The answer is quite simple: populism combined with a formidable organization. Diefenbaker claimed on many occasions to be a "House of Commons man" who loved Parliament. In truth, however, a great deal of his time as an MP was spent outside Ottawa. He had made his mark as a powerful orator, as a defence lawyer who could sway juries, and as a politician who could deliver a rousing stump speech to crowds in small towns or at large rallies. He made much of his desire to, in his words, act on behalf of the "average Canadian," protect civil liberties of his "fellow Canadians," and (in a jab pointed directly at the country's financial institutions centred in Toronto) look after the interests of "Main Street not Bay Street." In the process of speaking to Canadians in his first decade and a half in national politics, Diefenbaker not only gained both media and public attention but also laid the groundwork for a far more serious leadership run in 1956 than his two earlier attempts had been.

Ironically for a man who railed against his party's establishment ("the old guard"), Diefenbaker put together an impressive machine of his own. His victory demonstrated one of the essential lessons of politics: no candidate can win without a capable and engaged organization. It does not need to be large, but it needs to have plenty of contacts to call upon ("friends of friends") and the ability to sway votes towards the candidate. Three principal members of Diefenbaker's team, each of whom brought his particular expertise to the leadership campaign, warrant brief mention here:

- George Hees (1910–96) demonstrated considerable organizational skills in the campaign. A Second World War Army veteran, he was first elected to Parliament in a 1950 Toronto by-election. A handsome extrovert (dubbed "Gorgeous George" by friends) who had played football as a young man for the Toronto Argonauts, he travelled the country as president of the party from 1954 to 1956. Hees met with the Tory faithful in part to shore up the organization in advance of the election and in part to judge whether there would be enough support for him to seek the party leadership. He concluded that there was not and discovered that Diefenbaker had earned a devoted following among likely delegates to the convention. Hees took this into account and set about organizing for Diefenbaker.
- Gordon Churchill (1898–1985), an MP from Winnipeg, brought his training as a military officer to the strategic planning of Diefenbaker's leadership campaign and subsequently the 1957 general election campaign. His support for Diefenbaker came as something of a surprise to the candidate as he was generally considered to be part of the party's old guard. Churchill worked diligently on the Tory backbenchers in advance of the convention and was confident going into the leadership vote that 80 percent of them would support Diefenbaker.
- Allister Grosart (1906–84) was a party stalwart. He had served as George Drew's campaign manager during the 1953 election and had honed his skills in the advertising and public relations

business. He worked on campaign speeches and candidate literature, sometimes closely with Diefenbaker and sometimes with
only a small staff. As the 1956 Tory leadership convention was
the first to be broadcast on television, his role assumed greater
importance than it might otherwise have, as he was familiar with
the new medium through his business experience. He was enthusiastic about using television to the party's advantage, thinking
it a suitable way to capitalize on Diefenbaker's unique style of
campaigning and speech making.

These three were joined by other notables, mostly from the various provincial parties. Besides two close and trusted advisers from
Ontario – David Walker and Bill Brunt – Diefenbaker's machine
included Tory premiers, along with their organizations, from
Ontario, Nova Scotia, and New Brunswick, and the leader of the
Progressive Conservatives in Manitoba, who would soon become
that province's premier. There were even "discreet assurances"[37] of
support from the Union Nationale premier of Quebec. The stage
was set for the Tory leadership convention, and Diefenbaker won
decisively on the first ballot. It was clear that the party's old guard
had more than met its match.

3

The Players in 1957

CHAPTERS 3 AND 4 examine two parts of any election that are essential to explaining its outcome: the players and the issues. Although the issues, and some of the major political figures, were distinct to each occasion, both the 1957 and 1958 elections can be seen as two parts of a larger whole: the end of a period of Liberal hegemony (tentatively in 1957, decisively the following year) and, on the flip side, the two-stage rebirth of the Progressive Conservatives.

Political players are the men and women found in any party's election team. They slog it out – sometimes on transcontinental campaign tours; sometimes in the backrooms constructing and disseminating daily briefing papers; sometimes preparing rejoinders in what are now called "war rooms" to other parties' campaign claims; and sometimes mapping and/or altering their party's overall campaign strategies at a moment's notice. Still others are the backbone of any serious candidate's constituency organization. They are the volunteers who distribute candidate materials door to door, work the telephone banks, staff campaign offices and polling stations, and drive electors to polling stations on election day. They are the ones R.K. Carty has identified as working in "the trenches."[1] No party or candidate can do without them.

As important as "trench warriors" are to a party's campaign, this chapter looks at three different groups of players in the 1957 general election campaign: the party leaders, their principal colleagues in cabinet or on the front benches, and the parties' key campaign officials. Not all of them were familiar names then, nor have they become so with the passage of time. But all played a part in determining the outcome of the election and the fate of their party.

The Leaders

Placing their leader front and centre of their election campaign was by no means new to the older parties. Such had been the case from the time of John A. Macdonald's Conservatives in 1891 ("The Old Man, the Old Flag, the Old Party") to Mackenzie King's Liberals in 1935 ("King or Chaos"). But the 1950s proved to be different. Television arrived in mid-century at roughly the same time that public relations specialists were honing their craft, and the opportunities presented to party strategists by these twin developments were unprecedented. They could maximize television's potential for building a party's campaign around a single individual. Canadian parties have continued to make their leader the principal focus of their campaigns, invariably adapting their messages to the latest technologies to reach target audiences. That the politics of personality became so much a part of election campaigns and media coverage in the last half of the twentieth century and into the twenty-first owes much to the confluence of John Diefenbaker's rise, the advent of television, and the growth of the advertising profession.

"Uncle Louis"

Liberal leader Louis St. Laurent (1882–1973) was a study in contrast to his predecessor, Mackenzie King. The London *Economist* described him as possessing "most of the characteristics which were politically valuable in Mackenzie King, but also qualities of leadership which King never had."[2]

St. Laurent turned out to be an "ad man's dream, the perfect human material for the image merchants."[3] This was largely the result of his naturally genial manner and engaging personality. Voters found him approachable and easy to relate to. Canadians, as demonstrated in the 1949 and 1953 elections, both of which the Liberals won by comfortable margins, warmed to this avuncular man, whom they affectionately called "Uncle Louis" ("Papa Louis" in Quebec). He was a welcome change from his straitlaced bachelor predecessor, who, in the memorable words of poet F.R. Scott, was said to have "no vision to pierce the smoke-screen of his politics":

> *Truly he will be remembered*
> *Wherever men honour ingenuity,*
> *Ambiguity, inactivity, and political longevity.*[4]

Fluently bilingual, as was the first Liberal prime minister from Quebec, Sir Wilfrid Laurier, and the next, Pierre Elliott Trudeau, St. Laurent was, like both men, an ardent defender of both his native province and Canada. In his biography of St. Laurent, Dale Thomson relates an episode from young Louis's early years in rural Quebec that helps explain his fluency in both French and English. Louis "knew that his mother spoke to him in one way, his father in another, but assumed that all parents did so; only when he started school did he discover that he had been speaking two distinct languages. At table, the [St. Laurent] children asked for objects at their mother's end of the table in English, at their father's end in French."[5]

Born into a large family of modest means in the Eastern Townships, St. Laurent went on to become a successful Quebec corporate and constitutional lawyer. Late in 1941, he was asked by King to join the federal cabinet as minister of justice. Having served as

Louis St. Laurent |
Photographer George
Nakash, Library and
Archives Canada,
e010969218

president of the Canadian Bar Association earlier in his career, he
was known to, and respected by, the legal community across the
country. As a man whose values were "rooted in a traditional French-
Canadian mentality that respected authority and tradition,"[6] St.
Laurent "brought no political experience and even less ambition"[7]
to Ottawa. He accepted the prime minister's request out of a sense
of civic duty and attachment to his home province and to Canada.
No less critical to his selection by King, however, was the fact that,
unlike many Quebec Liberals, he was not opposed to military conscription should it become necessary during the Second World War.

St. Laurent succeeded King as Liberal leader and prime minister
in 1948. The convention at which he was chosen on the first ballot

approximated a coronation, for the retiring prime minister and several of his closest cabinet colleagues made no secret of their preferred choice for leader. Their preference aligned with that of the great majority of the 1,227 delegates. St. Laurent won with a decisive 69.1 percent of the vote, defeating long-time agriculture minister Jimmy Gardiner of Saskatchewan, who garnered 26.3 percent, and C.G. Power of Quebec, who got 4.6 percent. (Power, one of the great Liberal stalwarts of the first half of the twentieth century, quipped after the convention that so many delegates told him in confidence that they had voted for him that he should have demanded a recount!)

Under St. Laurent's watch, Canada ended appeals of court decisions to the Judicial Committee of the Privy Council in the United Kingdom. This amounted to a logical extension of the Statute of Westminster of 1931 and helped to further Canadian independence from "the mother country." Canada emerged from the Second World War with a stellar international reputation, and with the Cold War soon dominating East-West relations, the St. Laurent government adopted a resolutely anti-communist stance. Accordingly, the country enjoyed strong ties with its allies and played an important role in helping to establish the North Atlantic Treaty Organization (NATO) in 1949 and participating in the United Nations' defence of South Korea from 1950 to 1953.

On the domestic policy front, Canadians felt, on balance, that the St. Laurent government's stewardship of the economy had been a success. For all except the last year or so of his prime ministership, St. Laurent and his senior cabinet colleagues were seen by business leaders and senior public servants to be decisive, forward-thinking, and pragmatic. Like Mackenzie King's government, St. Laurent's was grounded in a certain political realism that comes with repeated electoral victories. (Or could it be that the repeated electoral victories were a product of a certain political realism?)

Within a year of becoming prime minister, St. Laurent played a critical role in negotiating Newfoundland and Labrador's entry into Confederation as Canada's tenth province. An overhaul of the Old Age Security Program in 1951 eliminated the "means test," which was widely considered to be demeaning. The program is now seen as one of the cornerstones of Canada's social security system. An astute observer of policy initiatives of provincial governments, St. Laurent was impressed with legislation in Saskatchewan, Alberta, and British Columbia in the late 1940s and early 1950s that established government-supported hospital insurance programs. Having received notice from Ontario that it would support a jointly funded federal-provincial hospital insurance program if certain conditions were met, the St. Laurent government shepherded the appropriate legislation through Parliament shortly before the 1957 election.[8]

During his last year or so in office, however, St. Laurent, who turned seventy-five before the 1957 election, was described as having become "old, tired, and – in the opinion of many – bored with the job ... going through the [motions] like a run-down automaton."[9] The fallout from the 1956 pipeline debate in Parliament, the Suez Crisis, and the finance minister's unwillingness to relax the purse strings had taken a toll. Added to these was the opposition's relentless chant of "Time for a Change." The Liberals may have been confident of being returned with a majority after twenty-two years in office, but this was not evident in the prime minister's wounded demeanour in the House as the election approached. By the middle of the campaign, it was apparent that he had become uncharacteristically irritable with the media and with the occasional demonstrator at political rallies. His dislike of television placed him at a disadvantage, especially against Diefenbaker, who delighted in the new medium.

When the votes were counted on election night 1957, it was clear that St. Laurent and the Liberals had won a larger share than the Progressive Conservatives (40.5 to 38.5 percent) but had come away with fewer seats (105 to 112). Quebec had saved the Liberals from total disaster, accounting for 62 of the party's 105 victories. The remaining 43 were spread among the other provinces and territories. There was nothing new about the Liberal strength in Quebec, for the province's allegiance to the party had remained steadfast since Wilfrid Laurier's time. What was new, and shocking for the Liberals, was how poorly they fared elsewhere.

St. Laurent acknowledged defeat and said the Liberals would soon relinquish office, even though constitutionally he could properly have tested his government's strength in Parliament. He wisely chose to step down, sensing that the two smaller parties would join forces with the Conservatives to bring down the government at the first available opportunity. He was right: they would have.

St. Laurent handed over office to the Conservatives on June 22, 1957, and announced his resignation as Liberal leader and retirement from politics soon after. Tributes flowed in from across Canada and abroad for a man who had distinguished himself in both domestic and international circles. St. Laurent had guided Canada through the postwar decade skillfully. Canadians were grateful for his contribution, but by the time the 1957 election came around, six out of ten voters indicated that they were ready for a change. When the Liberal Party executive called a leadership convention for January 1958, the winner was a foregone conclusion. The party's Louis St. Laurent decade had ended, and the Lester Pearson decade was about to begin.

Prairie Populist

David Smith has posed a question: if Canadians were asked which politician in the country's history best fits the description of a prairie populist, whom would they choose? His answer: "John Diefenbaker's name would confidently be proposed many times over."[10] About this there can be little doubt. Arthur Meighen, R.B. Bennett,

Joe Clark, and Stephen Harper – even Mackenzie King – were all in one way or another "prairie prime ministers" (or at least a prime minister elected in a Prairie constituency), but none had the *je ne sais quoi* of Diefenbaker. His was a decidedly different style of campaigning and governing.

It is helpful at this point to understand what constitutes "populism" and why Diefenbaker can be categorized as a populist leader. At its base, populism draws on a direct connection between a politician and the people that is "unmediated by institutions" and independent of a particular policy or set of policies.[11] Populist leaders are typically powerful orators who exhibit little interest in following established institutional norms or honouring organizational constraints unless by so doing they can advance their career, their cause, their mission, or (as many populists refer to it) their "vision." Populists are characteristically described as "outsiders," "loners," or "champions of the underdog."

Diefenbaker fit the bill. Speaking as a candidate to the party faithful across the country in advance of the 1956 Progressive Conservative convention and from time to time thereafter, Diefenbaker liked to remind his audiences that "Bay Street and St. James Street may be against me, but Main Street has always supported me."[12] His ability to connect with voters in 1957 and particularly in 1958 was, with the exception of Wilfrid Laurier, unprecedented to that point in twentieth-century Canadian politics. Countless voters came to believe that Diefenbaker had *their* particular interest at heart when he was speaking to them. At the conclusion of an enthusiastic election rally in Montreal in 1958, one admirer described Diefenbaker as "*un vrai homme du peuple.*"[13] Neither St. Laurent nor his successor, Pearson, could match that level of voter attachment, however fleeting it proved to be. Not surprisingly, many "average Canadians" remained loyal to Diefenbaker even after his government's defeat and his replacement as Conservative leader. They could "relate" to this man because he had "related" to them.

Unlike both St. Laurent and Pearson, Diefenbaker had a long political apprenticeship. Born in southwestern Ontario in 1895, he moved as a young child with his family to what was then the Northwest Territories, now Saskatchewan. Conditions were harsh, and with little in the way of financial resources, the family found, as did countless others at that time, that life on the virgin prairies "involved poverty, discomfort, hard work and disappointment," overcome only by "individual fortitude."[14] In 1906, Diefenbaker started school in a one-room rural school in which his uncle was the teacher. This was followed by high school in Saskatoon then enrolment at the University of Saskatchewan, where the student newspaper predicted he would one day become Canada's leader of the opposition. By all accounts, he was a determined and dedicated student. His studies were interrupted by a brief military stint in Canada and France. On graduation in 1919, he opened a law practice in Wakaw, Saskatchewan, a village of a few hundred people. In thirteen years, Diefenbaker had gone from a one-room school to a one-man law practice.

Diefenbaker's early years as a prairie lawyer unquestionably shaped both his understanding of Canada and his approach to adversarial politics. Wakaw was at the centre of a mix of immigrant homesteaders, farmers, and small-town merchants who typified the settlers moving onto the prairies in large numbers in the early twentieth century. The great majority were recent immigrants who had arrived from more than two dozen Eastern European and, in a few instances, Asian countries. The 1921 census found that Saskatchewan had nearly three times the national average of Canada's European-born (apart from English and French) population (39.14 percent, compared with 14.16 percent in the country as a whole). Manitoba and Alberta followed, with 33 percent and 31 percent, respectively.[15] Many of the Eastern Europeans, who spoke little or no English, typically put down roots in or near communities or farms where others from their home country or religious faith were clustering. They came to believe, according to Diefenbaker, in an "un-hyphenated Canada" – not "an English Canada" or "a French Canada" but (as he titled his memoirs) *One Canada*. This was a theme that he returned to countless times in his political career.

The Wakaw district was well suited to Diefenbaker's courtroom talent, although he freely admitted that his success in his first criminal case owed more to luck than to skill. Many of his clients among the "litigious and quarrelsome" local population were given to drunken fights in town on Saturday nights. Diefenbaker later recounted that he had defended one man accused of severely injuring and attempting to murder a trespassing youth. Even with "convincing evidence" of the man's guilt, the jury found him innocent. When asked how they could have reached such a verdict, members of the jury allowed, in the words of one of them, that they did so because "it is the kid's [Diefenbaker's] first case and his twenty-fourth birthday."[16]

However embellished this anecdote may have become in Diefenbaker's telling, the verdict nonetheless helped launch his legal career. It is reported that over the course of his thirty-eight years of practising law, he acted for the defence in twenty-seven murder trials and won acquittals in all but two of them.[17] In the next several decades, his reputation as a brilliant defence lawyer grew not only throughout Saskatchewan but in other parts of the country as well. He gradually emerged as a popular public speaker, often working into his remarks the theme of "One Canada" and a robust defence of civil liberties.

In tandem with his law practice, Diefenbaker made several forays into politics at both the provincial and federal levels, but, as noted earlier, he failed to win a single election. Finally elected to Parliament in 1940 for the constituency of Arm River, and subsequently for the city of Prince Albert, he won thirteen consecutive contests from 1940 to 1979, the last barely three months before his death.

As it turned out, the electoral defeats Diefenbaker suffered in the 1920s and 1930s were not his last. As a freshman MP, and indicative of how ambitious he was, Diefenbaker ran for the leadership of the newly named Progressive Conservative Party of Canada in 1942. Earning barely 9 percent of the vote, he placed a distant third behind the winner, Manitoba premier John Bracken. He lost again six years later, this time to the favourite of the party establishment, Ontario premier George Drew, who won on the first ballot with two-thirds of the votes. Drew was portrayed by the Diefenbaker campaign as a candidate of the "Old Guard" and "big interests," in contrast to Diefenbaker, who claimed to represent the "rank and file" of the party and the "average Canadian."[18] In the event, it did him no good. It can safely be said that as a member of the Tory establishment in Toronto, Drew was unquestionably on the Conservative side of the party, whereas Diefenbaker, as an outsider from the prairies, was in the Progressive wing.

Diefenbaker's third try for the Progressive Conservative leadership turned out differently. Upon Drew's unexpected retirement in 1956 because of ill health, Diefenbaker immediately let his name stand for his party's leadership. Although he had delivered some powerful speeches in the Commons that year, denouncing the St. Laurent government over the pipeline and Suez issues, Diefenbaker was not one of the primary Conservative spokesmen. His front-bench colleagues Davie Fulton, Donald Fleming, and Howard Green played that role. Diefenbaker's denunciations of the government were more often delivered in speeches across the country. This had the effect, intended or otherwise, of gaining considerable media attention and support among party activists at the constituency level, many of whom would serve as delegates at the 1956 convention.

Diefenbaker may have been a loner, but he proved to be a popular loner. He attracted as personal supporters many who were not in positions of power or influence. He played the "outsider" card with notable success, developing a following among other "outsiders" on

John G. Diefenbaker, MP, speaking in the House of Commons in
1948. | Photographer Louis Jacques, Library and Archives Canada, C-080883

the backbenches of the parliamentary party, the party's rank and
file in the country, and the general public. As a self-proclaimed
guardian of civil liberties, a champion of minority causes, a fighter
battling the power centres within his own party, an orator making
fiery, relentless attacks on the St. Laurent government, and one
who defended (in his own words) "the little people," Diefenbaker
showed that he was capable of appealing to a wide swath of people,
a number of whom, for a variety of reasons, felt socially or politically
marginalized.

Diefenbaker's third run at the leadership came in the face of powerful opposition within his own party. Yet shortly before the 1956 convention, one of Canada's leading political commentators noted that even Diefenbaker's "bitterest enemies concede[d] that if an election were held tomorrow, [he] would draw more votes to the Conservative party than any other leader in sight."[19] What he lacked in frontbench support, Diefenbaker more than made up – in numbers at least – from Conservative backbenchers. Some Conservative MPs supported him as a matter of personal political survival: "My people are for John," one of them explained in 1956. "If I were to oppose him, I'd probably lose the nomination and I'd certainly lose the election."[20] For others, only Diefenbaker as leader would provide them with the means to uproot and replace the party's old guard, who for so long had occupied the most powerful positions in the

Donald Fleming and Davie Fulton holding John Diefenbaker's hands aloft following Diefenbaker's victory at the 1956 Progressive Conservative leadership convention in Ottawa. | Photograph by Capital Press, University of Saskatchewan Archives and Special Collections, JGD/MG01/XVII/JGD 352 D

party. Three weeks before the 1956 convention, the Gallup Poll confirmed what members of the parliamentary party and the public suspected: Diefenbaker had the support of a clear majority of Conservative voters (55 percent), well ahead of other party notables whose names would appear on the ballot.[21]

The outcome was a foregone conclusion. As with Drew's and St. Laurent's election as leader of their parties in 1948, and with Pearson's election a decade later, Diefenbaker won the first ballot handily. The highly competitive leadership races that were settled only after four or five convention ballots were still a decade away: Robert Stanfield after five ballots at the Progressive Conservative convention of 1967 and Pierre Elliott Trudeau after four ballots at the Liberal convention of 1968. Diefenbaker's nominators were effusive in their praise. George Pearkes, a Victoria Cross veteran of the First World War and a British Columbia MP, went so far as to call Diefenbaker "the greatest living Canadian – a cross between Simon de Montfort and Benjamin Disraeli."[22] When the votes were tallied, it was clear that Diefenbaker had won handily on the first ballot with 60 percent of the votes cast (Table 3.1). He was finally where he longed to be – leader of his party, ready to do battle with the Liberals – and where his university yearbook had predicted he would be, leader of the opposition.

TABLE 3.1

First ballot results at the Progressive Conservative leadership convention, December 12–14, 1956, Ottawa

Candidate	Number of votes	Percentage of votes
John Diefenbaker	774	60.3
Donald Fleming	393	30.6
Davie Fulton	117	9.1
Total	1,284	100.0

Source: John C. Courtney, *The Selection of National Party Leaders in Canada* (Toronto: Macmillan, 1973), 152.

M.J. Coldwell |
Saskatoon Star-Phoenix,
a division of Postmedia
Network Inc., City of
Saskatoon Archives,
Saskatoon Star-Phoenix
Collection, S-SP-B-4266.

M.J. Coldwell

The two smaller parties, the Co-operative Commonwealth Federation (CCF) and Social Credit, were led in both the 1957 and 1958
elections by the same men who had led them for many years. M.J.
Coldwell had been at the helm of the CCF for seventeen years and
Solon Low of Social Credit for twelve years when the 1957 election
was called. The two men were as different as chalk and cheese.

M.J. (the name he was known by for his entire political career,
which stood for his two given names, Major James) was born in
1888 into a middle-class Conservative family in England. While
attending college in Exeter, he came to embrace the democratic
socialism of the fledgling British Labour Party. Emigrating to Canada in 1910 and armed with a teaching certificate, he headed along
with thousands of other immigrants straight to the prairies. As a
schoolteacher in small-town Alberta and Saskatchewan, then as a
school principal in Regina, he began a political career in the 1920s
that lasted until 1958.

As a young man, Coldwell showed considerable political drive and ambition that more closely resembled Diefenbaker's than St. Laurent's. From the early 1920s to his first election to Parliament in 1935, he held a variety of elected offices and sought, unsuccessfully, election to both Parliament and the Saskatchewan Legislative Assembly. He was elected president of the Saskatchewan Teachers' Federation for one year and of the Canadian Teachers' Federation for six. He served as an alderman on the Regina City Council from 1922 to 1925 and from 1926 to 1932. He ran as a Progressive candidate in Regina in the 1925 federal election but lost his deposit. He was elected president of Saskatchewan's Independent Labour Party, and then leader of the province's Farmer-Labour Party, but without a seat in the legislature. Coldwell was an active member of the CCF national executive when it adopted the Regina Manifesto at its founding convention in 1933. Soon after, he ran for the provincial legislature, only to be defeated. He served as the CCF's national secretary from 1934 to 1937 and its national chairman from 1938 to 1942. Upon the resignation of the party's first leader, pacifist J.S. Woodsworth, soon after the outbreak of war in Europe, Coldwell became the party's second parliamentary leader, a position that ended with his defeat in 1958.

Coldwell's career in federal politics was launched in 1935 with his victory in the federal election for the rural Saskatchewan constituency of Rosetown-Biggar. Re-elected there in the next five general elections, he gradually became a fixture in both provincial and federal politics. As a novice MP in 1935, he joined six others (including the future premier of Saskatchewan, T.C. Douglas) to form the tiny CCF caucus in the House of Commons under Woodsworth's leadership.

Once he became leader, Coldwell faced a seemingly unending organizational struggle unfamiliar to the leaders of the older and less doctrinaire parties. From the outset of the socialist movement in Canada in the early twentieth century, there had been major

CCF leader J.S. Woodsworth (centre) with members of his caucus, ca. 1940. T.C. (Tommy) Douglas is on the far left and M.J. Coldwell to Woodsworth's left. | Photographer Yousuf Karsh, Library and Archives Canada, PA-181423

differences among its competing factions. Those differences came to the surface during the Great Depression and in the postwar anti-communist frenzy in Canada. At the outset, the CCF was ostensibly a "movement" (Woodsworth's preferred term over "party"), but it really amounted to an amalgam of factions, including British Columbia trade unionists, prairie and Ontario farm organizations, Social Gospel advocates, modest socialists, radical socialists, followers of Social Credit monetary theories, and others. These disparate groups reflected the fact that, as the Regina Manifesto stated (perhaps "understated" is a better term) at the outset, the CCF was a "federation of organizations." Formally, it eschewed the usual party structure of leader at the top and numerous organizations at the federal, provincial, and constituency levels. These typically ranged from riding associations to clubs exclusively aimed at specific groups, such as women, young party members, and university organizations.

However, as the elections rolled around, as well as for internal day-to-day operations, the CCF had no choice but to accept the fact that it was competing in a partisan, federal, parliamentary institutional framework. Its intra-party structures needed to reflect that. These included a constitution, a national executive, and periodic party conferences; a salaried national staff; a defined command structure in the House of Commons (leader, ministerial critics, caucus whip, house leader, and so on); regional and provincial offices; and constituency organizations. Since party revenues were modest at the best of times, and active memberships varied considerably from province to province, not all the extra-parliamentary structures were feasible – certainly not in all parts of the country. In Quebec, where the party barely existed, the CCF nominated an average of only nineteen candidates per election from 1935 to 1958 – in a province electing between sixty-five and seventy-five MPs. Not a single CCF candidate was elected in Quebec between 1935 and 1958. The party managed to field candidates in twenty-two of the province's seventy-five districts in 1957 and in twenty-nine districts in 1958, but of those fifty-one candidates, only one received more than single-digit support (13.9 percent).

With few exceptions, the candidates in Quebec and several other provinces were of the "token" or "sacrificial" variety. They had little or no money, few volunteers, and (if they were lucky) a skeleton organization. As they could scarcely mount a serious campaign, their names were placed in nomination solely to "show the flag" for the party. Token CCF candidates were often the case not only in Quebec but also in much of rural Ontario, Atlantic Canada, and Alberta. All of this simply underscores the fact that CCF's organizational strength and electoral successes rested almost entirely on Saskatchewan, Manitoba, British Columbia, and parts of Ontario.

Organizational structuring awaited Coldwell's becoming leader in 1940. Not that the CCF lacked a formal structure under Woodsworth; rather, the party's inherently different interests were often at odds with one another. Members of farm organizations, for example, "wanted nothing more than a share of bourgeois affluence," in contrast to CCF intellectuals, who saw capitalism as perverting "the liberal democratic ideal" of socialism.[23] Such differences made central direction of the party apparatus difficult. In his biography of Coldwell, Walter Stewart points out that Woodsworth's strengths did not lie in his organizational ability. He describes the party that Coldwell inherited in 1940 as "at best, a swarm of impractical idealists, or, at worst, collectivists, crypto-Communists [and] Trotskyites."[24]

Neither had Woodsworth been considered a strong parliamentarian – instead, he was an eloquent crusader on a mission. Coldwell, on the other hand, was a dedicated socialist who was also a devoted parliamentarian, a talented debater, and an expert on parliamentary procedures. He and his colleague Stanley Knowles were arguably the outstanding procedural experts in the Commons in the 1940s and 1950s, followed closely by Davie Fulton of the Conservatives.

Stanley Knowles (1908–97) was one of a kind. An ordained Protestant minister, he succeeded Woodsworth in 1942 by winning a by-election in Woodsworth's old seat in north Winnipeg. He held that riding until his defeat in the Conservative sweep of 1958 but returned to Parliament four years later and continued as an MP until 1984. As noted, Knowles was a skilled parliamentarian and an expert on legislative rules and procedures. Soon after Diefenbaker became prime minister in 1957, he asked Knowles to become Speaker of the House. Knowles declined, feeling he would better serve his constituents and Canadians generally by sitting on the opposition benches and holding the government (of whatever stripe) to account.

The expertise of the half-dozen or so CCF and Conservative frontbenchers who had mastered the fine points of parliamentary procedure came into play during the heated exchanges over the Liberals' pipeline legislation in 1956, when together they roasted the government and the Speaker for their handling of the issue.

Coldwell, Knowles, and other CCF frontbenchers understood the (unstated) rules of adversarial, party-based politics much better than the fourth party in the Commons – Social Credit – and did not hesitate to use them when they sensed that it would work to their advantage.

In the 1956 pipeline debate, a side of Coldwell that had never been seen previously (and would never be seen again) came to the fore in the House and caught the attention of the media. One of the Speaker's egregiously partisan rulings so provoked M.J. that he was described as "boiling mad ... waving a clenched fist" at the Speaker as he stormed his way up the Centre Aisle of the Commons to the Speaker's Chair.[25] Otherwise, Coldwell was normally known to be a gentleman, respected by members on both sides of the House. His manner was Edwardian (not surprising for someone raised and educated in late Victorian and Edwardian England), and he was admired for contributing a sense of "reasonableness to the parliamentary traditions of [his] party."[26] In Diefenbaker's opinion, Coldwell was an able parliamentarian who added "eloquent lustre to the institution."[27]

Coldwell's own brand of democratic socialism was at first more on the radical side, but with time it mellowed and became more centrist. Although clearly principled, he could nonetheless be pragmatic, with a calm, rational approach to politics and public policy when the occasion demanded. There seemed to be wide agreement among colleagues and opponents alike that Coldwell's great contribution to his party was "common sense."[28]

In not a single election from 1935, when M.J. entered Parliament, to 1953 did the party manage to elect more than 28 MPs in a House of between 245 and 265 members. The party's share of the popular vote reached its zenith in that period when it received 15.6 percent in 1945. At its lowest, it was 8.5 percent. Yet the CCF could point to several successes in shaping Canadian social policy that more than offset its modest electoral performance. Over the life of the CCF (and its successor, the New Democratic Party), Canada's social safety net was created and expanded. The persistence of the democratic socialists in Parliament and on the campaign trail had much to do with this. Social policies in which Canadians now take pride owe a great deal to the doggedness of Woodsworth and Coldwell and their followers. From the introduction of old-age pensions in the 1920s, through the advancement of social reforms such as unemployment insurance, family allowances, and fair employment practices in the 1940s and 1950s, to a national health insurance program in the 1960s, the "radical" proposals of the left gained gradual acceptance. Such advances are now part of the fabric of Canadian society, but it was the governments of Mackenzie King, Louis St. Laurent, John Diefenbaker, and, later, Lester Pearson that introduced and shepherded such legislation in Parliament, not the CCF or the NDP.

King was a master at appropriating ideas when they suited his agenda and increased his government's chances of survival. He recorded in his diary in 1943, at the height of the CCF's popularity, that a fourteen-point reform program the Liberal Party's Advisory Council had recently approved likely "cut the ground in large part from under the CCF."[29] A succession of Liberal prime ministers, from King to Pierre Trudeau, can be said to have depended "on the CCF-NDP for innovations," whereas for the most part the CCF-NDP depended "on the Liberals for implementation of the innovations."[30]

Coldwell came to the conclusion that a reworking of the set of doctrinaire socialist principles set forth in the Regina Manifesto was badly needed. Starting in 1950, he and a group of his closest advisers, such as Stanley Knowles, Toronto labour lawyer and CCF national secretary David Lewis, and McGill law professor, poet, and CCF stalwart Frank Scott, worked on and off for several years to achieve the goal of making democratic socialism more acceptable to Canadians. The call for a new party was joined by the most electorally successful CCF leader in the country, Tommy Douglas (1904–86) of Saskatchewan. If the party did not adopt a program that would be more willing to accommodate private capital, Douglas warned the party's National Executive in 1956, the CCF would become "a diminishing group, a small, well-respected, highly thought-of minority, with increasingly less influence."[31]

Douglas was a popular figure, known for his oratorical wit and dedication to democratic socialism. Like Coldwell, he was born in Britain (Douglas in Scotland and Coldwell in England) and emigrated to Canada at a young age. Elected to Parliament twice (1935 and 1940), he resigned his seat in 1944 to lead the CCF to a massive win in the Saskatchewan provincial election that same year – a first for democratic socialists in North America. He led the provincial party to four more election victories before re-entering federal politics as first leader of the newly created New Democratic Party in 1961. Often called "the Father of Medicare," Douglas's standing nationally owed much to the fact that the CCF was instrumental in establishing Canada's first publicly financed universal hospitalization insurance plan in 1947 and and its first publicly funded health insurance (Medicare) scheme in 1962 in Saskatchewan.

The outcome of Coldwell's move to a less doctrinaire set of proposals was the Winnipeg Manifesto, the document prepared in advance of the 1957 federal election to replace the considerably more radical Regina Manifesto. Issued just a year before the election, it did little to improve the party's standing in terms of either the popular vote or elected MPs. In the election that followed nine months later, it was of even less benefit to the CCF, as Coldwell, along with all but eight of his fellow candidates, was defeated. The party's share of the popular vote slipped into the single digits in the 1958 election, roughly on par with its share of votes in its first federal election, in 1935. Following the 1958 election, the party's future direction (indeed, its continued existence) became a hotly debated topic among democratic socialists.

Solon Low

M.J. Coldwell had been an MP for ten years and his party's leader for five when Solon Low (1900–62) was first elected to Parliament in 1945. Low, president and national leader of the Social Credit Party, was at forty-five the youngest of the four party leaders in the Commons. He continued as MP for the Peace River constituency in Alberta and as Social Credit leader through the next five elections, but was defeated, along with all other Social Credit MPs, in the Diefenbaker sweep of 1958. Low's career in politics tells us a good deal about his party and the unique political culture of his province. He was born and raised in Cardston, a town close to the American border in southern Alberta created by followers of the Church of Jesus Christ of Latter-day Saints (the Mormons) who had travelled over wagon trails from Utah in the 1880s. Throughout his years in politics, Low was known to hold strong Christian beliefs, and references to the Christian faith were often sprinkled throughout his speeches and made their way to Social Credit election platforms.

The collapse of the Progressives after their moment in the sun in the 1920s, first on the federal scene and soon after in the United Farmers of Alberta government, left a political void in a province where grain farmers and small-town merchants harboured strong resentment of the banks, railways, and grain merchants. Collectively, these eastern businesses and institutions represented financial interests that many on the prairies felt were out to exploit them. The Great Depression, combined with the devastating drought of the 1930s, the foreclosure of countless farms, and the bankruptcies of many small businesses, made the simplistic economic remedies proposed by Social Credit attractive to thousands.

Social Credit as it was proposed in Alberta in the early years of the Depression was drawn loosely from the economic theories first advanced by an English engineer, Major C.H. Douglas, who was known for, among other things, his anti-Semitism and fascist leanings. At its core, Social Credit was based on the idea that the capitalist economy was inefficient because it denied individuals purchasing power equal to their contributions to the economy. To remedy this deficiency, a basic dividend should be paid to individuals by the state. This dividend, labelled "social credit," would enable people to buy the goods and services they had had a hand in producing.

Neither the Conservatives nor the Liberals could match the attraction of Social Credit in Alberta. A good part of the reason for this can be explained by the appeal of William Aberhart, the first Social Credit premier of Alberta. Prior to winning office in 1935, Aberhart was a Calgary schoolteacher and evangelist who in the early years of the Depression embraced the principles of Social Credit. Known for his Sunday afternoon province-wide radio broadcasts from his Prophetic Bible Institute in Calgary, "Bible Bill" Aberhart gradually worked into his sermons the supposed benefits of Social Credit. His proposal to have the province pay each citizen a basic monthly dividend of $25 found wide support among his impoverished listeners. In the 1935 provincial election, Social Credit swamped the United Farmers of Alberta government and the two older parties by winning fifty-six of the sixty-three seats and 54 percent of the popular vote. The party went on to monopolize provincial politics for the next thirty-six years, winning all nine elections over that period. In all but three of those elections, Social Credit received over 50 percent of the vote.

Starting in the 1920s, Aberhart capitalized on what was then a new and emerging technology to reach thousands of Albertans. Radio was a novel medium at the time, and radio receivers were as rare as they were expensive. It was not unusual for farmers and townspeople to gather around the one or two radio sets in a local library, town hall, or school gymnasium on a Sunday afternoon to listen to Aberhart's lectures/sermons broadcast over CFCN in Calgary, the most powerful radio station west of Montreal at the time.

New technologies can be used effectively by leaders to reach their intended audience. From Martin Luther and the relatively new movable-type printing press in the early sixteenth century – a technology that enabled him to publish thousands of broadsheets in the vernacular (German) denouncing the Roman Catholic Church – to Donald Trump's persistent reliance on his Twitter account, leaders exploiting a new communications medium can have a powerful impact on society. Aberhart belongs in that category. His effective use of weekly radio broadcasts to combine his evangelical and political messages paved the way for Social Credit's sweep in the 1935 provincial election.

Solon Low had been a part of the Social Credit movement from the beginning. Elected to the provincial legislature in 1935, he was soon named provincial treasurer (finance minister), a position he held until shortly before he entered the federal arena in 1945 as the MP for Peace River. He was known to be earnest, religious, and conservative, but, as his federal career demonstrated, he was unable to move his party much beyond its largely rural base in Alberta. As a party in the Commons totally dependent upon a small regional support base and unfamiliar with the adversarial politics inherent in a multi-party system in Parliament, Social Credit was in many respects an outlier in the institution. Its doctrines were readily dismissed by critics as "funny money," and its increasingly conservative views, coupled with its strong evangelical bent, meant it had little appeal in the more urban and cosmopolitan centres of Canada. Unlike the CCF, it could point to no major policy victories in Parliament. The CCF also invariably received a larger share of voter support than Social Credit (an average of 13 percent compared with 4.5 percent in the five federal elections contested by both parties from 1945 to 1958), and with MPs elected from four or five provinces, it had a more representational, more diverse, and less regionally dependent caucus than Social Credit.

Low was not a strong parliamentarian. As a debater in the House, he paled in comparison to prominent debaters and procedural experts in the other parties. Heading into the 1957 election, a schism

Solon Low, MP for Peace River, 1945–58, Social Credit party leader, 1944–61. | Photographer Arthur Roy, Library and Archives Canada, C-000700

developed between the more orthodox wing (Alberta and Solon Low, who remained true to what they considered Social Credit doctrine) and the more pragmatic, business-oriented wing (British Columbia's relatively new Social Credit government) that signalled a growing level of uncertainty within the party at large about what Social Credit stood for.

Social Credit's success provincially provided an organizational and support base from which to launch the federal party. In Alberta, it proved to be as successful federally as it was provincially, winning 72 of the province's 102 seats in the elections between 1935 and 1957. But that was pretty much it, for Social Credit won only a handful of seats elsewhere during that period, and all were from the adjoining provinces of Saskatchewan (2) and British Columbia

(10). The party's hope of becoming a player on the national scene never materialized.

With his and his party's defeat in 1958, Low's leadership came to an end. Not until the 1962 election did Social Credit resurface, when, in addition to a handful of MPs elected in the West under a new leader, the party's nascent Quebec wing burst upon the political scene under the leadership of a colourful populist from the northern part of the province, Réal Caouette. Social Credit's Quebec wing stunned many pundits and several old hands in Ottawa by winning twenty-six of the party's thirty seats in 1962. Caouette had turned the relatively new technology, television, to his advantage in rural Quebec just as Aberhart had done with radio in Alberta three decades earlier. With a pitch to voters based on what he depicted as the futility of voting for either of the older parties or the CCF, Caouette became something of an overnight sensation with his vacuous election slogan, "*On n'a rien à perdre.*" But once he left the scene a decade later, the party soon disappeared completely from federal politics.

The Teams

At election time, political parties rely on teams of policy experts, organizers, fundraisers, handlers, advance people, speechwriters, pollsters, and advertising specialists to manage particular aspects of their campaign. Several individuals and firms on contract may well have worked with or been engaged by the party in many prior elections; others will be relatively new to the game. So long as they coexist harmoniously, they are essential to the party's success. That said, harmonious intra-party coexistence is not always possible during the heat of an election campaign.

In 1957, as in earlier elections, the Liberals relied on the Cockfield, Brown agency to conduct their advertising campaign. Since the end of the Second World War, advertising had been an integral part of political campaigning, and a symbiotic relationship had developed between politicians and their ad experts. Cockfield, Brown was generally considered the best in the field of election marketing. An added benefit from the firm's standpoint was its close ties to many government ministers and party officials between elections, which ensured the flow of government advertising in its direction. In fact, the Liberals and Cockfield, Brown had such close ties that the general secretary of the National Liberal Federation, H.E. Kidd, was on "loan" from Cockfield, Brown for a decade, his salary paid for by the firm.

It was Cockfield, Brown that was responsible for cultivating the image of "Uncle Louis" St. Laurent. The Liberal campaigns of the late 1940s and 1950s fashioned their messages around a carefully crafted image of the prime minister. According to a memo summarizing a meeting of the Cockfield, Brown election advertising team in advance of the 1953 election, "in all [election] advertising it is desirable to incorporate a St. Laurent picture ... With the possible exception of [C.D.] Howe, cabinet ministers will not be featured."[32] The push to focus the party's print and television advertising largely on its leader came back to haunt the Liberals, however, when the Conservatives successfully borrowed from the image playbook and built their own campaigns around a relentless presentation of Diefenbaker under the leader-focused slogans "Time for a Diefenbaker Government" in 1957, and "Follow John" in 1958.

In both elections, the Liberals counted on a coterie of experienced organizers and speechwriters who, in most cases, had worked with the party for several years – in some cases several decades. This brought with it the obvious benefit of experience, but on the flip side it meant a greater likelihood of missing out on new and innovative ideas for advertising, campaigning, and organizing that could flow from younger, fresher minds.

Critical to any party's ability to mount a serious campaign is its fundraising capacity. The Liberals, unlike the other parties in postwar elections, carried out that part of their operation with consummate skill. Many of the party's principal self-styled "bagmen" were senators, appointed by either Mackenzie King or Louis St. Laurent. Their senatorial positions entitled them to attend party caucus meetings and brought them into close contact with ministers and their political staff. At a time when there were no statutorily defined contribution limits, spending limits, or disclosure requirements, Liberal fundraisers had free rein to tap (mostly) Toronto and Montreal corporations and executives. Sizable contributions came from relatively few donors. That was the way party financing worked in that era. As Ken Carty has noted, Liberal bagmen in the 1950s "instituted a system of kickbacks," whereby firms that had government contracts "were expected to make a financial contribution to the party that was proportionate to the amount of government business they were doing."[33] Exact expenditures by all the parties in the 1957 campaign have never been satisfactorily established. In his careful analysis of that election, however, John Meisel concluded that the Liberal Party likely spent two or three times its main rivals, somewhere in the order of $6–10 million, or between $60 and 101 million in 2022 dollars.[34]

The more visible players in the Liberal campaign, who delivered speeches at party rallies across the country, were drawn from the ranks of the senior cabinet ministers in 1957 and the official opposition front bench in 1958. In 1957, in addition to the prime minister, these included ministers C.D. Howe (trade and commerce), J.G. Gardiner (agriculture), Walter Harris (finance), Ralph Campney (defence), Paul Martin (health and welfare), Stuart Garson (justice), Lester Pearson (external affairs), Robert Winters (public works) and J.W. Pickersgill (citizenship and immigration). Pickersgill also worked closely with the prime minister on speeches and general election planning.

The 1957 Progressive Conservative campaign under John Diefenbaker was a more slapdash, less professional affair than the Liberals'.

Diefenbaker had been selected leader barely months before the election and understandably wanted to remake the party organization to reflect the change in leadership. Those closest to him during the campaign included Allister Grosart (vice president, McKim Advertising, who served as the Conservatives' national director and campaign manager in both 1957 and 1958); Merrill Menzies (an Ottawa economist who played a major role in drafting policies for both elections); Dalton Camp (speechwriter and strategist); and two of Diefenbaker's frontbench colleagues, George Hees of Toronto and Gordon Churchill of Winnipeg.

Besides Hees and Churchill, other prominent Conservative parliamentarians were called upon to speak at various rallies and events in both 1957 and 1958, including Diefenbaker's two leadership rivals, Donald Fleming of Toronto and Davie Fulton of British Columbia; Howard Green (Vancouver); Leon Balcer (Quebec); Ellen Fairclough (Hamilton); and Douglas Harkness (Calgary). Not all of them had supported Diefenbaker's leadership bid, but the prospect of gaining office in 1957 had a way of uniting a party known in the past for occasional, sometimes open disagreements among its leading spokespersons.

Partly in response to a report prepared by Gordon Churchill in advance of the 1957 election examining the allocation of scarce party resources to provinces and constituencies (the controversial campaign strategy outlined in that report will be examined in Chapter 5), the Conservatives' election team devised a scheme whereby each province would receive from the national organization an allocation of $3,000 per constituency in the province. The money was not allocated to individual ridings, however. Instead, it was transferred to the provincial campaign organizations (the amount varying according to the number of electoral districts in a province), on the theory that they would be better able to assess how the money should be spent. If constituencies needed additional funds for their local campaigns, that would be the constituencies' responsibility. In addition, roughly $800,000 was transferred to the provincial organizations. The party's national office spent approximately $1.7 million on the national campaign: the leader's tour, campaign rallies, national media advertising, and the like. In total, the cost of the Conservative campaign likely did not exceed $3.5 million, barely one-half of the Liberals' expenditures.[35] Nine months later, the Conservatives could – and did – spend considerably more money than any other party.

The CCF and Social Credit organizations and finances were modest compared with the two older parties. In Saskatchewan, British Columbia, and, to a lesser extent, Ontario, the CCF could count on hundreds of volunteers to staff campaign offices, prepare and distribute pamphlets and other party literature, and generally attempt to get out the vote on election day. Except for a few select pockets of support, such as North End Winnipeg and Cape Breton Island, the CCF barely existed in other provinces at election time. This was reflected in the fact that the party was unable to nominate even token candidates for about a hundred seats in both 1957 and 1958. The CCF scarcely registered with Quebec voters, garnering only 1.8 percent of the province's total popular vote in 1957.

In the 1957 and 1958 campaigns, M.J. Coldwell relied heavily on party stalwarts David Lewis (CCF national chairman), Tommy Douglas, Stanley Knowles, and Hazen Argue (an MP from Saskatchewan), McGill University law professor Frank Scott, and Quebec political activist Thérèse Casgrain. There had been little in the way of new blood in the party's national apparatus for some time. In all, the CCF spent a mere fraction of what the Liberals or the Conservatives spent, likely in the order of $200,000 and "certainly less than $250,000" in total for all national, provincial, and constituency associations.[36] The provincial parties in Saskatchewan and Ontario, together with several trade unions in British Columbia and Ontario, provided the bulk of the party's revenues.

In some circles, notably in Western Canada, the Social Credit party was seen in the months leading up to the 1957 election as a credible alternative to the Progressive Conservatives on the right of the political spectrum. Although the party had moved a considerable distance from the doctrines espoused by William Aberhart in the 1930s, it remained the political home for evangelical Christians, as reflected in the pool of Social Credit candidates nominated in 1957. No fewer than 11 of its 113 candidates were clergymen or lay preachers, a much larger share than in any of the other parties. In no small part because of the discovery of oil in Alberta in 1947, the provincial party had emerged as ardently pro-business. British Columbia's Social Credit government, which had been returned to office in 1956 with an increased majority, had also cornered the support of the province's business community.

Whatever hope Social Credit had of replacing the Conservatives came to an end when the latter chose John Diefenbaker as their leader. Social Credit had no one to match him on the hustings, nor did the parliamentary party have any frontbenchers with debating skills equivalent to those of Davie Fulton or Stanley Knowles. Less attention was paid to Solon Low and his colleagues, both in the Commons and on the 1957 and 1958 campaign trails; the media found little that was worth reporting about Social Credit. With a skeleton staff in its small national office and campaign organization, Social Credit fell back on the organizational efforts and financial support of the Alberta and British Columbia parties.[37] But as those two provincial organizations differed from one another in their commitment to Social Credit doctrines and in their election strategies, Social Credit had a difficult time being taken seriously as a national party.

Within months of taking office, Diefenbaker's cabinet ministers sensed that the public was increasingly supportive of the fledgling Conservative government. They were also convinced that the

Liberals, the CCF, and the Social Credit party were, as Denis Smith recorded, "tired, demoralized, and debt-ridden."[38] They were in no position to fight another election. Not surprisingly, the Tories were itching to call one – one that would give them a majority in Parliament, their first since 1930.

4

The Issues in 1957

THE 1957 GENERAL ELECTION proved the maxim that campaigns can make a difference. This was so not least because of the powerful and colourful campaign rhetoric of the Conservatives' new leader, John Diefenbaker. The 1957 and 1958 elections were *his* elections. He became the topic of conversation. among prospective voters, the object of media attention, and the principal focus of the Conservative campaign. The issues as he defined them were tailor-made for his style of campaigning.

The principal issues in 1957 related one way or another to how the St. Laurent Liberals had handled the great questions of the day, particularly in their final year in office: financing the TransCanada pipeline, responding to the Suez Crisis, increasing old-age pension payments, and supporting Canada's agricultural sector. These all became fodder for the opposition parties in what turned out to be an unruly final session of Parliament in advance of the 1957 election.

As we shall see in the next chapter, there was an additional, and in many ways more powerful, issue that played out in 1957, at least in the hands of the opposition: the length of the Liberal government's time in office. Bringing an end to the Liberals' twenty-two straight years in office became a cornerstone of the Conservatives', and to a lesser extent the smaller parties', 1957 campaign. Not surprisingly, their overall message was framed either as "Time for a Change" or, in the case of the Tories, "Time for a Diefenbaker Government." Other points of contention divided the Liberal government from the opposition parties, of course, but "Time for a Change" was a theme common to them all.

The Pipeline Debate

On rare occasions, a monumental debate in Canada's Parliament may lead a government to invoke closure to ensure a bill's passage. Two examples from Canadian history come to mind. In 1913, closure was used for the first time to force a vote (following two weeks of continuous, rancorous debate in the Commons) on the Conservative government's Naval Aid Bill, and the great flag debate of 1964 was finally ended with the imposition of closure after months of acrimonious debate in the Commons.[1]

The St. Laurent government's 1956 bill to authorize the construction and financing of a major pipeline joins the small group of "closured" bills that have entered the history books. Controversy arose not only because of the provisions of the bill itself but also because the notice of intent to invoke closure was given by the minister as he introduced the bill. In other words, closure was invoked *in advance of* any debate on the bill. This was (and remains) unprecedented.

The best way to understand why the pipeline debate shaped Canadian politics as it did in 1956 and subsequently is to learn about the fate of an earlier bill, the Defence Production Act (Amendment) Bill of 1955, and about the minister at the centre of both the defence production and pipeline controversies, the Honourable C.D. Howe. Howe was a power unto himself. In his twenty-two years in Parliament and as a cabinet minister, he had been responsible for five different departments, all of utmost consequence over the years: Transport, Munitions and Supply, Reconstruction, Trade and Commerce, and Defence Production.

Howe was blunt and straightforward, two not always endearing attributes in politics. He was not, in the judgment of one of Canada's leading historians, Donald Creighton, "a natural, instinctive parliamentarian."[2] This was unfortunate for a man upon whom the government placed so many weighty responsibilities. His colleagues and the public were aware of his short-tempered management of issues that were of great public importance and that deserved thoughtful scrutiny. Although he was held in considerable esteem by the business community for his leadership in mobilizing Canada's war effort and in transforming the postwar economy back to a free-enterprise one, Howe's handling of the defence production and pipeline bills gave the opposition a much-needed boost going into the 1957 election. In its own way, his management of both bills in the Commons contributed significantly to the fact that the 1957 and 1958 elections became "turning point" elections.

The longer Howe served in the cabinet, the more impatient he became with parliamentary and constitutional niceties. By the mid-1950s, his obvious frustration with normal rules of procedure and debate were capturing headlines. Several "Howe-isms" were quoted gleefully by opposition members in the House and on the campaign trail. When an opposition MP denounced Trans-Canada Air Lines (the forerunner to Air Canada, and one of the dozen or so Crown corporations for which Howe was responsible) as an example of "socialism," Howe snapped angrily, "That's not public enterprise; that's *my* enterprise."[3] Explaining that the role of his Department of Defence Production amounted to nothing more than that of a "purchasing agent," he declared that "if the [military] services say they need a gold-plated piano, it is our duty to buy it."[4] "Who would stop us?" he blasted across the aisle at an opposition member when questioned about the need for a particular government initiative, and in answer to an opposition question about possible abuse of power by the government, he declared that "if we have overstepped our powers, I make no apology for having done so."[5] Possibly the best-remembered "Howe-ism" was his scornful dismissal of an opposition member's question on budgetary estimates for the Department of Munitions and Supply, when he shouted, "What's a million?" across the aisle.[6] Creighton concluded his study of Canada from 1939 to 1957 by observing that Howe's manner in Parliament had become "rude" and "contemptuous," and that his "dictatorial powers" had "antagonized many members."[7]

In 1955, a bill to amend the Defence Production Act amounted to a request to Parliament to extend the act for a further five years. It could have been dealt with in short order, but it was not. The original bill had been drafted by Howe in 1951 after Canada's armed forces joined in the United Nations' defence of South Korea following an attack by communist North Korea. In addition to establishing a new department (the Department of Defence Production, of which Howe became the first minister), the 1951 act granted exceptional powers to the government and to the minister himself. It "revived most of the sweeping powers originally given the government in 1939 [at the outbreak of the Second World War], enabling it to mobilize the material resources of the country for an all-out military effort."[8] The minister could, if he deemed it necessary, "force manufacturers to make what he wanted, at prices set by himself," and "seize a manufacturer's premises and operate [the] business."[9] The bill stipulated that the powers were to be granted for five years and that they should not, according to Howe during the 1951 debate in the House, "be of a continuing nature."[10]

Those stipulations soon went by the board, however. The 1951 act was set to expire in 1956. Why the government chose to renew it in 1955 has never been adequately explained. The Korean conflict had ended with an armistice in 1953, and although the Cold War continued unabated, the need to extend the mandate of the Defence Production Act and, more to the point, the extraordinary "temporary emergency" powers of the minister a year before the act's expiration date was open to serious question.

Serious questioning? Perhaps "furious debates" would better describe what followed in the Commons as the Conservatives dug in their heels and were joined by the two smaller parties in proposing that a time limit be placed on the special powers granted to the minister.[11] Howe's bill called for those powers to be made permanent, and the opposition parties charged that he was acting like a dictator in seeking to prolong the grant of unparalleled peacetime powers to the minister and that the government was behaving in an arrogant and autocratic manner.

With the Tories determined to obstruct passage of the 1955 bill and the government (notably Howe) equally determined to have it passed without amendment, the stage was set for a conflict not seen in Parliament in many years. The Conservatives successfully mounted a filibuster that eventually prompted the prime minister and the leader of the opposition (George Drew) to meet in private and come to an understanding – while Howe was away from Ottawa – to work out a compromise to end the stalemate. They agreed that for the bill to overcome the opposition's objection, a relatively short extension would be an acceptable limitation of the minister's extraordinary powers. The concession infuriated Howe, but there was nothing he could do about it as the negotiated, bipartisan bill was quickly approved by Parliament.

The end of the stalemate was hailed as Drew's "hour of triumph in the House,"[12] and the Progressive Conservatives were said to have won "their greatest victory in twenty years in opposition."[13] Howe had lost the political clash over the Defence Production Act, but a much larger battle awaited him over his handling of the TransCanada pipeline legislation. The point of understanding the fate of the Defence Production Act is clear: emboldened by their parliamentary victory, the Tories, joined by the CCF, enthusiastically tackled Howe the following year.

The issue of financing of the pipeline played out as a case study in how a government should *not* conduct public policy. Described as an act of "atrocious political misjudgment"[14] and as a self-inflicted, "utterly ham-fisted" move on the government's part,[15] the Liberals' attempt to authorize the construction of a pipeline to carry natural gas from Alberta to Central Canada spelled trouble from the get-go. Against skillful parliamentarians such as Stanley Knowles and Davie Fulton on the opposition benches arguing points of order and procedure, the government was clearly outmatched.

The twofold purpose of Howe's push to authorize the pipeline was to ensure (1) that financial arrangements to build a gas pipeline from Alberta to Central Canada on an entirely Canadian route were in place, and (2) that construction could begin forthwith to take advantage of the best possible summer weather conditions. Given the treatment accorded their Defence Production Act in the House, the Liberals were certain that the Progressive Conservative front bench, working in close collaboration with the CCF leadership, would obstruct passage of the bill by way of filibusters and a never-ending succession of points of order. Speaking on a national radio address in early March 1956, Diefenbaker drew a comparison to the fate of the Defence Production Act: "That battle we won. But let me tell you that the fight we put on then will appear a mere skirmish beside the battle we will wage when the bill regarding the Trans Canada Pipeline comes before Parliament."[16] One CCF MP warned the government that "it ain't seen nothin' yet."[17] The debate on the Defence Production Act had turned out to be a dress rehearsal for the pipeline debate.

There was no question about the political support for construction of the pipeline, or any doubt that it should be built in Canada. The Conservative government of Ontario had given strong backing to the proposal and pledged $35 million to assist in the construction of the uneconomical northern Ontario section of the pipeline. The

Social Credit government of Alberta and all Social Credit MPs supported the project. The principal question that united the Conservatives and the CCF and engulfed the federal government and eventually the Speaker of the House of Commons stemmed not from the fact that a gas pipeline would be built but from the government's decision to force the bill through the House without adequate debate and consideration.

The CCF repeatedly called for the pipeline to be publicly, rather than privately, owned. The Tories viewed the financial arrangements, whereby the Government of Canada would advance up to 90 percent of the cost of constructing a portion of the pipeline to a predominantly American-controlled syndicate, as a sellout to American interests. The Liberals rejected the "socialist" alternative of public ownership advanced by the CCF as unfairly favouring one form of energy over others and denounced the Conservatives' objections to the financial arrangements as blind to the reality that the vast amounts of capital that were needed to ensure construction of the pipeline simply could not be provided by Canadian investors alone.

Closure was invoked in advance at every stage of the pipeline bill's progress through Parliament: introduction, first reading, second reading, committee stage, and third and final reading. The opposition denounced the process as a sham, as a violation of the rights of Parliament, and as a further demonstration of Liberal arrogance. Extended debates over procedures and adjournment were marked by heated exchanges between Liberals and the two largest opposition parties. At one point, with the Conservative and CCF leaders in the centre aisle shouting protests against the Speaker for overturning his own ruling of the previous day on a question of privilege, all semblance of order disappeared. A motion of non-confidence in the Speaker (unprecedented to this day in Canadian history) was defeated along party lines, even though no fewer than fourteen of the procedural Standing Orders of the House of Commons had been violated by the Speaker in one day. That day, dubbed "Black Friday" by the CCF and Progressive Conservatives, stands as arguably the low point of parliamentary decorum in Canada. The only moment of levity in the whole tawdry episode came as it was drawing to a close, when Liberal backbenchers attempted to drown out their opponents with boisterous renditions of "I've been working on the pipeline" (to the tune of "I've Been Working on the Railroad") and "There'll always be a pipeline" (to the tune of "There'll Always Be an England").

Generating headlines across the country, the topic dominated nearly five days of chaotic debate in Parliament and in the end contributed more than any other issue to the defeat of the St. Laurent government in the 1957 election. The prime minister, dubbed "Louis the Silent" for his failure to take any part in the day-to-day squabbling, sat dejectedly at his desk in the House. The parliamentary correspondent for the *Winnipeg Free Press* (a staunchly pro-Liberal newspaper) described St. Laurent as appearing "impassive" and "expressionless," concluding that "at a time of high controversy, prime ministers always dominate proceedings and lead their party. Mr. St. Laurent does neither." One of Canada's leading constitutional experts, Eugene Forsey, delivered a searing indictment of the government: "Canadian freedom is very sick. The sickness will not be cured till the Canadian people win back parliamentary government. The first step in the cure is to turn the Liberals out."[18]

In his study of the pipeline dispute, historian William Kilbourn observed that the debate amounted to "the stormiest episode in Canadian parliamentary history," in which the government's "right to continue in office was thrown into question as never before."[19] As if to bear this out, a post-election survey found that of those voters who switched from supporting the Liberals in 1953 to another party in 1957, 38.2 percent claimed that they did so "because of the pipeline debate." This amounted to the largest group of "switchers" in the survey.[20]

Of greater consequence to Canadian politics than its short-term political implications in 1956–57 is the pipeline issue's long-lasting effect on partisan behaviour in the House of Commons. Two leading scholars of the Canadian Parliament point out that the pipeline fiasco changed how Parliament later operated.[21] The opposition has become more obstructionist than in the past, and calls for "parliamentary reform" have surfaced as a regular talking point among political elites, editorialists, and academics. The Conservative refrain heading into the 1957 election, to the effect that the "Liberal cabinet had usurped the House's powers – and thus ... the country's liberties,"[22] struck a sympathetic chord with many Canadians. The question of the rights of Parliament became "entangled in the thorns of the pipeline question."[23] It is not a stretch to say that the pipeline debate helped prepare the ground for Diefenbaker's attempt to ensure – by way of his statutory Canadian Bill of Rights of 1960 – some measure of protection for the civil liberties of Canadians against, among other things, abuse of executive power.

At its base, the heated debate over the pipeline meant that the message transmitted to Canadians was that the Liberal cabinet had rammed legislation through the House and, in the process, had abused Parliament. The opposition parties, particularly the Progressive Conservatives and the CCF, following their victory on the Defence Production Act, relished the opportunity to take that message to the voters in the ensuing election. Supporting the government's pipeline initiative from its early stages, Social Credit MPs raised no serious objections on this issue during the election campaign, apart from noting that the matter was handled poorly by the Liberals. On balance, however, given the relatively little attention paid to Social Credit by the press and voters outside Alberta, their opinion scarcely mattered.

The 1956 Suez Crisis

Outside of wartime, Canada's international relations and foreign policies have rarely played a part in the country's elections. The 1957 election was a notable exception. Two almost simultaneous incidents dominated international affairs in the autumn of 1956, and the second proved to be of some value to the Conservatives during the 1957 campaign.

The two incidents were (1) the brutal suppression by the Soviet and Warsaw Pact armies of an unarmed citizens' uprising against the communist regime in Hungary in October 1956, and (2) an assault on Egypt the following month by the armed forces of Britain, France, and Israel. The Anglo-French-Israeli joint military action was a response to the recent nationalization of the Suez Canal by Egyptian president Colonel Gamal Abdel Nasser. Its aims were to return the canal's ownership to Western financial interests, to ensure unrestricted access to the canal, and to remove Nasser from office.

The two incidents tested the international order in a way not seen since the outbreak of hostilities in Korea in 1950. Along with its Western allies, Canada voiced strong opposition to the Soviet attack on Hungary and welcomed, according to the minister of citizenship and immigration at the time, an estimated 35,000 Hungarian refugees – more than any other country except the United States. They were admitted to Canada in late 1956 and the early months of 1957. Canada's official response to the suppression of the Hungarian Revolution had considerable support in the House of Commons and throughout the country, where arrangements were hurriedly made to provide housing, clothing, and provisions for the refugees as winter set in. Domestically, the Hungarian crisis did not become a divisive issue for either the country or the political parties.

Canada's response to the carefully orchestrated invasion of Egypt by Britain, France, and Israel played out differently, however. It gained prominence domestically as an important issue in the 1957 election but was scarcely mentioned in the election campaign the following year. The invasion backfired spectacularly. Although the United Nations Security Council was unable to end the conflict because of the British and French vetoes, the matter was successfully referred to the General Assembly, which approved a Canadian-sponsored resolution establishing the first UN Emergency Force (the forerunner of today's UN Peacekeeping forces).[24]

The attack on Egypt put the unity of the NATO alliance at stake, largely because the United States strenuously opposed it. Most of the Commonwealth countries also opposed the attack, but a few (notably Australia and New Zealand) voiced support for Britain. The future of NATO and of the Commonwealth hung in the balance as a serious schism developed between Britain and France and their closest allies.

Canada sided with the Americans in opposing the attack. In retrospect, this must be regarded as a watershed moment in the history of Canadian foreign relations, signalling the beginning of a shift from a basically pro-British bias to a pro-American one in Canada's international partnerships. From the joint Canadian-American initiative in establishing the North American Aerospace Defense Command (NORAD) in 1957, through various defence development sharing programs and the Canada-US Auto Pact of 1965, to the Canada-US Free Trade Agreement (FTA), the North American Free Trade Agreement (NAFTA), and most recently the US-Mexico-Canada (USMCA) Agreement, Canadian and American military cooperation and commercial and industrial integration have become hallmarks of the bilateral relationship. By 1960, it was obvious that the "British connection was no longer vital to Canada's international personality."[25] Canada's response to the Suez Crisis was the most powerful example to that point (1956) of the country's changing allegiances.

In the short run, however, the St. Laurent government's response to the crisis put fire in the Tories' bellies. It prompted the Conservative front bench to launch a full-scale assault on the Liberals

in the House of Commons for what they alleged to be an abandonment of Canada's two mother countries and the newly created state
of Israel. If nothing else, the condemnation of the government's
handling of the Suez Crisis brought forth colourful, media-ready
language from both the Liberals and Conservatives. The two
smaller parties differed in their responses but basically sat this one
out. The CCF supported the government for, in the words of party
leader M.J. Coldwell, by "making the move into the Suez ... Great
Britain largely forfeited [the] moral leadership" of the world,[26]
whereas Social Credit chose not to brand Britain and France as
aggressors. Both parties made few references to Suez during the
1957 campaign.

The Conservatives did not hold back, however, adopting a stri-
dently pro-British attitude in both Parliament and the subsequent
election campaign. In late November 1956, Prime Minister St.
Laurent defended his government's objections to the British-French-
Israeli attack and its strong support for the establishment of a UN
peacekeeping force, telling the House that the "era when the supermen of Europe could govern the whole world has and is coming
close to an end."[27] That was all the Conservatives needed to remind
voters of how, in their view, Canada had forsaken its allies. In a
well-received speech to the House on the Suez Crisis, Diefenbaker
declared that "such words should not have fallen from the lips of
a man who enjoys the respect the Prime Minister does."[28]

The label "supermen of Europe," together with the claim that
under the Liberals Canada had become "chore boy to the U.S.A.,"
entered the Tories' 1957 campaign lexicon and appeared in speeches
by candidates and prominent Tories across the country. The Conservatives accused the government of failing to stand up to some
"tin pot dictator" in Egypt. They attacked the prime minister for
leading a government that "did not have the backbone" to support
its allies as it was "so busy currying favour with the United States."
They described Canada as having knifed its "best friends in the

back" and of having become "the United States' chore boy." The favourable image of the prime minister as "Uncle Louis kissing babies" was said to have gone "out the window" with his government's handling of the issue.[29]

The verbal battle over the direction of Canada's foreign policy was joined just months before the 1957 election. In all likelihood, it had a modest though nonetheless positive impact on the Tories' support. According to one post-election survey, 5.1 percent of those who had voted Liberal in the previous election switched to an opposition party in 1957 because of the government's position on the Suez Crisis.[30] In his post-election assessment, however, St. Laurent's confidant and one of the Liberals' leading figures in the 1957 campaign, Jack Pickersgill, saw the Suez incident differently. He believed the Liberals' stand on the Suez invasion "may have [cost us] more seats than any other issue."[31]

"Six Buck Boys"

Government-financed old-age pensions had first been introduced in Canada in 1927 for men and women seventy years or more. J.S. Woodsworth deserves some of the credit for this because of his persistent pressure on the Mackenzie King's government. The original publicly funded old-age pension scheme included a means test to establish an individual's income level. To qualify for the $20 a month, the recipient had to be a British subject who had lived in Canada for at least twenty years. Status Indians were excluded. Benefits were restricted to those whose income, *including* the $240 pension, was less than $365 per year.

Over the years, the program was gradually expanded, and in 1952 a more comprehensive program was introduced. The Old Age Security Act of 1952 established the first universal pension scheme for Canadian citizens who had lived in the country for twenty years or more. The qualifying age remained at seventy years, but the means test was dropped, and Status Indians were included for the first time.

The monthly payment was set at $40, where it remained for four years until the Liberals raised it by $6 a month.

The three opposition parties were indignant. They criticized what they alleged was the stinginess of the $6 per month increase and accused the government of being tight-fisted and treating senior citizens in a demeaning manner. Moreover, "new Canadians" who had contributed to the support of the program through their taxes and who had reached the age of seventy were disgruntled because if they had not yet lived in Canada for twenty years, they were not eligible to receive any benefit from the program.

The CCF pledged to increase the monthly pension for those sixty-five and over to $75. Social Credit raised the ante by another $25 per month. As neither party stood a chance of forming the government, such figures could not be taken seriously. On the other hand, the Conservatives played their hand more cautiously by announcing that an increase of some unspecified amount in the old-age pension would be forthcoming should they form the government. The Liberals hung tough on the $6 a month increase, although there was strong pressure on the finance minister from within his own party to raise it by another $4, to $10 a month. The official reason for rejecting an increase was that any larger amount would be inflationary, but this failed to resonate with at least some of the electorate. A post-election survey determined that voters were keenly aware of this issue. Of those who switched from voting Liberal in 1953 to supporting another party in 1957, 26.7 percent cited the inadequate increase in old-age pensions.[32]

Supporting Canada's Agricultural Sector

The farm vote was a big deal in the 1950s, for obvious reasons. Every party courted farmers because they formed a significant part of the total Canadian population of 16 million. The 1956 census determined that 2.7 million people lived on farms, roughly 17 percent of the total population. An equal number were classified as "rural," that is, residents of small towns and villages adjacent to farms. Since then, Canada's total population has more than doubled to over 35 million, but its farm population has dropped by 90 percent, to 270,000, or less than 1 percent of the total population, and its small towns and villages have rapidly disappeared.[33]

A comparison of the number and location of electoral districts in the three Prairie provinces in the 1950s (provinces in which the number of rural residents constituted a major share of the total population) provides another way of looking at the dramatic shift from a rural to an urban Canada over the past six decades. At the time of the 1957 election, fewer than eleven of the forty-eight electoral districts in the prairies were in the region's five principal cities.[34] By the time of the 2021 election, the share of strictly urban seats in those three provinces exceeded 50 percent (thirty-two of sixty-two districts), with many others in mixed but predominantly urban districts.

In this light, it is understandable why government policies relating to the agricultural industry were such an important point of departure for parties competing in elections in the 1950s. The Liberals pretty much owned the farm vote in Atlantic Canada, Quebec, and Ontario. The Conservatives posed no serious threat in the rural parts of those provinces, and the smaller parties were not players east of Manitoba. Only in Western Canada did the Liberals face electoral challenges: in Alberta from Social Credit, and, intermittently, in Manitoba, Saskatchewan, and the hinterland of British Columbia from the CCF. The Conservatives had not been a factor in the non-urban parts of Western Canada since 1935.

Heading into the 1957 election, the circumstances were ominous for a party long in office, especially one as long as the Liberals at that point. Twenty-two years had taken a toll and their political antennae seemed to have been tuned out to the circumstances of many farmers, especially those on the prairies. By 1955, prairie farm net income had dropped by over one-half from just two years earlier, and American grain surpluses and export subsidies were taking a toll on Western Canadian farmers. In a word, the Americans were dumping their grain onto world markets at below-average prices, leaving Canadian farmers with little option but to store theirs in already bulging granaries.

The Conservatives and CCF rose to the occasion and hammered the government on this issue. Blaming the Liberals for the plight of farmers in general, they pressed in the House and on the campaign trail for cash advances on farm-stored grain. Rejecting that idea out of hand, C.D. Howe (who, along with his many other responsibilities, was minister in charge of the Canadian Wheat Board, the exclusive marketing agent for wheat and barley grown in Western Canada), countered with a proposal to increase government-guaranteed loan limits for farmers. This idea did not sit well with farmers, for the last thing they wanted was a loan. They needed immediate help. Even the pro-Liberal *Winnipeg Free Press* denounced Howe's scheme as "mere tinkering" with the problem. His biographers noted that Howe's "refusal to consider special subsidies only aroused further hostility" among farmers.[35] As a larger percentage of rural residents generally voted in an election than urban ones, the Liberals were at risk of losing a number of their seats on the prairies. They held one-third of the region's forty-eight seats going into the 1957 election, and although they thought they might lose a few, they had no idea what lay ahead.

The government played the farm card poorly, making a bad situation worse. The legendary Jimmy Gardiner (minister of agriculture for twenty-two years at that point, and former premier of Saskatchewan) had no success in getting his cabinet colleagues to approve construction of a major dam on the South Saskatchewan River, a dam that farmers in the area had long pushed for. He went into the 1957 election empty-handed, as it were. But more damaging to the Liberals was their deployment of Howe to speak at election rallies on the prairies. It is no accident that Howe was at the centre of the dust-up over Canada's agriculture policy. As "Minister of Everything" in the St. Laurent government, he was not popular for his "failure to sell Canadian wheat," as the opposition contended. There were unconfirmed reports of a Manitoba farmer blasting his television set with a shotgun when Howe's picture appeared on an evening newscast sometime in 1957. As we shall see, Howe was far from an ideal choice for the Liberals to send into boisterous meetings on the prairies during the campaign.

5

The 1957 Campaign

THE 1957 AND 1958 general elections can be summed up easily. The 1957 election was the Liberals' to lose. They did. And the election of 1958 was the Progressive Conservatives' to win. They did. Why did these elections turn out as they did? Were the outcomes determined before the campaigns began? The answer is no for 1957 and yes for 1958.

The outcome of the 1957 election was due to a confluence of four separate but interconnected realities:

- the Liberals' business-as-usual, complacent, arrogant, and testy approach to the campaign, combined with their uncharacteristically uninspiring performance
- John Diefenbaker's victory in his party's leadership race barely months before the election and his unleashing of a full-frontal attack on the Liberals, in which he laid claim to a "New National Policy"
- the Conservatives' surprisingly robust, albeit small, national organization
- the support of the federal party by Conservative premiers and their organizations.

The Liberal Campaign

Long known as "Canada's natural governing party," the Liberals had entered their third consecutive decade in office when they called the 1957 election. As the clear front-runner according to the Gallup Poll, the major national survey of voter intentions at the time, they appeared poised once again to win a comfortable majority of seats in the House of Commons. In his biography of Lester Pearson, John English notes the degree of confidence that pervaded the Liberal Party. They regarded as "certain" their return to office.[1] Perhaps most famously, *Maclean's* magazine ran a cover story a week before the election stating that Canada was about to re-elect the Liberals, and that the Liberals would form "one of the most powerful governments ever created."[2]

The Liberals had every reason to feel confident. A poll released less than seven weeks before the June 10 election showed that 74 percent of Canadians considered St. Laurent to be "doing a good job."[3] This was a remarkable figure considering that he had been prime minister for nine years at that point and his government had, just months earlier, been the target of relentless opposition attacks over its handling of the pipeline issue, old-age pensions, the Suez conflict, and federal-provincial financial relations. St. Laurent himself was confident of being returned to office. In the run-up to the election, he informed one of his colleagues that if the Liberals were facing off against George Drew, they would win, but facing John Diefenbaker increased their chances by a factor of ten.[4]

It was not hard to find examples of Liberal arrogance drawn in part from their self-perceived invincibility. One senior member of the party dismissed Diefenbaker out of hand: "Everybody [in the Liberals] felt the same way. Here was Dief. from way out west. What influence had he in central Canada, even the Maritime provinces? He was relatively unknown."[5] The Liberals were so certain of winning that they left sixteen Senate seats and a number of judicial positions vacant, no doubt looking forward to filling them once the dust had settled. It was not long before the Conservatives themselves filled those positions.

Remarkably for a party that had been in office for so long, the Liberals enjoyed a 19-point lead over the Progressive Conservatives at the start of the year: 50.6 percent to 31.7 percent. Not even Diefenbaker's recent selection as Tory leader had put a dent in their support. The January 1957 poll also found that, at 11 percent, support for the CCF had not budged from its share of the vote in 1953, but that Social Credit support had come close to doubling, from 5.4 percent in 1953 to 9 percent. Was Social Credit poised to make its long-awaited breakthrough out of Alberta? Was this a rogue poll? Or was this increased support a spin-off from the re-election in 1956 of the BC Social Credit government with a sizable increase in number of votes and seats? Social Credit's leadership appeared to believe that the party of Solon Low was on its way to better days.

The last Gallup Poll, released two days before the June 10 election, suggested that not much had changed for the two major parties

TABLE 5.1

Share of support from decided voters received by the Liberal and Progressive Conservative Parties, according to Gallup Polls before and during the campaign

Date	Liberal (%)	Progressive Conservative (%)
October 1956	49.0	32.7
January 1957	50.6	31.7
March 1957	46.0	32.9
May 4–10, 1957	46.8	32.9
May 28–June 1, 1957	43.3	37.5
June 8, 1957 (forecast)	48.0	34.0
June 10, 1957 (election)	40.5	38.5

Source: Adapted from John Meisel, *The Canadian General Election of 1957* (Toronto: University of Toronto Press, 1962), 190.

Note: Support for both parties was determined by Gallup Polls before and during the campaign commissioned by the Canadian Institute for Public Opinion (CIPO).

since January. With 48 percent support and a lead of 14 percentage points over the Conservatives, the Liberals appeared headed for an easy victory (see Table 5.1).

The Liberals could point to many positives as they began their campaign. The cabinet ministers, some of whom had held office for twenty-two uninterrupted years, were experienced and knowledgeable about their respective portfolios. They knew government operations well, and they had a close working relationship (critics often said it was *too* close) with senior members of the public service. The Mackenzie King and Louis St. Laurent governments had guided the economy and overseen its accomplishments through several difficult periods: the last half of the Great Depression, the Second World War, the postwar recovery, and the Korean War. After protracted negotiations between the federal and provincial governments, agreement had finally been reached on a publicly funded hospital insurance program. Barely weeks before Parliament was dissolved, legislation to establish such a program was approved unanimously in both the House and the Senate.

This should have been one of the parliamentary victories that the Liberals could point to in the campaign. The kicker, however, was that federal contributions to the provinces would take effect only when a majority of provinces representing a majority of the population had established hospital insurance programs themselves. As only Saskatchewan, Alberta, and British Columbia had existing programs, they would not be eligible for federal funding until this stipulation was met. Quebec was adamantly opposed to federal "intrusion" in provincial matters, such as health, so the practical effect was that Ontario and two other provinces would have to create plans that met the federal criteria before federal transfers would start. Needless to say, the three provinces with existing hospital insurance programs were anxious to see the stipulation dropped. They sensed that this was unlikely if the Liberals were re-elected.

In the first decade after the Second World War, thousands of jobs were created, largely in southern Ontario. On balance, Canada's postwar immigration and refugee policy was deemed a success, though it was unquestionably biased in favour of whites. Going into the election, the nationwide unemployment rate hovered around what the Liberals considered a respectable 4 percent, and for the first time since before the Depression, consumer spending had increased. In the first half of 1957, inflation was running at an annualized rate of 4 percent, but this, presented side by side with an annual increase of 7 percent in Canada's industrial output, led the minister of finance to paint "a rosy picture" of the country's economy.[6]

In hindsight, however, it is safe to say that the Liberals ran a flat (for them) election campaign. After twenty-two years in office, their banal campaign slogan, "Unity, Security, Freedom," lacked originality, signalling to old-hand Liberals that the party no longer had "an all-encompassing and powerful narrative" to live by.[7] This may have been true, but the "narrative" that the Liberals had been happy to present in the 1949 and 1953 elections was to a very large extent built around their leader, the avuncular Louis St. Laurent. They saw no reason not to make the prime minister the centrepiece of the 1957 campaign.

Once again, the Liberals planned a national advertising campaign and leadership tour built around St. Laurent's family-oriented, baby-kissing persona. Years earlier, this might have had the advantage of drawing a stark contrast to the straitlaced Mackenzie King. By 1957, however, King had been away from the political scene for ten years and dead for eight, which all but ensured that the contrast would be lost on newly enfranchised voters, many of them European immigrants. The image of a benevolent "Uncle Louis" might also have had the advantage of standing in marked contrast to George Drew, who his critics considered humourless and unbending. But with Drew stepping down as Conservative leader less than a year before the election, the Liberals were left exposed to the powerful campaign rhetoric of John Diefenbaker, who, as had been the case with the CCF's J.S. Woodsworth, was an accomplished crusader with a cause. St. Laurent was many things, but he was not a crusader.

Although St. Laurent was thought to have been in fine form and ready for battle at the outset of the eight-week campaign, it gradually became apparent that he lacked the stamina and personal warmth he had displayed as prime minister in the campaigns four and eight years earlier. He became increasingly and uncharacteristically impatient with the occasional heckler at his rallies. The previous year's unruly and acrimonious debates in the Commons over the government's handling of TransCanada pipeline issue (debates in which he was, as we have seen, not a participant but a disillusioned observer) had taken a toll. For several years, generally in the winter, he had also suffered from periodic fatigue, which was best treated by holidays away from Ottawa and the daily rigours of politics. St. Laurent was in his seventy-sixth year heading into the 1957 campaign, and although he appeared to some of his colleagues to have lost interest in politics, he was still seen by others as the Liberals' best bet for retaining office.

Traditionally the Liberal Party could be counted on to have the best campaign operation of any party. Its fundraisers ensured that it had the financial support needed for a campaign, and there were volunteers and, in some cases, paid organizers at the federal, provincial, and constituency levels. Unlike the other parties, the Liberals were capable of mounting a truly "national" campaign. The Conservatives, on the other hand, were weak in Quebec, the West, and parts of Atlantic Canada. Regardless of how much they had spent in Quebec in the past (the wisdom of which, as will be seen shortly, was called into question by one of Diefenbaker's closest campaign advisers) and their various attempts to achieve a breakthrough there, from 1935 to the 1953 election, they could count on winning scarcely any constituency besides a pocket of anglophone seats in Montreal. And no matter how the CCF and Social Credit attempted to fashion a winning national campaign from their respective areas of regional strength, they failed. Thus, the Liberals enjoyed a considerable organizational and financial edge for two decades.

After over twenty years in office, it is tough to campaign on "more of the same" in an open, competitive party system with an alert opposition and a press eager to pounce on mistakes. In the past, the Liberals had had a firm handle on elections, in part because of the largely ineffective and divided opposition, and in part because of Mackenzie King's demanding leadership. The Liberals' legendary dominance on the campaign trail continued during St. Laurent's first two elections as prime minister (1949 and 1953), even though his relaxed managerial style was markedly different from his predecessor's. With the shift from a circumspect prime minister like King, who was both wily in his day-to-day manoeuvres and in absolute control of his cabinet and party organization (both the lion and the fox of which Machiavelli wrote), to a more cordial and non-interventionist leader like St. Laurent, power moved from the party organization and the prime minister to individual cabinet ministers. Ministerial responsibilities included management of the Liberal organization and election apparatus in their respective province or region, candidate selection, and patronage appointments.

Regardless of the organizational prowess of individual ministers, however, Quebec was the enduring bastion of Liberal support that the other parties found it all but impossible to breach. A comparison of the numbers of MPs elected from Quebec and Alberta from 1935 to 1957 highlights the powerful presence of Quebec in Liberal electoral calculations. The total number of federal constituencies in Quebec from 1935 to 1957 was four times that in Alberta, 343 to 85. The Liberals' organizational strength in Quebec and relative weakness in Alberta is reflected in the fact that they won 303 of those Quebec seats, compared with only 19 of Alberta's. Looked at another way, nearly 40 percent of the parliamentary seats the Liberals won between 1935 and 1957 came from Quebec, a province with 24 percent of the seats in the House of Commons, whereas Alberta gave the Liberals only 1.5 percent of the total number of seats they won over the same period. Just as the Democrats in the United States at the time counted on their base in the "Solid South" to ensure a measure of control in Congress and possibly give them the presidency, the Liberals counted on their rock-solid support in Quebec to give them a firm base on which to build a majority government.

Had the 1957 Liberal campaign followed the established pattern, once the election was called, Liberal advertising would have begun, the leader's tour would have gotten underway, and party activists would have swung into action. This was how the party approached a campaign – with a degree of precision born of experience. Things were different in 1957, however. There were some national and local print and radio ads at the start of the campaign, once again featuring photos of Louis St. Laurent, but they lacked a distinctive message about what a post-election Liberal government would accomplish. St. Laurent did not begin campaigning until day ten of the fifty-nine-day campaign, a delay that enabled the other parties, notably the Tories, to get a head start as well as monopolize news coverage at the outset of the campaign.

Besides the shift in leadership style, the toll on senior party figures taken by years in office, and the devolution of political responsibilities to cabinet ministers, a fourth factor contributed to the Liberals' loss in 1957: the party's poor showing in recent provincial elections. In 1949, Liberals held office in five provinces and were in coalition in a sixth. By the 1957 general election, they were the governing party only in the two smallest provinces (Newfoundland and Labrador and Prince Edward Island) and part of a coalition government in Manitoba. As their level of popular support declined steadily in provincial elections, the electoral machinery of the provincial parties became progressively weaker. These were not good omens for the federal party. John Meisel summed up best the situation of the Liberal Party in 1957: "The Liberal campaign [gave] the impression that there was no high command regularly examining the party's strategy and tactics, comparing these with the efforts of the opposition, and providing the central leadership which would give the party the flexibility and dynamism required to counter effectively the activities of its opponents."[8] One of the Liberals' most experienced hands at electoral organization, Senator C.G. Power, sensed trouble ahead: "From the beginning of the year right to the date of the election, various incidents brought confirmation to my mind ... that there was no real co-ordination of efforts or team play amongst the [Liberal] party leaders."[9] On top of that, the Liberal campaign organization made a curious strategic move, dispatching C.D. Howe on speaking engagements in Western Canada. The choice summed up Liberal arrogance towards Western Canadian farmers, for Howe appeared tone-deaf to their concerns relating to the Canadian Wheat Board. To many, his flippant dismissals of criticism of government policies – such as "Who's going to stop us?" and "What's a million?" – demonstrated a defiant overconfidence on the part of the Liberals.

Howe's treatment of a questioner at an openly hostile campaign rally in Manitoba was widely reported in the press. Taking offence at a question about Liberal agricultural policy, he replied, "When your party organizes a meeting, you'll have the platform ... and we'll ask the questions." What he did not know was that the question had been posed by the president of the local Liberal association! Catcalls and jeers made him even testier as the meeting wore on. Finally, pressed for an answer to a question, he retorted, "Look here, my good man, when the election comes why don't you just go away and vote for the party you support? In fact, why don't you just go away?"[10] The Liberals, who had won eight of Manitoba's fourteen seats in 1953, lost seven of them in 1957. In the election the following

year, the Conservatives captured all fourteen. Anticipating one of
the conclusions of the final chapter, it is fair to note at this point
that the 1957 election marked the end of the Liberal Party's life as
a truly national political enterprise and the beginning of the pronounced regionalization of its support.

The Progressive Conservative Campaign

Three fundamentals underpinned the Conservative victory in 1957.
The first relates to the leader and his campaign, the second to two
parts of the strategy the party pursued, and the third to the support
that Conservative premiers and their organizations gave to the
federal campaign. Together, they go a long way towards explaining
why the Conservatives captured the plurality of seats in that election,
positioning them for a successful run at a majority in 1958.

If there is merit in the claim that in an election campaign a political party is an extension of its leader, few examples illustrate this
better than the Progressive Conservatives under John Diefenbaker
in both 1957 and 1958. From the early stages of the 1957 campaign,
Conservative posters as well as newspaper and television advertisements repeated the claim that it was "Time for a Diefenbaker
Government." The idea was to shift the Conservatives' advertising
away from any association with the past – whether it was George
Drew's sometimes bellicose leadership, or R.B. Bennett's five-year
tenure as prime minister in the early years of the Great Depression,
or the party's support for conscription during both the First and
the Second World Wars. The Tory campaign had one imperative:
to convince the country of the need to replace the Liberals with
something and, more important, someone new. "It's Time for a
Diefenbaker Government" was settled on as catchphrase that would
define the 1957 Conservative campaign.

The slogan was the creation of Dalton Camp's advertising agency,
Locke, Johnson, as a way of presenting the party in the hands a new
leader with a new agenda. Camp (1920–2002), described as "one

of the most brilliant public relations experts" of his time,[11] first became active in the Conservative Party in 1950. He was a strategist and advertising guru for the party federally and in several provinces over many years, and eventually a newspaper columnist and media commentator. Convinced following the Conservatives' second defeat in less than three years (1963 and 1965) that Diefenbaker should be replaced as leader, he staked his re-election as party president on the call for a leadership convention in 1967. In that, he succeeded.

Camp's advertising firm was one of four involved in planning and executing Conservative publicity in the 1957 election. (The number of advertising firms working on the campaign prompted Camp to quip that Diefenbaker had more advertising agencies working for him than General Motors.[12]) Diefenbaker appointed another ad man, Allister Grosart, as national director of the party and election campaign manager, positions he also held in 1958. As noted in Chapter 2, Grosart and MPs Gordon Churchill (Winnipeg South Centre) and George Hees (Toronto Broadview) formed the nucleus of a small group of advisers closest to Diefenbaker throughout 1956 leadership race. For the 1957 campaign, Camp served as a speechwriter, and Merrill Menzies, who had a doctorate in economics, came on board as a policy adviser. It was a remarkable group, consisting of some of the "old guard" Diefenbaker railed against as well as (certainly in the case of Menzies, who some in the party came to refer to as Diefenbaker's "muse") a measure of new blood.

Merrill Menzies (1920–99) brought something original to the Conservative Party. Perhaps "something old reconfigured" would be a better description, for Menzies's economic policies drew their inspiration broadly from John A. Macdonald's National Policy of the 1870s. An economist with his undergraduate degree from the University of Saskatchewan and a doctorate from the London School of Economics, Menzies was a key player in developing the program on which the Conservative campaign would be based. He was of the view that Canada had not fulfilled the challenge of Macdonald's policy of developing the Western part of the country, and that only by meeting this challenge could Canada be said to have achieved an "integrated national economy."[13]

Menzies was also convinced that the policies of the Liberal Party had "no character, no vision, no purpose – with appalling consequences to our parliamentary system and national unity."[14] He advanced a proposal that Diefenbaker heartily endorsed as it fit with his belief in government playing a positive role in national development and his stated concern for, in his view, the oft-overlooked parts of the country: Atlantic Canada, Northern Ontario and Quebec, the Western provinces, and the undeveloped North – in other words, pretty well the whole of Canada except for its metropolitan centres in southern Ontario and Quebec.

Though short on details, the New National Policy was promoted as a way of ensuring the construction of a national energy grid, the development of the resources of the North, the construction of the South Saskatchewan River Dam, and power developments on the Fraser and Columbia Rivers in British Columbia. It envisioned vast improvements in the forestry, agriculture, and fishing industries and called for the expansion of railways, highways, and waterways. On paper, it amounted to a truly heroic blueprint, and it became the centrepiece of Diefenbaker's stump speeches across the country in the 1957 campaign. In the 1958 election, the New National Policy was converted into a "vision" of Canada's future. "Vision" suited Diefenbaker's campaign style to a tee, for it approached something of a secular crusade.

Diefenbaker's powerful and dramatic delivery of campaign speeches in 1957 often included ending a sentence, after a carefully timed pause, with "and HOWE!" This invariably brought audiences to their feet, cheering and clapping. His was a captivating, some said spellbinding or mesmerizing, presentation. His speeches were delivered to crowds that grew larger and larger as the campaign progressed, signalling a change in Tory fortunes. Possibly no one captured the mood of Diefenbaker's 1957 campaign rallies better than Dalton Camp in recalling a rally in Amherst, Nova Scotia. The town

is now a little down at the heel, and the townspeople listen, fascinated, to Diefenbaker's comprehensive cataloguing of the area's problems – the chronic plight of the coal industry at Springhill, doomed to be shut down; the abandoned ferry service from Parrsboro to Wolfville; the loss of local industry; the decline of agriculture; the out-migration of the young; the plight of the old, and the problems that are being created as the life is slowly squeezed from the Cumberland towns and once-prospering villages along the Fundy shore.

In the close, damp stillness of the packed hall, the only sound is Diefenbaker's vibrant, emotive voice, his the only face in the crowd – his eyes lit by the ceiling lights and by the inspiration of his calling. He invokes Suez and St. Laurent's scornful "superman" epithet, directed at the British; he excoriates "the six-buck boys" who cheated the pensioners of their just deserts. "I love Parliament," he says, abruptly, turning to the mysteries of the pipeline controversy and the secrets of parliamentary procedure.

All these concerns, vaguely felt by wounded spirits, become focused on this single man, whose face quivers from the suppressed torments of having known and suffered the rape of Parliament, the despoiling of the British connection, the humiliation of the old, and the long, steady, inexorable decline in the prospects of Cumberland County and the town of Amherst. In Diefenbaker's passion is incorporated all the grievances of his audience; he absorbs their indignation and, at the end, after they have laughed with him, cheered him, felt their nerve-ends respond to his voice, they find that he has repossessed their hopes, and they believe in him as they have not believed in anyone in a long, long time, if even then.

I leave the hall, as the crowd's ovation begins, to find a taxi to drive me to Moncton. I sit in the back, remote and silent, discouraging conversation with my driver. It is a little like watching a nightly miracle, this recurrent chemistry between Diefenbaker and his audiences.[15]

Camp's account has been cited in its entirety for what it tells about one of dozens of speeches Diefenbaker delivered in the course of both the 1957 and 1958 campaigns: a receptive and welcoming audience ready to hear a message of hope; a chronicle of local grievances; a heartfelt attachment to Parliament as the ultimate defence against the unwarranted exercise of executive power; and a promise of better days ahead with a Conservative government – all wrapped up in a style of speaking (and finger pointing) that Diefenbaker had perfected as a defence lawyer in prairie courtrooms. From the time he became Tory leader barely six months before the election, the press occasionally, and more frequently as the campaign progressed, sensed the changes afoot, calling them a "Diefenbaker Revolution." What began as a movement for change in early 1957 built gradually to the point where, in 1958, it produced, in relation to the size of the House of Commons at the time, the largest single electoral victory in Canadian history.

"Charismatic" is a term too often mistakenly applied to political leaders who happen to be popular and who enjoy widespread admiration from a substantial part of the electorate. As its name suggests, however, charisma means something more than simple popularity. It signifies a special aptitude, a personal quality that holds out a promise of deliverance for people in distress.[16] In politics, it captures the personal magnetism of an authoritative crusader whose cause is to wrest control of elected office for "the people" (in Diefenbaker's case, "the average Canadian") from those who have abused it. Diefenbaker's method of delivery was sometimes described as that of a revivalist preacher who felt the pain of those in

Diefenbaker campaigning in Quebec City, 1957. | University of Saskatch-
ewan Archives and Special Collections, JGD/MG01/XVII/JGD459

attendance and who could lead them to a better future. That is an apt comparison.

But personal charisma can also be fleeting, as it was in Diefenbaker's case. If the expectations of the followers are not met, then whatever authority might have come from identifying concerns and offering hope to address those concerns disappears. Diefenbaker's ultimate fall from office in 1963 can be seen in that light: although his government delivered on a number of promises made in 1957 and 1958, some of which (as will be seen in the concluding chapter) have had a long-term impact on Canadian society and politics, the downturn in the economy combined with the prime minister's indecision about critical matters and his growing distrust of those around him in his final years in office brought the "Diefenbaker Revolution" to an end in 1963.

The Conservatives' victory in 1957 owed much to the powerful campaign mounted by Diefenbaker and those in his immediate circle. But the party's electoral chances were also enhanced by the application of two strategies. The first had been outlined in a memorandum prepared in advance of the party's 1956 leadership convention by frontbench Winnipeg MP Gordon Churchill. The second came from the realization of senior party organizers that to win, the party needed to appeal to voters who had hesitated to vote for the Conservatives in the past but who might well be persuaded to vote for them this time. As it turned out, some of the results of the second strategy are evident to this day.

In his memorandum, Churchill analyzed his party's fortunes in federal elections since Confederation. The basic premise underlying the memo was that the Conservatives should follow the advice of gamblers, athletes, and military officers (of which Churchill had been one), and "play to your strength." He pointed out that based on the four instances when a Liberal government was defeated by the Conservatives between 1878 and 1930, the outcome was not determined by the number of seats the Tories had won in Quebec: "the great changes that result in the downfall of a [Liberal] government occurred not in Quebec but elsewhere in Canada." One of his central points was that "Quebec should not be ignored [in the Conservative campaign], but it is extremely unlikely that it will be decisive." Churchill concluded that to win office with at least a minority government, the Tories needed to increase their support in other parts of the country. This meant that in Ontario, Atlantic Canada, and the four Western provinces, the party would have to retain the 49 seats they held and win at least 60 of the 141 seats they did not hold in those areas. If they succeeded, they could form a minority government. If Quebec were to produce 20 seats, a Conservative majority could be assured.[17]

Taking account of Churchill's memo, the party's national campaign committee agreed in 1957 to abandon the recent practice of spending a disproportionately large share of its campaign funds in Quebec. With George Drew as leader in the 1953 election campaign, 45 percent of the party's national funds had been expended in Quebec, yet the Conservatives elected only four MPs from the province. The formula devised for the 1957 campaign was simple and equal: the same amount of $3,000 per federal constituency in a province would be allocated to each provincial organization. They, in turn, would decide how best to distribute the money among the various constituencies.

The other strategic move undertaken by the Conservatives in 1957 was to recraft the party's image so as to dispel a common perception of the Conservatives as a pro-business, right-of-centre group drawn largely from Toronto financial elites. Like most images, this was not entirely accurate, but in the public eye (and in Diefenbaker's mind), the Conservative Party was composed overwhelmingly of the old guard, mostly from southern Ontario. Unless the party polled at least 8–10 points above the 30 percent level of support it had averaged since 1935, the Conservatives stood no chance of forming a government. With this in mind, senior party officials moved to "broaden the base" of support by crafting the campaign and its advertisements in such a way as to attract voters who had previously not supported the Conservatives. It was determined that the most likely pool of potential Tory voters would be found among those who had previously not voted at all or, if they had voted for another party, were sufficiently dissatisfied with the Liberals that they would welcome a change as long as it was not the Tory old guard. The campaign's emphasis, in terms of both policy announcements and advertisements such as "It's Time for a Diefenbaker Government," fit the occasion perfectly. This was an unorthodox marketing approach for the party, but it matched the kind of outsider image that Diefenbaker was confident with as he waged his election battle on behalf of the average Canadian. The following year, "Follow John" was the logical extension of this almost non-partisan approach to electioneering. As well, by the policies they espoused in both elections, the Progressive Conservatives played up the "Progressive" part of their name while playing down the "Conservative" part.

The Conservative strategy of expanding their pool of voters paid off handsomely by tapping into new voters, particularly recent arrivals in Canada. The postwar immigrant and refugee population had grown by 1.5 million by the time of the elections. Over half were eligible to vote in 1957 and 1958. The new voters tended to live in the suburbs adjacent to major cities. The expanding suburban population in the period leading up to 1957 is demonstrated graphically in the case of Canada's two principal metropolitan areas.

York County, surrounding the city of Toronto, increased its seat count from four to seven over the previous decade, with the three districts created in the redistribution of 1949 (York Centre, York-Humber, and York-Scarborough) averaging 46 percent growth in their electorates between the elections of 1953 and 1957 (range: +11.6 percent to +86.9 percent). By contrast, the eleven electoral districts within the city of Toronto saw their electoral populations decline by an average of 9.7 percent (range: +3.7 percent to –14.2 percent) over the same period. The populations of similar ridings, such as Mercier, Jacques-Cartier-Lasalle, and Laval on the fringes of the city of Montreal, increased by an average of 41.7 percent (range: +31.5 percent to +51 percent) between 1953 and 1957, whereas a group of four east-end Montreal districts (Sainte-Anne, Saint-Jacques, Saint-Laurent-Saint Georges, and Sainte Marie) experienced an average decline over the same period of –12.3 percent (range: –8.2 percent to –14.1 percent).

In his study of the 1957 election, John Meisel determined that there was a "99 to 1" certainty that the increase in the Conservative share of the total vote was directly and positively linked to the increase in areas of strong population growth.[18] The same point can be made about the Conservative success in the 1958 election. The Tories had won three of the seven York County seats in 1953;

they won all seven in 1957 and 1958. In Jacques-Cartier-Lasalle, Laval, and Mercier, the Conservative candidates were a distant second 1953. In 1957, they won one of those three Island of Montreal ridings, and in 1958 they captured all three districts with sizable majorities.

Meisel offered a plausible explanation for the Tories' success in suburban Toronto and Montreal in 1957 (and by extension, 1958). It hints at the types of campaigns the two principal parties waged in that election. Diefenbaker's "aggressive" campaign style and "vigorous" development policies appealed to the more "expansionist" and forward-thinking communities. The Liberals, by contrast, drew their support from "sleepier and less alive" (and, it might be added, slower growing) parts of Canada. The Conservatives' new-found support was unquestionably linked to the growth in a constituency's electorate, much of that growth driven by postwar immigration to the suburbs of the major cities.[19]

But the Conservatives had another trick up their sleeve: targeting "new Canadians" and ethno-cultural clusters in inner cities. In 1957, the party deliberately sought votes in select electoral districts, and it paid off. The Liberals had enjoyed the support (and the votes) of many immigrants and their descendants going back to Wilfrid Laurier's time. With their "frequent anti-immigrant posture,"[20] the Conservatives had never been a match for them on that front. Diefenbaker set about changing this. He was comfortable with Canadians of non-British, non-French ancestry, and his belief in "One Canada" ensured receptive audiences. At the outset of the 1957 campaign, strategists made a point of trying to sway opinion leaders, for example, by having Diefenbaker meet with editors of a variety of Ontario and Manitoba ethnic publications – quite possibly a first for any Tory leader. By "intelligently target[ing] this collection of influencers,"[21] Diefenbaker paved the way for local campaigns to seek the support of ethno-cultural groups composed in many cases of new Canadians. At a minimum, his resolute anti-communism drew the serious attention of editors of publications distributed to the 200,000 or so refugees from Soviet bloc countries.

Two Toronto constituencies provide examples of how effective the Tories' ethno-cultural strategy proved to be. Parkdale had been won by the Liberals by comfortable margins in 1949 and 1953, and High Park had been Liberal since the end of the Second World War. Thanks to rapid immigration in the 1950s, the ridings' populations had changed markedly. By 1957, Parkdale, for instance, was said to be "50 percent new Canadians," but its Liberal MP was reported to have "neglected the ethnic vote" in the lead-up to the election. Not so for the Conservative candidate: Arthur Maloney, a popular Toronto lawyer, ran for the Tories and made the "recruitment of new Canadian voters, with an emphasis on Ukrainians and Poles," the focus of his campaign. He hosted a St. Patrick's Day party attended "by more than one hundred representatives from a dozen ethno-cultural communities," and in his door-to-door canvassing, he typically "said a few words [to prospective voters] in their own language." The following year, Maloney held a rally days before the election at which the leaders of several local groups, including those from the "Croatian, Czech, German, Hungarian, Italian, Latvian, Polish, Lithuanian and Ukrainian" communities, spoke on his behalf. He beat the incumbent Liberal by 2,100 votes in 1957 and went on to capture 52 percent of the vote to the Liberal opponent's 33 percent the following year. In High Park, an area with a high Eastern European population, the Conservative candidate was a local physician and president of the Ukrainian Council of Canada. He defeated his Liberal opponent by 2,200 votes and was re-elected in 1958 with over half the vote.[22] In both elections, Conservatives won in parts of Metro Toronto that had not gone their way in many years.

There is little doubt about the third element that contributed to the Conservative victory in 1957. Displeased over the state of federal-provincial relations (particularly with respect to transfer payments to the provinces), Ontario premier Leslie Frost threw the

Diefenbaker endorsed by Ontario premier Leslie Frost in the 1957 campaign. | Photograph by World Wide Photos, University of Saskatchewan Archives and Special Collections, JGD/ MG01/XVII/JGD 365

full support of the formidable provincial Conservative organization into the campaign. Testifying to its organizational prowess was the fact that the party had been in office for fourteen years at that point – and had almost twenty-eight more to go before being defeated. Frost, who in the past had rarely taken part in federal campaigns, played an active role in both 1957 and 1958, attending many rallies at Diefenbaker's side and speaking glowingly of the federal party. The Liberals criticized the "Frost-Diefenbaker alliance," but that hurt neither the two leaders nor their parties. There was general agreement following the 1957 election that the "unqualified and invaluable support of Premier Frost" was one of the major factors in the Conservative victory.[23] In Ontario, the Progressive Conservatives jumped from 40.3 percent of the popular vote and 33 MPs elected in 1953 to 48.8 percent of the vote and 61 MPs in 1957.

TABLE 5.2

Progressive Conservative seats and percentage of the vote in four Conservative-led provinces, 1953, 1957, and 1958 elections

	1953		1957		1958	
	Seats	Vote %	Seats	Vote %	Seats	Vote %
Ontario	33	40.3	61	48.8	67	56.4
Nova Scotia	1	40.1	10	50.4	12	57.0
New Brunswick	3	41.9	5	48.7	7	54.1
Manitoba	3	27.0	8	35.9	14	56.7
Total seats	40		84		100	

Source: Data from Howard A. Scarrow, *Canada Votes: A Handbook of Federal and Provincial Election Data* (New Orleans: Hauser Press, 1963), 145–88.

The federal Conservatives also won strong endorsements from the Tory premiers of Nova Scotia (Robert Stanfield) and New Brunswick (Hugh John Flemming), as well as the soon-to-be-elected Tory premier of Manitoba (Duff Roblin). All three had defeated provincial Liberal Parties to gain office, in the process creating strong organizations that were placed at the service of the federal party in 1957 and 1958. Like Leslie Frost, they looked forward to a more favourable federal-provincial financial arrangement under a Diefenbaker government. The Maritime premiers also expected targeted adjustment grants for their provinces, and Manitoba expected cash advances on farm-stored grain. Diefenbaker delivered on both issues prior to the 1958 election.

Table 5.2 shows how provincial support of the federal party paid off handsomely in both 1957 and 1958. In the two Maritime provinces, Ontario, and Manitoba, the Conservatives more than doubled in 1957 (84 seats) what they had won in 1953 (40 seats), and reached 100 seats the following year. The jump in Conservative support in the four provinces does much to explain the party's success in 1957. Nationally, the Conservatives went from 51 seats in 1953 to 112 in

1957. Of the 61 new seats, all but 15 came from the four provinces with strong organizations, demonstrating the truth of Gordon Churchill's maxim of "playing to your strength."

The importance of television to the Conservative campaign cannot be minimized. Television arrived on the scene in Canada in 1952, when CBC-TV and Radio-Canada began broadcasting in Toronto and Montreal. Within a few years, television replaced radio as the dominant electronic news and information medium across the country. The strong economic growth of the first half of the 1950s, along with attendant high rates of employment, led to a level of consumer purchasing power not seen since the 1920s. A television set became a must-have item for families. There were an estimated 146,000 sets in Canada in 1952; by the time Diefenbaker was chosen as Tory leader in December 1956, the number had jumped sixteen-fold, to 2.3 million.

Party organizers (particularly those running the Conservative campaign) recognized that constituency meetings and leaders' rallies attracted mainly the party faithful, whereas television could reach vastly larger numbers of uncommitted or undecided voters. Responding to the new reality of news, information, and entertainment transmission, the parties made the 1957 election the first television election throughout much of Canada. Public relations teams began scheduling events around the times of local and/or national newscasts in a bid for daily television news reports of a leader's speeches or statements by notable candidates – a classic illustration of an institution adjusting to a different, much desired mode of communication.

Parties advertised in the print media both locally and nationally as their funds permitted, but nothing matched the free time provided by CBC-TV and Radio-Canada for party broadcasts. Parties could use their allotted free time as they saw fit. The amount of time varied according to a formula determined by the network, with the Liberals and Conservatives getting the lion's share of the shows (eight and seven, respectively) and the two smaller parties proportionately fewer shows. The leaders spoke on a number of the programs, sometimes accompanied (as was Diefenbaker on the French-language shows) by a party notable from a particular province or region. It is difficult now, with the vast array of telecommunication and Internet options available to Canadians, to imagine the wide listenership of the free radio and television programs. In many parts of the country – and not necessarily remote parts either – it was pretty much the only available public affairs program.

Prime Minister St. Laurent did not take well to television. He made "few concessions to the new medium" and his performances came across as wooden and unexciting.[24] By contrast, Diefenbaker was a natural on television. At the end of the 1957 campaign, the consensus was that his vibrant performance and ease with the camera made Diefenbaker much better at attracting and holding his audiences. His messages were not always fully scripted or logically coherent, for he had a habit anytime he spoke (televised or not) of interspersing his policy announcements with themes he was most comfortable with: "Speaking for the Average Canadian," "Vision of Northern Development," "A New National Policy," "Love of Parliament," "Liberal Arrogance," and so on. But for campaigns carefully crafted by party strategists around a personality ("Time for a Diefenbaker Government" in 1957 and "Follow John" in 1958), the arrival of television was a godsend. In its own way, Diefenbaker's success with television calls to mind the phenomenal rise in popularity of Social Credit's William ("Bible Bill") Aberhart, who, in the lead-up to the 1935 Alberta provincial election, used the then-new medium, radio, to great effect.[25]

The CCF and Social Credit Campaigns

Heading into the 1957 election, the CCF and Social Credit had hopes for a breakthrough. Both parties had leaders seasoned to the rigours of campaigning, the Liberals had had a bad year in the House of Commons, the Conservatives had just chosen a new (and un-proven) leader, and, with early signs of a weakening economy, voters might well be persuaded to turn to one of the two smaller parties.

The CCF was clearly more national in reach and better known. At dissolution, it had twenty-three MPs from five provinces; in addition, it had held office in Saskatchewan since 1944 and had members of legislatures in five other provinces. The party fielded candidates in every province in 1957, 162 in all, and (while not flush) it had sufficient funds for a leader's tour and a measure of national advertising. At 27,500, party membership was at its highest level since 1949. The CCF had traditionally relied on a variety of in-house publications circulated to party members between elections, so it is not surprising that its "educational" reach was by far the most impressive of the four parties. It had volunteers in many parts of the country, some of whom had first joined the party in the 1930s. They could be counted on to promote their party's cause and canvass enthusiastically in the weeks leading up to and during an election campaign. Perhaps best of all for the CCF was that, in contrast to Social Credit, it could point to policy achievements since its first MPs were elected in 1935. The party had made an indelible mark on Canadian social policy for, as noted earlier, Mackenzie King and Louis St. Laurent saw to it that if a CCF proposal suited their government's agenda (and its political survival!), they would implement it.

Social Credit, on the other hand, could point to no major policy successes at the federal level, and Solon Low was the least known of the four party leaders. His fellow MPs came entirely from two provinces. His undistinguished parliamentary career meant that the national media paid him and his party little attention. He had not shone during the fiery pipeline debate of 1956, unlike George Drew and senior Tories and the CCF's M.J. Coldwell and Stanley Knowles. Throughout the 1957 campaign, Low had no notable parliamentarian at his side, unlike St. Laurent with his bevy of cabinet ministers, or Diefenbaker with his (formerly reluctant) parliamentary colleagues, or Coldwell with his trusty sidekick Knowles. Social Credit MPs contributed minimally to debates on national issues, and the party had little to offer that was of any relevance to the improvement of existing programs. As members sometimes gave "vent to their prejudices" (notably anti-Semitism), the party remained a marginal and occasionally controversial presence on the federal scene.[26]

Throughout the 1957 campaign, the CCF had to counter the Conservatives' claim that "a vote for the CCF is a wasted vote." The implication was clear: to defeat the Liberals, it made sense for voters to back the only party that stood a chance of doing that – the Conservatives. The "wasted vote" refrain is an old and familiar one that smaller parties have had to contend with when competing against two or three larger parties in a first-past-the-post election. To refute the claim, the CCF pointed out that in terms of their pro-business agendas, there was little difference between the Liberals and Conservatives: "Tweedledum and Tweedledee," as Tommy Douglas liked to describe them. Thus, the CCF argument went, a vote cast for the CCF would be a vote against both old-line parties. Besides, as the CCF leadership repeatedly stated, it was the Conservatives who were not even the "third party" in Western Canada: they were the fourth. In 1953, the Tories had won only nine of the seventy seats in the four Western provinces, compared with twenty-five for the Liberals, twenty-one for the CCF, and fifteen for Social Credit.

The replacement of the Regina Manifesto by the Winnipeg Declaration in 1956 led to some moderation in the CCF party platforms in 1957 and 1958. The party continued to call for increased social welfare services as well as a national medical care insurance program, but it no longer advocated doctrinaire socialist principles such as the nationalization of key industries and a stated aim of replacing capitalism that had been championed in the 1933 manifesto. The more pragmatic program was attacked by militant members of the party for its apparent shift to the right and to appeal to Canada's growing organized labour movement.

There was truth in such criticism, but, as senior party members who supported moderation, such as Stanley Knowles, David Lewis, and Frank Scott, argued, the best road ahead for Canadian socialism was for the CCF to become more relevant to the times and to reach a practical accord with the labour movement. This, they claimed, would advance the cause of both the party and organized labour. Although originally cool to the idea of the idea, Coldwell headed into the 1957 campaign as an ardent supporter of a CCF-labour link. He had come to the conclusion that the agreement would ultimately lead to a party similar to Labour parties in Britain, Australia, and New Zealand. The shift towards a more moderate program, combined with the move to incorporate organized labour into the party, proved to be a lasting legacy of the party's ideological and organizational repositioning in advance of the 1957 election. Once this repositioning culminated in the creation of the New Democratic Party in 1961, Canada's democratic socialist movement had reached a point in its history from which there would be no turning back.

6

A New Parliament, a New Leader, and Another Election

THE 1957 ELECTION RESULTS stunned the country. The Liberals were reduced to 105 seats, a drop of 66 from four years earlier, and the Tories more than doubled their representation, from 51 to 112. The CCF added 2 seats, for a total of 25, and Social Credit 4, for a total of 19, but clearly neither party made the breakthrough they had hoped for. Nine members of the St. Laurent cabinet were defeated, including the ministers of defence, finance, and justice, and, to the delight of the Tories, C.D. Howe.[1] Nationally, the Liberals won a greater share of the popular vote than the Conservatives (40.9 percent to 38.9 percent), but that was a reflection largely of their continuing strength in Quebec, where they beat the Tories decisively, 57.6 percent to 31.1 percent. Apart from Saskatchewan and Alberta (where the smaller parties remained dominant) and Newfoundland and Labrador (staunchly Liberal), in all other provinces either the two parties were tied in the popular vote or the Conservatives won comfortably. Notably, in vote-rich Ontario, the Tories gained 28 seats and increased their share of the popular vote by 8 percentage points over their 1953 totals. For their part, the Liberals lost 30 seats in the province and their electoral support dropped 9 percentage points. (See the map on page 2 for the 1957 election results. Appendix 3, Table A1, presents the complete province by province breakdown by votes and seats.)

In seven of Canada's forty-four elections from 1867 to 2021, one of the two principal parties has won more votes but fewer seats than its leading opponent. The 1957 election was one of them.[2] The St. Laurent government need not have resigned, for it was entitled to "test the waters" in the House of Commons at the first available opportunity to see whether it could command majority support. According to one of Louis St. Laurent's senior staff members, the prime minister would have none of that. His "first and only reaction" was to "hand over the reins of power to John Diefenbaker as promptly and in as orderly a fashion as possible."[3] It was all but certain that he would resign as party leader shortly thereafter.

The Liberal defeat resulted from a variety of factors: the party's lacklustre campaign, combined with an overconfidence and sense of entitlement that comes with repeated electoral success; the unexpected vigour of the Tory organization; John Diefenbaker's commanding presence on the campaign trail; the appeal of the Conservatives' imaginative New National Policy platform; and the vigorous support of Tory premiers and their provincial parties.

An increased level of voter participation also played an important role in bringing an end to the Liberals' period in office. Voter turnout jumped to 74.1 percent – a full 6.6 points over the 1953 figure. But what really mattered was *where* the vote increased. There was a marked jump in turnout in constituencies with growing numbers of first-time voters. Some were newly enfranchised and others had not previously voted. Both were attracted to the Tories in 1957. It was in those faster-growing constituencies that the Tories defeated incumbent Liberals, often by sizable margins, which led John Meisel to note an inverse relationship: "the greater the increase in turnout [in the new areas], the greater ... the Liberal party's loss."[4]

Voter turnout in federal elections is never uniform across Canada. The 1957 election was no exception, as can been seen in turnout levels in Canada's two largest provinces. Compared with the rest of their province, the two major metropolitan areas recorded among the lowest levels in the country: 68.7 percent in Metropolitan Toronto (including neighboring York County), compared with 76.3 percent in all other parts of Ontario; and 63.7 percent on the Island of Montreal, compared with 79.6 percent in the rest of Quebec. Of special note is the fact that in Canada's smallest riding at the time, Îles de la Madeleine in Quebec, 90.9 percent of the 5,052 registered electors voted, a record high for the country in that election.

The election's surprising outcome owed much to the campaign waged by the Tories. It was crafted in such a way as to hold both the CCF and Social Credit at bay and to make the Conservatives the chief beneficiary of the opposition's united call of "time for a change." For this to work, the Conservatives needed a performance from their leader that would command positive media and public attention across the country. As the campaign wore on, they got what they hoped for – increasing media attention and greater "buzz" in the proverbial coffee rows about the new, different leader of what no longer looked like an old party. Diefenbaker's crowd-pleasing rallies and skillful use of television set him apart from the other leaders and turned 1957 into a "Diefenbaker election," as many in the press and leading politicians in other parties acknowledged, sometimes grudgingly. Dalhousie University political scientist Murray Beck, whose studies on Canadian elections included 1957 and 1958, pointed to Tory posters of upcoming political rallies as proof of the party's leader-centred campaign. Diefenbaker's portrait was featured prominently, with a reference to "Progressive Conservative Party of Canada" only in small print at the bottom. The Conservative campaign became a "one-man show."[5]

Unlike elections in many other Western democracies, since the Second World War those at the federal level in Canada where the governing party was defeated have sometimes been a bloodbath for the losing party and a massive win for the victorious party. Two such elections in the past forty years illustrate this. The end of the Pierre Trudeau/John Turner governments in 1984 brought the Conservatives, led by Brian Mulroney, to office. Reduced to only 40 seats, the Liberals suffered the worst defeat in their party's history, whereas the Conservatives gained 108 seats and ended up with the largest number of seats ever won by any party in Canada – 211 out of 282. Nine years and one intervening election later, the massive Tory presence in the House was wiped out when the Conservatives were reduced to 2 seats. The Mulroney/Kim Campbell era came crashing down as the Liberals under Jean Chrétien swept to office with 177 MPs, an increase of 137 over their 1984 standing.

The Diefenbaker government's tenure, beginning in 1957/1958 and ending in 1963, was similar in one respect but not in another. In 1953, the Conservatives had won only 51 ridings to the Liberals' 171. Five years later, in the second of the two consecutive elections with Diefenbaker as leader, the tables were turned, with the Tories winning 208 seats to the Liberals' 49. The Diefenbaker government's defeat in 1963 was not of the same magnitude, however, in contrast to the abrupt end of the Trudeau/Turner and Mulroney/Campbell governments. As will be seen in the concluding chapter, the turning point elections of 1957 and 1958 brought about a reconfiguration of the party system that survived the defeats of 1962 and 1963 and, with modifications, is with us still.

A consequence of periodic massive changes in party standings, as in 1957/58, 1984, and 1993, is that Canada, unlike the United Kingdom and the United States, experiences both a rapid turnover in the composition of the House of Commons and, apart from a relatively few veteran MPs on the front benches, a dearth of experienced parliamentarians. In the United Kingdom, 70 percent of MPs serve at least ten years, regardless of changes in government. The proportion of newly elected MPs rarely exceeds 20 percent, which means that when a transition does take place, the prime minister has seasoned parliamentarians to call on in constructing a cabinet. Turnover·in the US House of Representatives is even rarer than in the United Kingdom. Roughly 90 percent of members of Congress typically run for re-election, and of that group 90 percent are re-elected. By contrast, Canadian MPs serve on average half as long as their British counterparts and considerably less than members of the US Congress, and they are far more likely to lose their seats when their party is defeated.[6]

A New House, a New Cabinet

It is sometimes said that a prime minister has little choice but to assemble a cabinet of his enemies. This was only partially true in Diefenbaker's case. Some of his ministers had been known opponents; others were among his supporters. Two of Diefenbaker's opponents in the leadership race were given important ministries: Davie Fulton (Justice) and Donald Fleming (Finance). Leon Balcer, the president of the Progressive Conservative Party, who had openly opposed Diefenbaker for leader, became minister of mines and solicitor general and, later, transport minister. Ellen Fairclough, a member of the party's old guard who told Diefenbaker she had voted for Davie Fulton for the leadership became secretary of state and subsequently minister of citizenship and immigration. Howard Green, who supported Donald Fleming at the 1956 leadership convention, was given Public Works, followed by External Affairs. Two veteran MPs who were part of a group of Tory frontbenchers who considered Diefenbaker temperamentally unsuited for leadership also entered cabinet: George Nowlan (minister of national revenue) and J.M. Macdonell (minister without portfolio).

Before entering Parliament through a 1950 by-election, Ellen Fairclough (1905–2004) had been a city councillor and an accountant in Hamilton, Ontario. She was the sixth woman elected to the Commons and the first to be appointed a cabinet minister. Hers was a strong voice in cabinet for Canada's Indigenous people, and,

John Diefenbaker and Ellen Fairclough at a desk once belonging to Sir John A. Macdonald. Prime Minister's Office, Centre Block, Parliament Buildings, 1960. | Photograph by Batten, University of Saskatchewan Archives and Special Collections, JGD/MG01/XVII/JGD 3431

as will be seen in Chapter 8, as minister of citizenship and immigration, she was instrumental in ushering legislation through Parliament that reformed Canada's immigration system.

Howard Green (1895–1989), a veteran of the Canadian Army in the First World War, was first elected to Parliament in 1935 and re-elected in every federal election until his defeat in 1963. Respected on both sides of the House for his skill as a debater and his familiarity with parliamentary rules and procedures, his unyielding opposition to arming Bomarc missiles with nuclear warheads on Canadian soil contributed to the turmoil and collapse of the Diefenbaker government in 1963. When choosing his cabinet shortly after the 1957 election, Diefenbaker rejected a suggestion that Green be named minister of justice, saying: "Not Howard. He'd hang every prisoner in the country."[7]

A roughly equal number of Conservative MPs who made it into the cabinet had either openly backed Diefenbaker for the party leadership or sensed, once the leadership race was underway, which way the winds were blowing. Among them was recent party president and MP George Hees (Transport, subsequently Trade and Commerce), who was thought by Diefenbaker to be both a "glamorous hunk of a man who look[ed] like a Hollywood actor" and an "intellectual lightweight" but who nevertheless deserved to be one of two Toronto cabinet ministers because of his support in the leadership contest. Hees had put his money where his mouth was in the 1957 campaign by signing a promissory note for $85,000 with a Toronto bank in order to provide $1,000 to each of the eighty-five Conservative candidates in Ontario.[8]

Other MPs who had backed Diefenbaker in 1956 and made it into cabinet were Douglas Harkness (briefly Northern Affairs and National Resources, followed by Agriculture, then National Defence); William Hamilton, one of two Quebec MPs (along with Balcer) named to cabinet at the outset (postmaster general); George Pearkes (National Defence until his appointment in 1960 as Lieutenant-Governor of British Columbia); Gordon Churchill (Trade and Commerce, later Veterans Affairs); and Michael Starr (Labour).

Michael Starr (1910–2000) was the son of Ukrainian immigrants. In addition to English, he spoke fluent Ukrainian, which proved to be a great asset when campaigning for the Conservatives in Western Canada. First elected to the Commons in a 1952 by-election, he was a popular and well-liked MP who was known to have close ties to many ethnic and cultural organizations. As minister of labour, he extended unemployment insurance benefits to women and seasonal workers.

The cabinet sworn in on June 21, 1957, had been assembled hurriedly in the short time between the election and Diefenbaker's departure for a Commonwealth Prime Ministers' Conference in London within hours of the first cabinet meeting. It seems that those close to Diefenbaker had spent little time on the transition of power from the Liberals to the Conservatives and on the complexion of the new cabinet. Some ministers found out only at swearing-in ceremony at Rideau Hall which department they would be responsible for. On the whole, the ministers were younger than those in the St. Laurent government, and – apart from Quebec and the usual mix of lawyers and businessmen that typically made up Canadian cabinets – this can be seen as an early move towards assembling a cabinet more representative of Canada's increasingly diverse population. The media noted favourably the fact that for the first time the cabinet included a female minister (Fairclough) and a minister of non-British, non-French descent (Starr).

Of the 112 Conservatives elected in 1957, 68 were new to the House of Commons. Only one of those 68 (W.J. Browne of St. John's, elected to Parliament in 1949 but defeated in 1953) made it to Diefenbaker's initial cabinet, a clear indication that Diefenbaker relied on those he knew best, his colleagues in the parliamentary party. Eleven of the sixteen cabinet ministers appointed in 1957 had served in the armed services during either the First or Second World War or both, compared with nine of twenty ministers in the defeated Liberal government. Such military experience meant little, however, when the ministers failed their biggest test five years later – remaining united over the issue of nuclear missiles on Canadian soil.

Like the cabinet, the Conservative caucus was more broadly representative (again, except for Quebec) of the general population than it had been leading up to the 1957 election – or than the Liberals had been even while winning election after election. It was almost certainly the most diverse government caucus to that point in Canadian history. The only two female MPs elected in 1957 (and again in 1958) were both Conservative.[9] Among the MPs elected for the first time in 1957 was "a Jung, a Jorgenson, a Mandziuk, a Kucherepa, and a Martini,"[10] who were of Chinese, Scandinavian, Ukrainian, Polish, and Italian descent, respectively. Such diversity demonstrated Diefenbaker's appeal to a wider electorate than had typically supported his party (or any other party, for that matter) in the past and contributed to the Tories' "new look." The Conservatives won the support of more non-French Catholics in 1957 than they had in some time and, despite its modest showing in Quebec, succeeded in getting more French Canadians elected than at any time since 1930. The party had started to branch out from the Anglo-Saxon-Protestant-Toronto–dominated party it had been through much of the twentieth century.

By contrast, the Liberals added little new blood to their parliamentary party in the 1957 election. All but 10 of the 105 Liberals elected in 1957 had been members of the previous Parliament. With 60 percent of their 105 MPs from Quebec, the Liberals were more heavily dependent on that province than at any time since the conscription election of 1917. This, along with the string of cabinet ministers who were defeated, was a blow to the party that for many years had billed itself as Canada's natural governing party, capable of winning support – admittedly in varying degrees – from every region of the country.

The Liberals' failure to win any of Prince Edward Island's four seats, their almost complete wipeout in Alberta, Manitoba, and Nova Scotia, and their overreliance on Quebec meant that the party had little choice but to rebuild from the ground up following the 1957 election. That would entail, at a minimum, a new set of policies, a revamped organization, successful fundraising, and, given St. Laurent's resignation shortly after the election, a new leader.

Time was not on their side as it appeared certain that Diefenbaker would welcome any excuse to call an election at the first opportunity. As it turned out, the rebuilding could not get underway until St. Laurent's successor had had time (very little, as it turned out) to settle into his new position as party leader.

By definition, a prime minister and his cabinet are the public face of the government. They are the members of the political executive who present, explain, defend, and usher through the House of Commons and its committees the legislation advanced by the government. In any cabinet, there are capable and reliable ministers who manage their departments skillfully and competently, while others are ill suited to or uncomfortable in their positions, or are weak parliamentarians, given to mistakes, or possibly scandal prone. Among Diefenbaker's more capable ministers for a great part of his government's six years in office were Fleming, Fulton, Hees (despite Diefenbaker's impression of him as an "intellectual lightweight"), Harkness, and Alvin Hamilton, who was added to the cabinet two months after it was initially sworn in. Less stellar were Churchill, Pearkes, Balcer, and two or three other Quebec ministers.

A Whirlwind Start

The new ministers hit the ground running. Knowing they would almost certainly be back at the polls within months (if the election hawks in the party had their way, and they seemed to include almost everyone), they set about loosening the public purse strings. Seasonal unemployment benefits were increased, as were those of old-age pensioners, veterans, and blind and disabled persons. More than 100,000 federal public servants received pay increases. Central Mortgage and Housing Corporation received $150 million for loans on low-cost housing. The same amount was allocated to Western farmers as a cash advance on their farm-stored grain. The fishing industry on both coasts was assisted, and unconditional regional adjustment grants to the Atlantic provinces were increased by

$25 million a year for four years. Personal and corporate tax rates were lowered, and $100 million was added to the export credit loan program to aid small and medium-sized businesses. Federal transfer payments to the provinces were increased over and above what had been agreed to by the previous government. There were announcements of additional spending on student scholarships and bursaries, grants for municipalities, additional credit on farm development loans, and increases in family allowances and veterans' disability payments. Few Canadians came away empty-handed. Would all of this additional spending be a hard sell with the public in the 1958 election? Apparently not. Even such a normally Liberal newspaper as the *Montreal Star* found the Conservatives' tax proposals "moderate ... sensible, and ... appealing to the voter."[11]

Most of these moves had been part of the Conservatives' election platform in the lead-up to the 1957 election. Cabinet approval was also given to begin construction of the massive South Saskatchewan River Dam. In an example of political irony, when the dam was officially opened a decade later by Prime Minister Lester Pearson, it was given the name "Gardiner Dam," after one-time provincial premier and long-serving federal agriculture minister J.G. Gardiner. Gardiner had championed the project for a number of years, as had Diefenbaker, but the St. Laurent government had never acceded to Gardiner's entreaties.

Two influential Royal Commissions were appointed by the new government: one on Energy in the wake of the bitter pipeline debate of 1956, and the other on Transportation, charged with, among other matters, the shortage of railway boxcars to move prairie grain. A Federal-Provincial Conference was convened, at which an agreement on the final details of the national hospital insurance program was finalized. A team charged with increasing overseas markets for Canadian grain was sent to Europe in the late summer. A fifty-member mission led by the new minister of trade and commerce, Gordon Churchill, was dispatched to England as a follow-up to the

Commonwealth Prime Ministers' Conference. At the time of the conference, Diefenbaker had made an offhand remark at a press conference that Canada would divert 15 percent of its trade from the United States to the United Kingdom. According to one trade expert, the prime minister's proposal "smacked of naïveté and nostalgia."[12] The proposal never came to fruition, nor could it. It was too late for a shift of that magnitude. Since the Second World War, Canada had moved increasingly out of the Imperial/British economic, cultural, and social orbit and into the American one.[13]

In all, the first seven or eight months between the 1957 and 1958 elections amounted to nothing less than a whirlwind. Compared with the final years of the St. Laurent government, Diefenbaker's was seen to be vigorous, attentive to public concerns, and sympathetic to the needs of Canadians. By the end of 1957, heading into what would almost certainly be an election year, the Tories were seen as having achieved as "impressive [a record] as any new government in Canadian history."[14]

Nonetheless, economic storm clouds were gathering. The government did not acknowledge that a recession had begun, and there were indications of sharply increasing unemployment ahead.[15] The Liberals, now in opposition, tried to make the most of this by goading the new government (and in the process reminding the public) with a slogan harking back to the Depression: "Tory times are tough times." In choosing to ignore the taunt, the Conservatives exuded a confidence not seen in the party for decades. They had set the stage for an election in early 1958, and they were not to be disappointed. Shortly after his defeat, Louis St. Laurent resigned as leader of the Liberal Party. The race to succeed him was on, but in truth it was not so much a race as a coronation. Lester Pearson led from the get-go, and his only competitor, Paul Martin Sr., the outgoing health and welfare minister who had served in Parliament since 1935, never had a chance.

The New Player: "Mike"

Lester Pearson was the archetypical public servant–turned–politician. As a teenager in the First World War, he served with the Royal Flying Corps, where he was given a nickname that stuck with him the rest of this life – "Mike." Following studies at the University of Toronto, he found employment for two years at the meat processing firm Armour and Company. Renowned through his entire career for his wit and self-deprecating humour, Pearson liked to recount during the Cold War that the Russians claimed he had once worked in the armament industry!

Following two years at Oxford University in the 1920s, where he had starred in both lacrosse and ice hockey, Pearson returned to Toronto and taught for four years at the University of Toronto before accepting a position with the Department of External Affairs in 1928. His career in the foreign service took off. He was posted first to London, before and during the early years of the Second World War, then to Washington for the remainder of the war. Named ambassador to the United States in 1945, Pearson had the demeanour of a slightly rumpled professor (and "innocent intellectual," in the view of his colleague Walter Gordon[16]), whereas in fact he was often singled-minded and determined. He was also quietly ambitious – not ruthless, just quietly ambitious. His international experience developed in him diplomatic skills that came in handy at critical moments in international affairs and later in politics.

Pearson was one of the central players in the establishment of the United Nations Relief and Rehabilitation Administration (UNRRA) in 1943 and the United Nations (UN) and the Food and Agriculture Organization (FAO) in 1945. Within four years of the end of the Second World War, he had made the transition from the public service to political life, joining first Mackenzie King's cabinet and then Louis St. Laurent's as minister for external affairs. In that role, he played a major part in establishing NATO in 1949, served

Lester Pearson speaking at the 1958 Liberal leadership
convention at which he was chosen party leader, Ottawa,
January 14–16, 1958. | Photographer Duncan Cameron, Library
and Archives Canada, PA-110786

as president of the United Nations General Assembly in 1952–53,
and engineered a way of bringing an end to the Suez Crisis in 1956
through the establishment of the United Nations Emergency Force.

Mike Pearson had unquestionably made his mark internationally.
His diplomatic skills had been put to good use, and he had made
many friends for Canada among allies and in the Commonwealth.
Being awarded the Nobel Peace Prize for his role in bringing about
a ceasefire in the Middle East was, in a manner of speaking, the
icing on the cake in advance of the 1958 Liberal leadership convention. The question remained, however: how would he fare in domestic
politics? There was little doubt among Liberals that Pearson would
succeed St. Laurent as party leader. Many in the party subscribed to

Lester Pearson, Louis St. Laurent, and Paul Martin Sr. before the balloting at the Liberal leadership convention, Ottawa, January 14–16, 1958. | Photographer Duncan Cameron, Library and Archives Canada, PA-110785

the notion that the party had an established French/Catholic to English/Protestant tradition of leadership alternation: Edward Blake to Wilfrid Laurier, to Mackenzie King, to Louis St. Laurent. Thus, the thinking went, it was time for a Protestant (Pearson's father had been a Methodist minister in southern Ontario), English-speaking leader.

But there was more to Pearson's selection than alternation. He had earned his bona fides internationally and brought considerable credit to Canada in the process. He was popular with Liberals and with Canadians in general, and this showed in capital fashion when delegates chose their leader at the January 1958 convention in Ottawa. Pearson won even more decisively than St. Laurent had a decade earlier. Of the 1,380 delegates, 1,074 (77.8 percent) chose Pearson, compared with only 305 (22.1 percent) for his only serious challenger, Paul Martin Sr. One vote was cast for a candidate few delegates had heard of – the mayor of Portage la Prairie, Manitoba, Lloyd Henderson.

In contrast to Diefenbaker, Pearson was anything but an outsider, rogue, or renegade in his party. He had been very much in the mainstream of the Liberal Party during his decade as an MP and external affairs minister, although his early years as a career diplomat had trained him to eschew partisan politics as long as he served in the diplomatic corps. Pearson emerged as a major player on the international scene as St. Laurent's principal spokesman on foreign affairs. The international crises of the 1950s gave him a platform that in the end served his interests well in Canada.

As it turned out, however, Pearson's strength on the international scene was also his weakness, for it soon became apparent after he became the Liberal leader that he was no match for Prime Minister Diefenbaker in the House of Commons or, more critically, in the general election that year. Within days of becoming leader, he made a strategic blunder that, in Diefenbaker's hands, brought nothing but grief to the Liberals. In his maiden speech to the House of Commons as Liberal leader and de facto Leader of Her Majesty's Loyal Opposition, he called on the government to resign so that his party could return to office and implement Liberal policies. The proposal had been laid out for him by his colleague Jack Pickersgill, a parliamentary tactician who would normally not have made such a blunder. It was at one and the same time both unprecedented and calamitous, and Pearson admitted as much, acknowledging after delivering his speech that his "first attack on the government had been a failure, indeed a fiasco."[17] It was arguably one of the most unusual and politically naive moves by an opposition leader so new to that position.

"Was there a more perfect demonstration of Liberal arrogance?" asks Denis Smith in his biography of Diefenbaker.[18] The prime minister stood in the House just after Pearson's motion and launched a blistering attack on the unremitting "arrogance" of the Liberals for their craven attempt to return to office. It was widely regarded at the time as one of the most powerful parliamentary speeches in memory. Paul Martin claimed that Diefenbaker's response to Pearson's call for the government to resign was the prime minister's "great hour ... [It] was one of the greatest devastating speeches" he had ever heard.[19] To Pickersgill, Diefenbaker's roasting of Pearson amounted to a "torrent ... in which Pearson was figuratively torn limb from limb."[20] Diefenbaker had been itching for an excuse to call an election, and he got it.

Within days, Diefenbaker asked the Governor General to dissolve Parliament. The 1958 election was underway. In his response to Pearson's proposal in the House and in the subsequent election campaign, the prime minister was in his element. As it turned out, however, that campaign was the pinnacle of Diefenbaker's electoral history. By contrast, after a rocky start as opposition leader and a disastrous election campaign, Pearson seemingly had nowhere to go but up – which he did. Years later, he was judged by a panel of experts as the best of the six Canadian prime ministers from St. Laurent to Jean Chrétien to have governed for more than four years, whereas Diefenbaker was ranked last.[21]

If the 1957 election campaign was fought on a series of issues – the government's handling of the TransCanada pipeline, Canada's reaction to the Suez Crisis, support for the agricultural sector, old-age pension increases, Liberal arrogance – the 1958 campaign was fought almost entirely on promises. In the early months of 1958, the Liberals were in no position to repeat the Conservatives' claim in the previous election that it was "time for a change," so they turned to what can generously be described as a grab bag of promises. There was also nothing of any serious consequence from the Conservatives' brief time in office for the opposition parties to attack and turn against the government.

Throughout the campaign, the Liberals understandably made much of Pearson's newly awarded Nobel Peace Prize. They had little else to go on. The once-popular Louis St. Laurent was gone, several of their leading cabinet ministers had been defeated in 1957, their organization was much weaker than it had been in many years, party coffers had shrunk, and they had had no time to craft new policies and assemble a team of outstanding candidates. For the Liberals, there could scarcely have been a less propitious time to fight an election.

The Liberals also failed to capitalize on two related developments that they could have turned into election issues, thereby saving at least some of their seats. The first had to do with rapidly growing unemployment, possibly fuelling fears of an economic recession ahead; the second was the questionable release of a "secret" report by Diefenbaker in his attack on Pearson following the latter's inaugural speech in the House of Commons after he became the Liberal leader.

There was little doubt about where the employment figures were heading. In 1956, the last full year of the St. Laurent government, 197,000 persons were unemployed in Canada. In 1957, this number rose by 80,000, and in 1958 it was 432,000, more than double the 1956 level. The annual percentage of unemployed shot up from 3.4 percent in 1956 to 7.1 percent in 1958.[22] Economic indicators were unfavourable. "Tory times are tough times" was heard again and again from Liberal candidates on the campaign trail, but it failed to resonate with voters. The striking increase in the number of unemployed should have played a greater role in the election but was lost in the excitement over having a new government and what the Conservatives billed as a new course of action in the hands of an energetic group of ministers and a dynamic prime minister. The

Liberals were never able to turn unemployment into an election issue, possibly because when the Conservatives hurriedly assembled a winter works project to deal with the jump in those looking for work, it reassured Canadians that their new government was working to solve the problem.

The second development that the Liberals failed to capitalize on was the release by the new Conservative government of what it alleged was a "secret" or "hidden" report prepared for the St. Laurent cabinet. The report laid out details of an expected downturn in the economy in 1957–58. In January 1958, Diefenbaker delighted in quoting from the report while attacking Pearson for his effrontery in suggesting that the Conservatives resign and hand power back to the Liberals. It essentially forecast rising unemployment coupled with a worsening domestic economic situation in the year or two ahead. "Why didn't you tell the people these things?" Diefenbaker thundered in the House.[23] The Liberals offered little in reply apart from expressing dismay that the Diefenbaker government had breached a long-standing convention of one government not revealing a document prepared by the public service for an earlier one. Diefenbaker was undeterred. The Liberals objected loudly, but, as Pickersgill admitted after the dust-up in the House, their "protests were ignored by the public."[24] What might have worked to their advantage did not.

The 1958 Conservative Campaign

The 1958 campaign was as easy for the Conservatives as it was difficult for the other parties. The Tories had delivered on most of their previous election promises, thus building up a measure of public trust in a short period. No less important to their success was the "Follow John" theme, which caught on in all parts of the country as the campaign progressed. Audiences at Tory rallies swelled as Diefenbaker shuttled from city to city, sometimes by train on whistle stops but increasingly by airplane. The intensity of the

John Diefenbaker's 1958 election campaign was launched in Winnipeg on February 12 with a speech to a packed Winnipeg auditorium. Denis Smith writes in *Rogue Tory* (Toronto: Macfarlane Walter and Ross, 1995) that "the auditorium was jammed with noisy enthusiasts. When the doors to the hall were closed, crowds outside surged and broke them down" (279). | University of Saskatchewan Archives and Special Collections, JGD/3573/XB

campaign all but guaranteed considerable print and television attention. The Liberals did not attempt to match it.

Shortly into the campaign, Quebec premier Maurice Duplessis threw his powerful Union Nationale organization behind the Conservatives. Known widely in his province as *le Chef,* Duplessis (1890–1959) was a force unto himself. From his early years as a Conservative in Quebec provincial politics to his later founding of the Union Nationale, he made a pronounced mark on the province over his eighteen years as premier. His government fought to protect and enhance areas of provincial jurisdiction, dealt ruthlessly with striking resource-sector workers, maintained close ties with the Roman Catholic Church, and, by expanding hydroelectric grids through much of the province and financing various public works projects, laid the foundation for modern Quebec.

Duplessis's machine did its job well. Large crowds of Quebecers, the great majority of whom had likely never voted Conservative in their lives, turned out to see and hear Diefenbaker. At one rally in Montreal, the crowd of several thousand "just tore the roof off in a frenzy" following a fiery introduction by one of the Conservative candidates in advance of the leader's speech. "It was one of the few times when Diefenbaker's quality of oratory met a real challenge," said a member of his cabinet.[25]

In rally after rally across the country, Diefenbaker was in crusader mode. In a typical campaign speech, he challenged his audience to become part of the movement he was leading. Promising "a new sense of national purpose," he implored his audience to "catch the vision! Catch the vision of the kind of Canada this can be! ... I've seen this vision; I've seen this future of Canada. I ask you to have faith in this land and faith in our people."[26] An evangelist could not have done better.

One example captures the mood of the country heading into the 1958 election. As noted earlier, labour minister Michael Starr was of Ukrainian descent. He was dispatched to Western Canada for a few days to speak to voters in small communities with sizable Ukrainian populations. He later reported on one event where he addressed a crowd of over 500 packed into a town hall at 10 p.m. He spoke for twenty minutes in English and then switched to Ukrainian. He saw tears running down the cheeks of many in the audience. "Now I can die," one man said. "I have met a minister of Ukrainian extraction." Diefenbaker was mobbed when he addressed such meetings, Starr recalled. People swarmed him "just to touch his hand."[27]

The coup de grâce of the campaign was the unveiling of a novel proposal by the Conservatives calling for the development of

Canada's North. Dubbed "The Northern Vision," the slogan perfectly suited Diefenbaker's style of campaigning – a forceful, passionate style that, as the campaign progressed, captivated more and more Canadians and gained increasingly attentive media coverage. It was a study in contrast to the campaigning styles of the three successive Liberal leaders that Diefenbaker campaigned against in federal politics: Mackenzie King, Louis St. Laurent, and Lester Pearson. It is revealing that he chose as the title of the first of his three-volume memoir *One Canada: The Crusading Years,* covering his life up to the 1957 election. He genuinely believed that his time in the political wings and his eventual winning of the leadership of his party amounted to a victorious crusade. The 1957 and, especially, the 1958 campaigns confirmed his view of the electioneering gifts he could employ.

The 1958 Liberal Campaign

Ministerial control of the Liberal Party and its election and fundraising apparatus that had been perfected under St. Laurent came at considerable cost to the party once it was out of office. Fundraising was no longer easy, nor did it bring in nearly the level of financial support that had defined the party's period in government. The national organization was a shadow of its former self. A small election organization group was patched together under the direction of two senators, J.J. Connolly and C.G. Power, but it had markedly less money available for the national and local campaigns. There were reports of defections from provincial organizations in the face of an expected Conservative win, and with fewer volunteers in many constituencies, it was by far the most organizationally challenged of any Liberal campaign since 1930. There was even a scramble to field a complete roster of candidates (265), for in addition to the 72 MPs defeated in 1957, 19 of those elected that year chose not to run again the following year.

The Liberals' slogan was "Vote the Pearson Plan ... For Jobs ... For Peace," and their platform had something of a rushed look about it. All in all, their promises suggested that if elected they would turn on the spending taps in support of a variety of government programs, but this rang hollow for it stood in direct contrast to their tight-fisted control of expenditures during the St. Laurent years. They promised that a Pearson government would expand the Canadian economy and multilateral trade with the aim of achieving full employment, but no specifics were given on how these goals would be accomplished. It would cut income taxes by $400 million, improve the unemployment insurance scheme, establish a national scholarship and bursary program to support 10,000 post-secondary students, introduce a farm development bank and a national health insurance scheme, broaden the eligibility criteria for the old-age pension program, build a rail link to Great Slave Lake, and continue the South Saskatchewan River Dam project initiated by the Tories. Even normally Liberal newspaper editorialists found the proposals excessive, commending the Conservative government's plans as "more moderate and ... more sensible."[28]

The 1958 election was not Lester Pearson's to win. It is difficult to conceive of any Liberal leader winning against the Conservatives at that point, for John Diefenbaker was likely in his finest hour in 1958. Television proved to be of little help to Pearson either, as Diefenbaker was found to be "by far the more attractive of the two men from the [TV] viewing public's point of view."[29] Senator Connolly later admitted that "looking back I think the party never had a chance."[30] The election was tailor-made for Diefenbaker's style of campaigning: accusatory of the Liberals for what he portrayed as a litany of sins; visionary about Canada's bright future under a Conservative government; and inclusive of all Canadians, without distinctions based on region, language, or religion, under his oft-repeated mantra "One Canada."

The Smaller Parties' Campaigns in 1958

The back-to-back elections took a heavy toll on both smaller parties. They had the Conservative Party strategies and the apparent magnetism of the Tory leader to contend with; they were strapped for money; Social Credit was divided over strategy and policy, while the CCF leader had health issues that kept him from campaigning as robustly as in the past; and public opinion had swung strongly in favour of the Conservatives.

Many voters were also determined that the Liberals would not make a comeback, and the Conservatives got the majority they wanted. Saskatchewan premier Tommy Douglas recalled that voters in his province who would normally have supported the CCF at both the federal and provincial levels abandoned the federal party in 1958. "We will vote for you provincially," Douglas said they told him, but they wanted to take no chance "on Jimmy Gardiner and C.D. Howe coming back."[31]

As with the Liberals, not much could be done to save the two minor parties, for the election had become akin to a referendum on Diefenbaker. It mattered little what they had to offer in 1958. Against the Liberals with their newly chosen leader, and the Progressive Conservatives led by the new Prime Minister, the two smaller parties could scarcely make an impression on the voters. The CCF called for a planned economy, full employment, and a comprehensive social security program, but in calling for a contributory pension plan separate from the government old-age security program, the party was ahead of its time. (St. Laurent had once described the CCF as "Liberals in a hurry.") Such a program came into being a decade later with the implementation of the Canada/Quebec Pension Plans under a Pearson government.

Social Credit's platform included low-interest, long-term loans to farmers, a new tax regime to assist small businesses, lower-interest loans to assist in the construction of homes for Canadians, and a general reduction in taxes to reduce consumer prices and induce consumer spending. Neither the CCF nor the Social Credit plans gained serious attention for, unlike previous elections, the 1958 election was clearly a two-party contest. Or, perhaps more accurately, it was a one-party contest with the only unresolved questions being how many votes the Conservatives would get and how many seats they would win.

Social Credit's 1957 motto had a hollow ring to it: "On to Ottawa." If it was meant to suggest forming the government, that was a pipe-dream of considerable magnitude as the party managed to field only 115 candidates, well short of a theoretical majority even if every one of them had won. Even forming the official opposition was little more than fanciful thinking in 1958, when Social Credit fielded 33 fewer candidates.

With a second election barely months after the first, and with favourable press coverage of the Conservatives' claim of needing a majority government to carry out their mandate, prospects were grim for the CCF and Social Credit. The CCF had depleted its coffers in 1957 and had just over $20,000 to spend on the 1958 campaign.[32] Its leader, M.J. Coldwell, then in his seventieth year, had suffered a mild heart attack shortly before the election in June 1957, but, against the advice of his caucus colleagues and many other senior party officials, he joined a Parliamentary Association delegation on an exhausting tour of India that autumn. This left his constituency of Rosetown-Biggar unattended in the lead-up to the widely expected 1958 election and, more worrisome for the party, his parliamentary caucus leaderless in a minority Parliament. Normally a vigorous campaigner, Coldwell reluctantly turned over several scheduled events in both 1957 and 1958 to two seasoned campaigners, Tommy Douglas and Stanley Knowles.

Social Credit, which had even at the best of times a skeleton "national" organization, focused on saving as many seats as possible in Alberta and British Columbia. Candidates in both provinces were told they would have to finance their own campaigns in 1958.[33]

The Social Credit platform in both elections consisted mainly of a pro-business, anti-government list of actions the party would take should it win office. It opposed government support of the arts, particularly the National Film Board and the recently created Canada Council. It frequently attacked the CBC, although it had no objection to using the free radio broadcast time made available to all parties by the national broadcaster. Internal bickering over election strategies at the local level led some constituency executives and candidates to resign.

The cabinet ministers and senior party officials in the only two provinces with Social Credit governments understood their political movement differently. In Alberta, the party traced its origins to the Depression, William Aberhart, evangelical Christianity, and a pur-ported variant (modified, not surprisingly, after the discovery of oil in the province) of Major Douglas's Social Credit economic theories. In British Columbia, by contrast, Social Credit had a much more fiscally conservative bent from the start. After unexpectedly winning office in 1952, the party provided a convenient home for former Liberals and Conservatives intent on holding the CCF at bay. What it brought to the federal party was a "pro-business, private enter-prise" orientation, not unlike that of the Progressive Conservatives and Liberals in Ottawa. It was a far cry from the "funny money" plans of the 1930s.

As the 1958 general election approached, it was apparent that little stood in the way of a Tory majority government, the first since R.B. Bennett's in 1930. After their minority win in 1957, everything appeared to favour the Conservatives when the election was called early the following year. Lester Pearson's unwise call on the govern-ment to resign gave the Tories the pretext they needed to call an election, and it confirmed for many voters their impression of the federal Liberals as arrogant. The three opposition parties fared poorly in 1958 largely because of Diefenbaker's powerful campaign per-formances, evoking images of "visions" and "Crusades"; a surprising measure of media support for the Conservatives; the collapse of the Liberal election machine that had been controlled by Louis St. Laurent's cabinet ministers; the abandonment of the smaller parties by their usually dependable electorate; the straitened finances of all three parties running against the Conservatives; and the continued support of the organizations deployed by provincial Conservative premiers and party leaders, now joined by Quebec's Union Nationale. The final pre-election Gallup Poll of voting intentions showed where things were headed on March 31, 1958: Progressive Conservative, 52.9 percent; Liberal, 27.5 percent; CCF, 7.4 percent; Social Credit, 2.0 percent; and Undecided, 10.2 percent.[34] Some in the press claimed that the election was over before it began.

The Results

The polls got it right. The Conservatives won with 53.6 percent of the vote and captured all but 57 of the seats in the 265-seat House of Commons. They won every seat in four provinces (Alberta, Manitoba, Nova Scotia, and Prince Edward Island) and a comfortable majority of them in all other provinces, save Newfoundland and Labrador where, once again, the Liberals prevailed. (See the map on page 3 for the 1958 election results. Appendix 3, Table A2, shows the popular vote and seats won by party for the provinces and territories). The 1958 election was an outlier in Canadian election history in many ways. It produced a Conservative victory of gargantuan proportions; reduced the Liberals to an unfamiliar place on the opposition benches with a much-diminished caucus; returned the CCF to levels of seats and votes roughly equivalent to when they first entered Parliament in 1935; and eliminated the Social Credit party completely.[35]

Voter Turnout in 1958

The election was distinctive in one further respect: voter turnout reached an all-time high in Canada in 1958. In Figure 6.1, voter

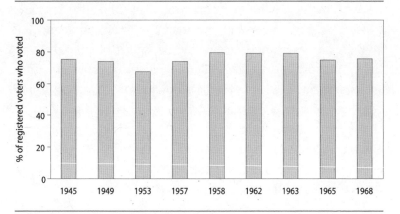

FIGURE 6.1

Voter turnout, 1945–68

Source: Reports of the Chief Electoral Officer of Canada (Ottawa: 1945–68).

turnout between 1945 and 1968 is expressed as a percentage of the number of registered electors who voted. In the two postwar federal elections, it averaged 74.5 percent, dipped in 1953 to the second-lowest level to that point in the twentieth century, jumped to 67.5 percent in 1957, then reached its highest level in Canadian history, 79.4 percent, in 1958. The 1962 and 1963 elections – the last two in which John Diefenbaker was prime minister – followed closely at 79 and 79.2 percent, respectively. Turnout then fell back to its pre-Diefenbaker levels in the mid-70 percent range. The positive relationship between higher turnout levels and Tory electoral success that was first detected in 1957 appeared to be true of 1958 as well.

Apart from Newfoundland and Labrador, the provinces with the smallest populations recorded the highest levels of turnout in 1958. Prince Edward Island topped the list with 85.4 percent, followed by Nova Scotia, New Brunswick, and Saskatchewan with an average of 81.2 percent. All others (including the territories) were in the mid-70 percent range. Newfoundland and Labrador, at 51.9 percent, further distinguished itself on several fronts. Except for St. John's,

where the Conservatives won the city's two seats, party competi-
tiveness (one of the variables contributing to voter turnout) in the
rest of the province was minimal to non-existent. The victory of all
five Liberal candidates outside St. John's was never in doubt. One
was elected by acclamation (the only member of the new House to
be chosen unopposed); three defeated their Tory opponents by
winning on average 70 percent of the popular vote; and long-time
Liberal MP and cabinet minister Jack Pickersgill was re-elected in
his Bonavista-Twillingate constituency with a stunning 87.2 percent
of the vote – the largest share of the vote of any of Canada's 265
MPs. Pickersgill's riding also distinguished itself by recording the
lowest voter turnout level in Canada, 43.5 percent. This inverse
relationship highlights the link between the degree of voter engagement and the elector's perception of the utility of casting a vote.[36]

Not surprisingly, the turnout rates in 1957 and especially 1958
are associated positively with increased voter interest in the election
outcomes. The themes of "Time for a Change" in 1957 and "Elect
a Majority Government" in 1958 clearly struck responsive chords.
Voter interest levels in 1957 jumped by 9 percentage points over
1953 (from 49.2 to 58.6 percent), and in 1958 they hit a high of
70 percent. Diefenbaker's appeal in both elections and his emphasis on majority government in 1958 were said to be the principal
causes of the heightened public interest.[37] It also helped that in
1957 the argument for change was echoed by all three parties opposing the St. Laurent Liberals, which gave the claim greater res-
onance than if it came from only a single party. But in 1958 only
the Conservatives were in a position to appeal for a majority government, and none of the others could make a strong case for a
change in government.

An Expanded Cabinet

With time and a larger pool of Quebec MPs to draw from following the 1958 election, Diefenbaker brought two of them into his

cabinet that year and another one in 1959. In all, nine Quebec Conservatives headed ministries over the government's six years – some for a short time before the government's defeat in 1963, and one – Leon Balcer – for the entire six years. It was widely conceded in Ottawa and by the Quebec press, however, that by the end of Diefenbaker's tenure, none of his Quebec ministers ranked in the top tier of the cabinet, nor had any been given a top-notch position in the past six years.

Cabinet ministers were added from time to time, including David Walker, a trusted Diefenbaker ally from Toronto, to Public Works; Sidney Smith, who was persuaded to leave the presidency of the University of Toronto to become, before his untimely death in 1959, minister of external affairs; and Hugh John Flemming, former premier of New Brunswick, who was co-opted as the first forestry minister following his government's defeat in the province's 1960 election. In the waning days of the government, Wallace McCutcheon, a successful Toronto businessman, was appointed to the Senate the day he was named to cabinet as minister without portfolio to ease relations with the increasingly concerned financial community.[38]

Alvin Hamilton (1912–2004) of Saskatchewan joined the cabinet in midsummer 1957. A Diefenbaker loyalist, he was a ball of fire who seemed to have ideas about how best to solve any number of problems. A loquacious high school teacher and leader of the Saskatchewan Conservative Party, he had served as a navigator and flight lieutenant in the Royal Canadian Air Force during the Second World War. Like Diefenbaker before him, he tried several times to win a seat in the provincial legislature and in Parliament, failing six times before finally making it to the House of Commons in 1957. He was named minister of northern affairs and national resources, and in 1960 he replaced Douglas Harkness (1903–99) as agriculture minister.

Like Hamilton, Harkness was a schoolteacher who had served overseas with the armed forces during the Second World War, receiving the George Medal for bravery in the 1943 Sicilian campaign. He was also a farmer and one of two Conservatives elected from Alberta in each of the three elections from 1945 to 1953. Respected by MPs of all parties as a man of honour dedicated to the task at hand, he believed strongly in a country's living up to its international (notably defence) obligations, and it was therefore no surprise that he should have stood up to Diefenbaker. Eventually resigning from cabinet in 1963 over the issue of accepting nuclear armaments on Canadian soil, he continued to serve in the Commons for nine more years.[39]

Together, the 1957 and 1958 elections revived the Conservatives and brought them to a level unseen since John A. Macdonald's time. The question was whether this renewal would last. As the 1962 election approached, Diefenbaker and his colleagues could point to several accomplishments over their five years in office. These, together with the legacies of the Diefenbaker government, will be discussed in the final chapter. Even with its successes, however, the government faced several challenging problems, some of them of its own making. How they handled these problems determined their fate in 1963.

7

Challenges, Failures, Defeat, and Regrouping

ASKED BY A REPORTER what causes a government to be thrown off course, British prime minister Harold Macmillan famously quipped, "Events, dear boy, events." It is axiomatic that every government faces unforeseen circumstances and challenges. It is how they deal with them that becomes the test of governing – and a test of how long they will retain power.

Governments may be in office for years because they have managed to dodge potentially fatal bullets (Mackenzie King's), others for mere months because they have not (Joe Clark's). Some are defeated at the polls because of their sense of invincibility (St. Laurent's), others on a vote of no-confidence in the House of Commons followed by defeat at the polls because they became fractious and unruly (Diefenbaker's).

By 1962, and certainly by 1963, the Diefenbaker government had become sufficiently unravelled that its defeat was simply a matter of time. The Tories lost nearly 90 seats in 1962, compared to what they had won four years earlier, and a further 21 in 1963. Although they did not match the numbers elected during Louis St. Laurent's and Mackenzie King's heydays, Lester Pearson's Liberals nonetheless bounced back from where they had been in 1958. They more than doubled their representation in the House of Commons – from 49 MPs in 1958 to 100 in 1962 and 129 in 1963. It was enough to turf the Conservatives out of office and to confirm in the view of some commentators (and many Liberals!) that the party was back where it belonged as "Canada's natural governing party." Of the two smaller parties, Social Credit fared the better largely because of a breakthrough in rural Quebec, where it won 26 seats in 1962 and 20 the following year. By contrast, the newly created NDP got off to a disappointing start by electing only 19 MPs in 1962 and 17 in 1963. (See the map on page 3 for the 1962 election results. Tables A3 and A4 in Appendix 3 show the popular vote and seats won by party for the provinces and territories in 1962 and 1963.)

But the big story of 1962 and 1963 was the defeat of a government that had had such a resounding victory a few years before. Countless explanations (and excuses) have been offered for the government's collapse and defeat. Principal among them were:

- the government's (especially Diefenbaker's) failure to capitalize on the opportunity the 1958 election provided to make serious inroads in Quebec
- the fallout from the cancellation of the Avro Arrow
- the worsening economy and the attempt to fire the governor of the Bank of Canada
- NORAD, Cuba, nuclear warheads, and JFK.

Quebec

The Tories' failure for decades to have any bench strength from Quebec in their parliamentary party, together with the sudden influx of novice MPs from the province in 1958, was not a good combination. By the halfway point of the Diefenbaker government's tenure, knowledgeable Quebec media commentators and intellectuals were taking a dim view of the part that Quebec ministers were playing in the government. Writing in *Le Devoir*, the influential Montreal daily newspaper he edited, André Laurendeau commented in 1960 that not since R.B. Bennett had French Canadians "felt themselves so distant from the country's business as they are under Mr. Diefenbaker."[1]

Besides the fact that none of his Quebec ministers was an outstanding cabinet member, Diefenbaker had never shown any particular interest in or knowledge of Quebec. With the death in 1959 of Union Nationale leader Maurice Duplessis, followed soon after by the death of Duplessis's successor, Paul Sauvé (whom Diefenbaker briefly considered a possible successor as federal Tory leader), the door was opened to the Quebec Liberals under Jean Lesage. Their victory in the 1960 provincial election put wind in their sails and they set about changing the province.

The ensuing "Quiet Revolution" (which in some respects had begun under Sauvé) moved the province in a direction Diefenbaker neither knew nor understood. He liked to remind audiences that it was his government that had introduced French-English simultaneous translation to the House of Commons and Senate, that had ordered Government of Canada cheques to be issued in both English and French, and that had appointed the distinguished military veteran and diplomat Georges Vanier as Governor General. The suggestion seemed to be, "There! I have recognized Quebec's importance." These token moves were scarcely noticeable in the face of the profound social and political changes Quebec was undergoing at the time.

Diefenbaker became increasingly out of touch with the social and economic transformations that marked Quebec in the 1960s. His large cohort of MPs from the province, many of whom were in Ottawa thanks to the organizational efforts of the Union Nationale in 1958, provided no protection from losses in the ensuing elections. Four years after their massive victory in Quebec, the Tories were reduced to fourteen seats from the fifty they had won in 1958. In the 1963 election, they lost a further six.

The Avro Arrow

The cancellation of the Avro Arrow program in 1959 has entered the pages of Canadian history (and mythology) as one of the most debated issues of the postwar era. Coming out of the Second World War and heading into the Cold War, Canada had much to offer its NATO partners in the way of aerospace expertise. In 1953, after years of deliberation, the St. Laurent government contracted with A.V. Roe (Canada) to produce 500–600 supersonic fighters at $1.5–2 million per plane (plus development costs) to replace the Royal Canadian Air Force's CF-100 jets and possibly to sell to Canada's allies. The delta-winged two-manned Arrow was state-of-the-art for its time. It would be capable of intercepting in the Canadian Arctic Russian bombers carrying nuclear bombs in an attack on North America.

Much changed, however, in the six years between the Arrow agreement in 1953 and the program's cancellation in 1959. Cost overruns were considerable, the order was reduced to 100 planes, and production delays pushed back the delivery date to at least 1962. The United States dashed any hope that Canada had of selling the Arrow to them when they began producing their own single-engine, cheaper, and lighter supersonic aircraft. In the wake of Russia's successful launch of the Sputnik satellite in October 1957 (ironically, the very day that the first Arrow rolled out of its hangar at Malton, Ontario), it became clear that the days of manned bombers were numbered and that the age of intercontinental ballistic missiles (ICBMs) had begun.

Whom to criticize for the way this whole unfortunate episode unfolded? The debate continues. It is not unusual for newly elected governments (as Diefenbaker's was in 1957) to place squarely on the shoulders of their predecessors the blame for all the ills that had befallen the country and the new government. Accordingly, the Diefenbaker government charged that the St. Laurent government had been fully apprised of the excessive costs, extended delivery deadline, and absence of international sales in advance of the 1957 election. The Conservatives believed that the Liberals had chosen to reveal as little as possible before the election because of the possible negative consequences for the party.

Regardless of who was to blame, all the project's anticipated problems mentioned earlier came to pass in the early years of the Diefenbaker government. After much discussion by cabinet, the government announced the cancellation of the Arrow program in February 1959. Overnight an estimated 25,000 jobs were lost directly in A.V. Roe's research and production facilities and indirectly among contracted suppliers, mostly in the Toronto area. Engineers and skilled technicians headed to the United States, where many found employment with NASA. With the cancellation of the project, Canada's military aerospace industry, which had been an essential part of the country's war effort, was, if not over, markedly diminished.[2]

The blow to a sector of the economy employing a highly skilled workforce was significant, and the Tories paid a heavy price in metropolitan Toronto. The party had won every one of the eighteen seats in the city of Toronto and surrounding York County in the 1958 election, with an average of 57.5 percent of the vote. Four years later, they were reduced to three seats in the region and 36 percent of the vote; the following year, they were winless and garnered just 27 percent of the vote. Leslie Frost, the Conservative premier of Ontario, summed up the damage to the federal party: the cancellation "was the beginning of the decline of the Diefenbaker government ... The overwhelming vote of confidence of March 1958 was completely lost."[3]

Could the political damage caused by the cancellation of the Arrow have been avoided? Possibly some of it. First, a more experienced and seasoned government would almost certainly have had a better-prepared public relations message to manage the fallout when the cancellation was announced. Second, the Diefenbaker

government had undertaken no large-scale interdepartmental review of foreign and defence policies upon assuming office. It is
reasonable to assume that had it done so, and had the review been
released to the media, both the government and the public would
have better understood the likely consequences of abandoning
the Arrow program. Third, since the cancellation would be a major
blow to a highly skilled sector of the economy, a well-crafted labour
force adjustment program could have provided assistance to those
who lost their jobs overnight.

The Economy and the Coyne Affair

Large-scale European immigration, coupled with expanding construction, manufacturing, and mining and resource sectors, kept
the economy strong for the first decade after the Second World
War. On the eve of the Diefenbaker upset in 1957, however, the
economy was slowing, possibly heading into a recession. From a
postwar average of 2.5 percent, the unemployment rate climbed
to an average of 4.2 percent between 1954 and 1957. It rose to 6.7
percent between 1958 and 1960, and reached 8 percent in 1961, the
highest level since the Great Depression. Over the same period, the
annual gross national product fell by 150 percent, from 5 percent
to 2 percent.

The government, specifically Finance Minister Donald Fleming,
whose fiscal policies attempted to address the economic realities of
the time, had a falling out with the governor of the Bank of Canada, James Coyne. Appointed by the St. Laurent government in
1955, which fed into Diefenbaker's suspicion of him as a Liberal
partisan, an "unregenerate Grit,"[4] Coyne was openly critical of the
government's handling of the economy in several speeches and
statements in 1960 and 1961. He took exception to the government's fiscal policies, specifically deficit financing as a tool to
stimulate the economy, calling instead for measures that would
restrict the economy: tight money, reduced imports, limits on

foreign investment, and higher taxes. According to economist Merrill Menzies, the effect of Coyne's monetary policies was to maintain a "grossly overvalued Canadian dollar," which had negative consequences for both exports and employment.[5]

The stage was set for an unprecedented battle between the government and the governor of the central bank. Coyne's seven-year term was ending soon, but in the first half of 1961, Fleming, who had for some time strongly defended Coyne's independence, concluded, along with Diefenbaker, that Coyne should be removed forthwith. Ostensibly, the issue was a 40 percent increase in Coyne's pension that the Bank of Canada board had approved. In reality, however, the decision to remove him resulted from a clash of personalities and disagreement over the extent of the bank's independence and the monetary and fiscal policies best suited to the circumstances. Coyne stubbornly refused to resign. (It is important to note that calls for his resignation came not only from the Conservatives but also from several noted economists and some senior Canadian bank officials.)

In June 1961, the government introduced a one-sentence bill in the House of Commons declaring that upon the bill's coming into force, the Bank of Canada's governorship would be immediately vacant. The bill easily passed the House, where Coyne was accused by some Conservative backbenchers of being "an anarchist" and a "Communist in sheep's clothing." Coyne's request to testify before a House committee was denied. The Liberal-dominated Senate's Standing Committee on Banking and Finance granted him that opportunity, however, and Coyne charged that it was the prime minister with "unbridled malice and vindictiveness" who was the "evil genius" behind the whole sordid affair. With its Liberal majority, the Senate defeated the bill to fire Coyne, who, viewing this as a vindication of his stance, resigned forthwith.[6]

After the dust from the Coyne Affair settled, editorialists and many in the Canadian public sided with Coyne, for (in the words of opposition leader Lester Pearson) the Diefenbaker government had denied him "the fundamental right of justice and fair play."[7] Parliament subsequently enacted legislation that made clear what should have been established some time before, that in the event of a fundamental policy disagreement between the Bank of Canada and the government, the government would be ultimately responsible for monetary policy.

Soon after Coyne's departure, the Canadian dollar "dropped like a stone in financial markets,"[8] temporary import surcharges were introduced, and $1 billion was borrowed from the International Monetary Fund, the US Federal Reserve, and the Bank of England. These measures helped restore a measure of confidence in the Canadian dollar, reassure international financial institutions about the health of the Canadian economy, and aid in economic recovery. But as a final humiliation for the government, a run on the dollar midway through the 1962 election campaign led the government to peg the dollar (which had been trading at par with the US dollar) at US$0.925. The Liberals seized on the move and distributed a political prop (dubbed a "Diefenbuck") symbolizing what they described as the government's mishandling of the economy and its struggle with the governor of the central bank. The entire Coyne incident, in Peter Newman's account of Diefenbaker's years in politics, turned out to have been the "least admirable crusade of his career."[9] It expended a great deal of the government's political capital and undoubtedly worked against the Conservatives in their first nationwide test at the polls since their massive win of 1958.

NORAD, Cuba, Nuclear Warheads, and JFK

Diefenbaker cherished his warm relationship with Dwight Eisenhower, whose last years as US president coincided with Diefenbaker's first three and a half years as prime minister. Diefenbaker has been described as having fallen for a combination of Eisenhower's "charm, flattery, and considerateness, and ... his own hero-worship."[10] Several jointly sponsored American-Canadian initiatives helped "Ike" and "Dief" cement the long-standing friendly relationship between the two countries. These included the 1958 agreement to integrate the US-Canada air command through the establishment of NORAD, the opening of the St. Lawrence Seaway in 1959, and the signing of the Columbia River Treaty in 1961, just days before Eisenhower left the White House.

Diefenbaker's relationship with Eisenhower stood in stark contrast to his subsequent association with President John F. Kennedy. That relationship was testy at best, openly hostile at worst. Often thought by his critics to harbour a latent anti-Americanism, Diefenbaker frustrated his American allies on two critical defence issues. In both cases, his hesitation to join the United States on matters of mutual defence and military mobilization had wider implications, for it indicated a hesitancy and indecisiveness that is, to say the least, unhelpful in situations that call for swift executive action.

Diefenbaker visited Kennedy in Washington on February 20, 1961, their first meeting after Kennedy assumed office. To an aide, he described Kennedy as a man with "a far-sighted judgment on international affairs." Kennedy, on the other hand, found Diefenbaker "insecure and untrustworthy." He told his brother Robert that he did not want "to see that boring son of a bitch again."[11] Nevertheless, he visited Ottawa months later for further meetings with the prime minister. Publicly the meeting was said to have gone well, but privately Diefenbaker became suspicious of what he regarded as Kennedy's gratuitous and condescending attitude towards him. Accompanied by his attractive and stylish wife, Kennedy upstaged Diefenbaker at every turn. An American briefing note accidentally left behind was discovered following the meeting. It contained talking points for the president, each stating that Kennedy should "push" Diefenbaker to accept or approve various initiatives favoured by the Americans, including Canada's joining the Organization of

American States (which Diefenbaker had already told Kennedy he strongly opposed) and increasing its foreign aid budget. The note allegedly had "SOB" scribbled by hand in a margin. Rather than having it returned to the American Embassy, as would have been correct protocol, Diefenbaker reportedly kept it in a vault, for possible use as blackmail against the Americans should the occasion arise.

By 1963, Diefenbaker's dislike of Kennedy had given way to a more troubling obsession: he was convinced that the president wanted him voted out of office and replaced by Lester Pearson, with whom Kennedy had a warm relationship. A leading Democratic pollster, Lou Harris, advised Pearson on campaign tactics. This, together with the Liberals' use of advertising techniques similar to those employed in Kennedy's successful presidential bid in 1960, confirmed in Diefenbaker's mind that Kennedy contributed to the Conservatives' defeat in the 1963 election.

Like Canadian-American relations in general, the operational command structure of NORAD was severely tested by the Cuban Missile Crisis of October 1962. The Soviet Union was discovered to have stationed nuclear-armed missiles in communist Cuba, posing a threat to both the United States and Canada. Kennedy mounted a naval blockade of Cuba and demanded that the Soviets dismantle the missiles. The threat of nuclear war between the two superpowers was palpable.

The Americans called on Canada to place its forces on standby in the event rapid mobilization was needed. Such was the obligation of both countries under the terms of the joint operational command structure of NORAD. Diefenbaker, over the objections of Defence Minister Douglas Harkness, who urged immediate mobilization, hesitated for two days before grudgingly agreeing to the American request – adding to the White House's list of grievances with the prime minister. The crisis ended thirteen days after it began, with

Soviet ships turning around, the missiles being dismantled, and both superpowers making concessions, but the damage to Canadian-American relations took longer to heal.

To the White House, the Cuban Missile Crisis had shown the Diefenbaker government to be an indecisive and unreliable ally. Kennedy was reported to have been so furious with Diefenbaker that he was determined "never [to] see or speak to him again."[12] With ministers divided and uncertain over their defence obligations, the Canadian cabinet was ill prepared to deal with the next defence issue, which, in the end, sealed the fate of Diefenbaker's government.[13]

Both Canadian and American air operations had become aligned according to NORAD regulations and policies following the hasty approval of the agreement that Diefenbaker had signed soon after taking office in 1957. In keeping with the terms of the agreement, Canada approved the deployment of fifty-six Bomarc B anti-aircraft missiles on Canadian soil. When it became known in 1960 that the missiles would be equipped with nuclear warheads, demonstrations protesting the move broke out across Canada.

The cabinet, quarrelsome and divided on the issue, delayed final approval for the delivery of the warheads, which led to further displeasure on the part of the Kennedy administration. In January 1963, the State Department made the extraordinarily undiplomatic move of issuing a press release contradicting several of Diefenbaker's statements. The press release, in the opinion of the Douglas Harkness, was nothing less than "a piece of complete stupidity."[14] The External Affairs Minister Howard Green, emboldened in his opposition to the warheads, claimed that Canada should not join the "nuclear club" in the midst of disarmament talks. For his part, Harkness was equally adamant that Canada should live up to its commitments to an ally.[15]

Cabinet ministers were at loggerheads with each other, and with Diefenbaker seemingly incapable of stopping the ministerial drift or coming to a definite decision, the government went into free fall.

Harkness resigned, followed within days by Associate Defence Minister Pierre Sévigny, and then by Trade Minister George Hees. All three had supported Diefenbaker's bid for the leadership in 1956. The government was in shambles a mere six years after assuming office. Not surprisingly, the Conservatives were defeated in early February 1963 on a vote of confidence that briefly united the three opposition parties. In the ensuing election, on April 7, the Liberals added 29 seats to the 100 they had won ten months earlier but fell 4 seats short of forming a majority government. The Conservatives lost 21 of their 116 MPs, and both the NDP and Social Credit held the balance of power, with 17 and 24 seats, respectively. Thus ended the Diefenbaker government.

Pearson, whose party at a policy convention the year before renounced nuclear weapons, reversed course heading into the 1963 election. He pledged that a Liberal government would live up to Canada's defence obligations and accept nuclear warheads. The Liberal leader was alleged to have said that having changed directions on the nuclear issue, he at last became a politician.

The Reconstituted Liberals, CCF, and Social Credit

The 1958 general election had been devastating for the three parties that lost a second time to the Progressive Conservatives. Their task was clear: if they were to again become players of any significance or seriously contend for office at the national level (only the Liberals could come anywhere near to doing this at the time), rebuilding was the name of the game.

Lester Pearson set about making his party as strong an opponent of, and as viable an alternative to, the Conservatives as his reduced numbers allowed. He was joined on the front bench by three seasoned MPs. Paul Martin and Lionel Chevrier were first elected to Parliament in 1935, and both served in the Mackenzie King's and Louis St. Laurent's cabinets. J.W. (Jack) Pickersgill had been King's special assistant for seven years and joined St. Laurent's cabinet upon his election to Parliament in 1953. He was one of the House's legendary figures. An able parliamentarian and debater, he would often jump from his seat to raise a point of order or ask a question – so much so that one of his nicknames was "Jumpin' Jack." Martin, Chevrier, Pickersgill, and Pearson were known as the "Four Horsemen," leading spirited attacks on the Diefenbaker government over the cancellation of the Avro Arrow, the attempted dismissal of James Coyne, the Cuban Missile Crisis, and the nuclear warhead issue.

By 1960–61, cracks had begun appearing in the Diefenbaker government. The Liberals were inching up in the polls at the Tories' expense, the economy was weakening, and, to some of his colleagues and several members of Ottawa's press corps, the prime minister appeared indecisive and defensive. The Liberals gained three more MPs through by-election victories in seats the Tories had won in 1958; the party's fundraising started to pick up; its organizational structure was enhanced in parts of the country, notably in vote-rich Ontario; and Toronto's Keith Davey (who went on to become a legendary political organizer known to everyone in politics as "the Rainmaker") was appointed national campaign director in advance of the 1962 election. Pearson also took steps to rejuvenate the party by, in effect, copying from the Conservative playbook and reaching out to non-British, non-French Canadians. The party hired an "ethnic liaison officer," with responsibility for attracting minority groups to the Liberals just as they had been attracted to the Diefenbaker Conservatives.[16]

No less important was Pearson's decision to convene what became known as a "Thinkers Conference" in Kingston, Ontario, in 1960. The conference accomplished its two goals. First, new blood. With few MPs in attendance (at Pearson's insistence), the door was opened to new supporters. It was hoped that some of the participants might become candidates and, if the party succeeded electorally, join a Pearson government in some capacity. In the event, fully one-quarter of the 196 men and women who participated went on to hold senior (either elected or appointed) positions in Pearson's government.[17]

Second, a new direction. In the short run, the media were not impressed with what they heard about the party's plans should it return to power, but eventually the consensus changed. The cautious, incremental approach to public policies of the King and St. Laurent governments to public policies would be left behind. Instead, a Pearson government would become activist, slightly left-of-centre, and moderately nationalistic, intent on introducing a national pension scheme, a universal health insurance program, improved social assistance programs, limits on foreign control of the economy, and a distinctive Canadian flag.

The Liberal policies, many of which came out of the Kingston conference, had Pearson's full support. They amounted to a major rebranding of the party in advance of the 1962 election. With a host of new, younger candidates, the Liberals transformed themselves into a more expansionist and radical party than the one that had governed for twenty-two straight years under King and St. Laurent. In turn, the change in direction made the party attractive to "a set of highly educated urban professionals [who] came to play a leading role both as [party] strategists and political candidates."[18] This turned out to be one of the cornerstones in the process of making the Liberal Party attractive (increasingly so in the coming decades) to urban Canada. For Pearson, the Kingston conference amounted to, in his own words, the "beginning of our comeback."[19] It also signalled a major turning point in the history of the Liberal Party and, by definition, of the party system.

The squeeze was on the CCF, just as it had been in 1957 and 1958 when a revived and activist Progressive Conservative party burst onto the scene. Like the Liberals, the CCF used the period between 1958 and 1962 to reconstruct the party. It turned out to be a major overhaul. From early 1956, the year the Winnipeg Manifesto was issued, leading CCF members thought it imperative to forge links with organized labour. The intent – which found favour among executive officers of the newly constituted Canadian Labour Congress and leading CCF figures such as Stanley Knowles, David Lewis, Frank Scott, and T.C. Douglas – was to form a party that would bring under one roof CCF adherents, farm organizations, and labour. "New Party" clubs were formed at the constituency level in several parts of the country following the 1958 electoral disaster, and in a 1960 by-election a "New Party" candidate took an Ontario seat that had been won by the Conservatives only two years earlier with two-thirds of the vote. Once again, the future looked promising for democratic socialism.

The founding convention of the new party was held in Ottawa in 1961. It made three significant decisions. First, by preferential voting among the delegates it chose "New Democratic Party" as its name. Second, Tommy Douglas, then in his seventeenth year as premier of Saskatchewan, was overwhelmingly chosen leader. Third, reflecting the important role that labour was expected to play in broadening the party's support in Central Canada, the party platform was less doctrinaire than the CCF's had been.

The breakthrough the NDP hoped for failed to materialize in the 1962 election, however. By moving the Liberals to the left, Pearson had stolen the NDP's thunder on issues such as a national health insurance scheme. Although organized labour contributed financially to the NDP campaign, it failed to deliver as many votes as party strategists had hoped. Moreover, not all farm organizations and CCF activists favoured formal links with organized labour. The two had not always seen eye to eye on policies and electoral arrangements in the past, and this continued for the next few years, especially in the CCF's traditional stronghold of Saskatchewan, where the provincial party waited several years before reorganizing under the NDP name.

As if to bear out the party's shifting support base, the share of the vote the NDP received on the prairies – apart from two

T.C. (Tommy) Douglas at the 1961 New Democratic Party convention where he was chosen as the first leader of the federal party, Ottawa, July 31 to August 4. | Photographer Duncan Cameron, Library and Archives Canada, C-036222

constituencies in Winnipeg – dropped to levels lower than the CCF had ever reached. MP Hazen Argue, who had succeeded M.J. Coldwell as CCF leader but lost to Tommy Douglas in the 1961 NDP leadership race, defected to the Liberals early in 1962. The final blow to the NDP was Douglas's defeat in the 1962 federal election in his home province of Saskatchewan. Winning only nineteen seats and 13.5 percent of the national vote in 1962 and seventeen seats and 13.1 percent of the vote in 1963, the NDP got off to a rocky start.

Social Credit was not about to give up after its 1958 wipeout. Determined to remain a player at the federal level, the party attempted to build on what had been its base in Alberta and reach out to eastern Canada, notably Quebec. A new constitution and a new set of policies (which were very similar to the old) were drafted in 1960. A new leader, Robert Thompson, was selected the following year. Thompson had long been active in Alberta Social Credit circles, and there were those in his province, including the premier, who thought he could broaden the party's base nationally. Thompson was not known outside Alberta, however, which meant that during the 1962 election, which took place soon after he became leader, he was competing for headlines and news coverage against three established political figures – Diefenbaker, Pearson, and Douglas.

Thompson's rival for the Social Credit leadership was Réal Caouette, a firebrand on the hustings. A car dealer from Rouyn, Quebec, he had long been supportive of Social Credit ideas. Named associate leader after his loss to Thompson, he made effective use of television coverage of his events in northern Quebec. His powerful speeches and dynamic presentations advancing the case for his brand of social credit capitalized on the unpopularity of the Conservative government, uncertainty about Pearson's Liberals, and the socialist solutions of the newly created NDP.

The 1962 election gave Caouette an opportunity few politicians have. Social Credit elected thirty MPs: two each in Alberta and British Columbia, and twenty-six in Quebec. The balance of power within the party had clearly shifted. In 1963, Social Credit retained its four seats in the West but slipped to twenty in Quebec. Within months, internal disagreements led Caouette and a dozen other *créditistes* to quit the party and establish their own. This left Thompson and his colleagues with just eleven seats – one less than the threshold for recognition as an "official party" under parliamentary rules. Neither party lasted long. By the early 1980s, both Social Credit and the Ralliement créditiste had disappeared from the federal scene, unlike the NDP, which now has an established presence both federally and provincially.

With the eventual disappearance of Social Credit, the transformation of the CCF into the NDP, the emergence of a more activist and moderately nationalist Liberal Party under Lester Pearson, and the westward shift in the Conservatives' principal support base, the groundwork for a changed political landscape had been laid over the course of six years.

8

Legacies

WHAT DID THE CONSERVATIVES leave behind? Were there any ac-complishments and legacies we should acknowledge as having come from Diefenbaker's six-year prime ministership, or was it all merely a flash in the political pan? As with most governments, the Conservatives under John Diefenbaker left a mixed record after six years in office. Before examining this record, however, it is import-ant to look at what happened to bring down a government that people had placed such hope in at the outset and that seemed so full of ideas and energy compared with the Liberal government that preceded it.

The Unravelling

Things fall apart; the centre cannot hold.

— W.B. YEATS

The end of the Diefenbaker era came not with a bang but a whim-per – a prolonged whimper. Not that it was without noise and controversy and accusations and recrimination. There was plenty of that from all sides following the government's defeat in 1963 and the Conservatives' failure to make anything more than marginal gains in seats and popular vote share in 1965. The Tories, according to the Gallup Poll, had suffered a precipitous decline in public support in the wake of the Avro Arrow decision and the increasingly weak economy, falling from 59 percent shortly before the Arrow announcement in 1959 to 38 percent in September 1960. In its remaining years, the Diefenbaker government never got over 40 percent.

Diefenbaker loyalists in the general public defended him staunchly. They were, on balance, older and from less urban parts of the country – the Maritimes, rural Ontario, the interior of British Columbia and, especially, the prairies. They remained fiercely loyal to "Dief the Chief." Diefenbaker critics, on the other hand, tended to be younger, from Quebec (particularly francophone Quebecers), and from major urban centres in Ontario and British Columbia. There were clearly regional, linguistic, and age differentials on the question of support for the Tory leader from which the party did not recover under his watch.

Following the 1962 election, critics, including a few MPs and cabinet ministers, wanted Diefenbaker out. In at least one instance in early 1963, a group of cabinet ministers (a "cabal," in Ellen Fairclough's opinion[1]) attempted a ministerial coup. Diefenbaker fended them off by rallying support in the Tory caucus. All but a handful of major newspapers, including the two Toronto dailies (the *Globe and Mail* and the *Toronto Telegram*) that had previously supported Diefenbaker either withheld their support in the 1963 election or backed the Liberals. Finally, many individual Canadians, who in some cases could trace their engagement in Canadian politics to Diefenbaker's messianic appeal in his early years as leader, sensed the futility of his continued leadership. In the words of one Tory supporter from Atlantic Canada, "I'm not a turn-coat. But things are in a hell of a mess. It all seems to be pulling apart."[2]

So, what went wrong that led to the Diefenbaker government's defeat in 1963? Possibly at the top of the list would be the prime minister's failure to recognize that his familiar refrain of "One Canada" may have resonated with some but certainly not all, especially in the increasingly nationalistic quarters of Quebec. By the early 1960s, much of the province had come to embrace "*deux nations*," a concept Diefenbaker would never accept and would rail against for the rest of his life. As his leadership wore on, he grew increasingly out of sync with the new Quebec, a province he had never understood well to begin with.

Under Diefenbaker, the Quebec wing of the parliamentary party had become dispirited, and morale among the large Tory contingent in Parliament slipped dramatically during their four years of majority government. Many of the Quebec MPs had arrived on Parliament Hill in 1958 thanks to a combination of Maurice Duplessis's organization and Diefenbaker's sudden popularity in the province. On the whole, these new MPs were unfamiliar with Ottawa and federal politics, and Diefenbaker did not make it any easier for them to become part of his team. He gave no Quebec MP a senior cabinet portfolio, he did not name someone approximating a deputy leader from the province, and he prohibited the Quebec MPs from meeting as a separate caucus to discuss federal matters germane to their province. On resigning from the Conservative Party to sit as an Independent MP months before the 1965 election, Leon Balcer, who had held various portfolios in Diefenbaker's cabinet, told the press that "there is no place for a French Canadian in the party of Mr. Diefenbaker."[3] The opportunity that the 1958 election had provided the Conservatives to create a strong, lasting presence in Quebec had been wasted.

Then there were Diefenbaker's skillful attacks on C.D. Howe, Jimmy Gardiner, and others in the St. Laurent government that worked at the time but belonged to a bygone era. Those men were no longer on the scene. Fittingly, during Diefenbaker's tenure, the Liberals and CCF/NDP regrouped under different leaders, candidates, and policies. The Tories did not. As a result, Diefenbaker and his government now became the targets on the 1962 and 1963 campaign trails, proving the adage that "what goes around, comes around."

In addition, Diefenbaker had grown increasingly suspicious and distrustful of some of those around him, notably cabinet colleagues, party officials, and senior public servants. A few even detected what they considered a streak of paranoia in his dealings with the press, bureaucrats, and some members of cabinet. Diefenbaker was given to occasional fits of temper and to embarrassing ministers in front of their colleagues. Such incidents, combined with his widely acknowledged unwillingness (or inability?) to make tough decisions, his almost complete lack of understanding of Quebec at a critical moment in the province's development, his falling out with the Americans over mutual defence responsibilities, and his increasingly testy relationship with the press, led to growing pressure to force him out of the leadership.

Diefenbaker had entered executive office with few of the organizational, managerial, and political skills an accomplished leader needs to hold together a coalition of contending interests, regions, and egos. Practising law for two decades, often on his own, he had few opportunities to delegate responsibility or work closely with associates or partners. Parties, especially those in power, depend on a generous measure of collegiality and teamwork if they are to function properly. Descriptions of cabinet meetings near the end of Diefenbaker tenure suggest deep concern on the part of many ministers about the government's lack of focus and, equally troubling, the prime minister's inability to bring prolonged, inconclusive cabinet debates on matters of vital importance to a definitive conclusion. In the words of Defence Minister Douglas Harkness, Diefenbaker had a "pathological hatred of taking a hard decision."[4] This view was shared by others in cabinet.

The first two years of Diefenbaker's government, when it was at the height of its popularity, suggest that the prime minister may not always have been as indecisive. But it is fair to say that he had an easy time of it given the political situation then. The opposition was in disarray, Canadians were tired of Liberal governments, and the new prime minister's popularity was unmatched. From 1957 to early 1959, the government acted with a resolve and a degree of unanimity that had completely disappeared by its sixth year in office. Could the economic and political fallout from the cancellation of the Avro Arrow program in 1959 (for which Diefenbaker stated publicly on several occasions he assumed full responsibility) have taken its toll on his capacity for concluding decisively the matter at hand? It is tempting to think so, but one can only speculate.

The Diefenbaker government took office more or less at the same time that an economic recession hit the country. Over the next few years, unemployment reached levels unseen since the Great Depression. In the short run, Diefenbaker's preferred option was to blame the St. Laurent government for creating the conditions giving rise to a recession. This could go only so far, however. As we have seen, the dispute with Bank of Canada governor James Coyne over monetary policy dominated the political agenda in early 1961, causing uneasiness in the domestic and foreign financial communities and putting nearly constant pressure on the dollar. This situation, together with the lacklustre economy, lasted through the 1963 election and gave rise to genuine concern in financial circles over the government's ability to manage the economy.[5]

Legacies

Forced out of office by the 1963 election, the Diefenbaker government left behind a decidedly mixed record. It had fumbled the ball – sometimes badly – on matters of national and international importance. At the same time, however, Diefenbaker and his ministers undertook various initiatives for which they have not always received full credit and that are now an accepted part of the country's social, economic, and political fabric.

At one level, they include the obvious. Diefenbaker started the slow and still far from complete process of making federal institutions more representative of Canada's population. By the 1950s, white, mostly middle-aged (or older) men had long monopolized electoral politics, a fact reflected in membership in the House of Commons, the Senate, and cabinet, as well as in appointments to the courts and federal agencies and boards. The mould was broken (and the glass ceiling cracked ever so slightly) with a few of Diefenbaker's appointments to such institutions and with a more diverse set of Tory election candidates than the usual mix of businessmen and lawyers. Justin Trudeau's boast about his gender-equal cabinet ("Because it's 2015") can be seen as the logical heir to the move first taken in 1957.

The Diefenbaker government tackled several institutional and constitutional reforms that had either been avoided by previous governments or had failed to gain the necessary agreement from the provinces. Not all were completed during its tenure, but, if nothing else, they were placed on the to-do list for future governments. Legislation requiring mandatory retirement at age seventy-five for federally appointed provincial superior court judges comes to mind as an example of an institutional reform that the Diefenbaker government introduced. It was adopted in 1961, bringing the retirement age in line with that established in 1927 for the Supreme Court of Canada.

The right to vote was extended to Status Indians in 1960. They were the last Indigenous Canadians to be enfranchised, and Diefenbaker was determined to set that right. It should come as no surprise to learn that First Nations saw Diefenbaker as "their great champion"[6] in Parliament for his handling of the Indigenous file and his appointment of James Gladstone of the Blood Reserve in Alberta to the Senate, the first Indigenous person named to that body. Diefenbaker liked to remind audiences and colleagues that as a youngster growing up on the prairies, he had come to know

James Gladstone, the first Indigenous person appointed
to the Senate, 1958. Gladstone was a member of the
Blood Tribe of the Blackfoot Nation in Alberta. |
University of Saskatchewan Archives and Special Collections,
JGD/MG311/3864

and respect many local Indigenous Peoples, among them the
legendary Northwest Rebellion Métis leader Gabriel Dumont,
who frequented the Diefenbaker family's modest home. This was
an experience that no previous party leader had had, and in its own
way helps to explain his understanding of Native concerns.

Diefenbaker's record of promoting the cause of Indigenous
Peoples was acknowledged at various points in his career. He was

On May 27, 1959, Wa Pa Ha Ska (Whitecap Dakota First Nation) Chief
Little Crow granted Prime Minister John Diefenbaker the honorary
name "Walking Buffalo" at the inauguration of the construction of
the Gardiner Dam near Outlook, Saskatchewan. | Provincial Archives of
Saskatchewan, Saskatchewan Government Photographic Services photo 59-090-06

named an Honorary Chief by the Union of Saskatchewan Indians
in 1953 ("Chief Eagle") and by the Whitecap Dakota First Nation
in 1959 ("Walking Buffalo"). And following the passage of the
legislation extending the right to vote to Status Indians, he was in-
ducted into the exclusive Kainai Chieftainship by Alberta's Blood
Reserve.[7]

On a related matter, Ellen Fairclough, whose responsibilities as
minister of citizenship and immigration included the Indian Affairs
branch, was given the green light to introduce legislation that would
establish an Indian land claims commission. Initially recommended
soon after the Second World War by a special joint committee of
Parliament, the idea got nowhere until the report of a second joint
parliamentary committee (co-chaired by Senator James Gladstone)

was issued in 1961. In a handwritten note to Fairclough, her deputy minister recommended having Parliament approve the establishment of a three-member independent commission to settle various long-standing grievances, including British Columbia and Oka land titles, noting that the move "had the support of Indian and non-Indian organizations" and would do much to "regain the confidence of the Indians." Fairclough's handwritten response was short and to the point: "Ok. Let's do it then."[8] Bill C-130 to create such a body received first reading in early 1962 but died on the order paper when the election was called. Not until twelve years later was an Office of Native Claims (ONC) established.

Many opposition members and party leaders dating back to 1903 had called for an end to electoral boundary readjustments by the federal cabinet, but no government had taken up the task. It was difficult for governments to relinquish a power that made it possible to minimize opponents' election chances and enhance their own. As an MP on the opposition benches, Diefenbaker bore a particular grievance against Agriculture Minister Jimmy Gardiner, whom he held responsible for eliminating ("Jimmymandering," Diefenbaker called it) his Saskatchewan electoral district in the 1947 redistribution. The move was easy to read: it was an attempt by the Liberals to "rid the House of an annoying antagonist."[9] Diefenbaker, like others on the opposition benches before him, promised to end the practice of partisan redistricting if given a chance. Once in office, he became the first prime minister to introduce a motion calling for the establishment of independent, arm's-length commissions to draw riding boundaries. Nothing came of it as the 1962 election and 1962–63 minority government intervened, but Lester Pearson picked up the ball, and in 1964 his government ushered through Parliament the Electoral Boundaries Readjustment Act, which entrusted redistricting to ten independent commissions, one for each province.

Diefenbaker chaired four federal-provincial conferences during his six years in office. Three major decisions came out of them. First, the Atlantic Adjustment Grants were intended to benefit a less prosperous region of the country. Such a program had been a feature of Diefenbaker's 1957 election platform. It was approved with the valuable support of Ontario premier Leslie Frost,[10] setting a precedent for subsequent financial assistance programs targeted at specific regions, such as the Department of Regional Economic Expansion (DREE), created in 1969.

Second, the initial requirement of the national hospital insurance program – that a majority of the provinces with at least a majority of Canada's population had to sign on before federal funding would begin – was dropped. This meant that federal contributions to the three provinces with existing programs – Saskatchewan, Alberta, and British Columbia – could begin receiving funds at once. Tommy Douglas, Saskatchewan premier at the time, thought that eliminating the original condition was very much to Diefenbaker's "credit," and that without the change Canada "would not have had hospital insurance for many years."[11] Ontario soon signed on, and by 1961 all ten provinces were on board. The acceptance of a universal hospital insurance program helped pave the way for the publicly funded medical care insurance program that was adopted in the mid-1960s.

Third, the equalization formula that had come out of the final federal-provincial conference of the St. Laurent era (1956) proved to be contentious. Ontario voiced strong opposition to the plan and sought to have it replaced. This figured prominently in Premier Leslie Frost's backing of the federal Conservatives (who had promised to revisit the issue) in the 1957 election. The upshot was the replacement of the "tax rental" agreement that had been in effect since 1941 with a system of block grants and tax "abatements" whereby the federal government would leave "room" for the provinces to introduce their own personal and corporate taxes and succession duties. In Frost's opinion, the new arrangements were a "substantial improvement" over the old.[12]

Davie Fulton was one of the more talented and effective of Diefenbaker's ministers. As minister of justice, he undertook a constitutional initiative that came close to being accepted but ultimately fell short of unanimous agreement when both Quebec and Saskatchewan (for quite contradictory reasons) opted not to support it. The plan was to "patriate" the British North America Act by making it a Canadian, not a British, document and to defer the question of designing an acceptable constitutional amendment procedure until the act was "domiciled" in Canada. The patriation issue had bedeviled governments and policymakers of all stripes for the better part of the century. Since the last attempt to marshal unanimous approval for the move had ended in failure over a decade earlier, Fulton felt that the passage of time may have resulted in sufficiently new and favourable conditions and players to make approval possible. This turned out not to be the case, but it did spur a new generation of scholars and federal and provincial politicians and officials to carry the torch on the question of Canada's constitution. The "Fulton Formula," as it was dubbed, was picked up by Lester Pearson's justice minister, Guy Favreau, soon after the Liberals returned to office in 1963. And from the "Fulton-Favreau Formula," it was only a matter of time before Pierre Trudeau brought the matter to a head with the 1980–81 constitutional negotiations and ultimately the 1982 patriation of the BNA Act and the adoption of the Canadian Charter of Rights and Freedoms.[13] In its own way, the Fulton Formula was part of a "thread of continuity."[14]

Diefenbaker took pride in his defence of civil liberties, whether in the courtroom, on the campaign trail, or in Parliament. In countless speeches, he revealed a singular dedication to fighting for this cause. He helped alert Canadians to the fact that part of a government's responsibility is first to ensure that citizens have the means to protect their rights and freedoms, and second to work on the international front to end blatantly discriminatory practices that violate civil liberties. Domestically, what Diefenbaker considered his "greatest achievement"[15] was the Canadian Bill of Rights, adopted with unanimous support in Parliament in 1960. As bold and clear a statement of rights and freedoms as it was, the Bill of Rights was nonetheless a statutory document, not an entrenched part of the constitution. Diefenbaker had indicated that if agreement could be reached with the provinces on an entrenched bill of rights he would willingly accept that, but as such an agreement was not a realistic possibility, he settled for the second best option.[16] Because the Bill of Rights' scope was limited to matters under federal, but not provincial, jurisdiction, and it was a statute rather than a constitutionally entrenched document, it was judged by leading constitutional authorities and the Canadian Bar Association to be of little more value than a bold statement of principles. At one level, the critics were right. Over the course of the next two decades (until the adoption of the constitutionally entrenched Canadian Charter of Rights and Freedoms in 1982), it played scarcely any part in court decisions. In the end it was seen as having little more than interpretive value, and in only five of the thirty-five court cases where it was cited did it constitute part of the decision.[17]

In another respect, however, the Bill of Rights proved to have both educational and propaganda value, and it shed light on the need to remedy the failure of the Diefenbaker initiative at some point in the future. The question of how best to protect rights and freedoms became a talking point among Canadians who had paid little or no attention to civil liberties in the past. Twenty thousand copies of the Bill of Rights were distributed to schools across the country, and its contents found their way into the pages of law journals and into lectures and discussions in university classes in law, political science, and history, where topics such as "provincial and federal jurisdictions," "entrenchment," and "constitutional amendments" were discussed, often for the first time.

Ultimately, the Diefenbaker package helped pave the way for the adoption of the Canadian Charter of Rights and Freedoms. When the Trudeau-initiated proposals for patriation of the constitution and entrenchment of the Charter were argued, challenged, and approved in the early 1980s, it was fair to say that the path had been made somewhat easier, or at least more comprehensible at the public level, for those who favoured adoption of the Charter. At a minimum, supporters could point to the Tories' Canadian Bill of Rights as a means of addressing concerns with the Trudeau package that were voiced by some Conservatives nearly two decades later. At the same time, they could also argue that the case had been made for constitutionally *entrenched* protections of rights and freedoms *because* of the obvious inadequacy of statutory guarantees. In its way, the Canadian Bill of Rights was part of another "remarkable thread of continuity"[18] dating back to the 1930s that pointed to the need to protect civil liberties and the best way of going about it.

With respect to a government's international obligation to respect civil liberties, the Diefenbaker government focused a good deal of attention partway through its six years in office on one issue – South Africa's policy of apartheid. Diefenbaker and his colleagues found racial segregation repugnant, and the prime minister used the occasion of two Commonwealth meetings in London (1960 and 1961) to express Canada's official view on the subject. He was uncomfortable with the notion of expelling South Africa from the Commonwealth for, as he told the House of Commons, there would be "no merit in such action."[19] Yet his fear of a split between "white and non-white" Commonwealth members at the 1961 meeting prompted him to join an initiative of the newly independent Commonwealth countries that in the end led South Africa to withdraw from the organization. Canada had not been the principal actor on that front – this role fell to the non-aligned countries, notably India – but as the only "white" Commonwealth country to side with them, its "involvement did influence the outcome."[20] It also signalled a shift in foreign policy from one that was based largely on Canada's relations with European and American allies to one that also embraced the African continent and the Far East.

It has been credibly claimed that "South Africa's departure from the Commonwealth is one of the most notable developments of the Diefenbaker years."[21] This event took on a life of its own over the next several years. Diefenbaker's opposition to apartheid was singled out years later by Nelson Mandela, and still later by former prime ministers Brian Mulroney and Joe Clark, as a key moment in Commonwealth history. On the occasion of his becoming the first-ever honorary citizen of Canada in 1990, Mandela singled out Diefenbaker's stand on apartheid in his address to Parliament: "I would ... like to pay special tribute to the Prime Minister of this country, Brian Mulroney, who has continued along the path charted by Prime Minister Diefenbaker who acted against apartheid because he knew that no person of conscience could stand aside as a crime against humanity was being committed."[22] Mulroney, in turn, commented favourably on Diefenbaker's role in ending apartheid in a personal reflection about Mandela following the latter's death in 2013.[23] Joe Clark, recalling his service in the Mulroney cabinet as external affairs minister, was asked why the Progressive Conservatives made apartheid a "Canadian cause." He found his answer in Diefenbaker's promise to South Africa in 1961 to shine a "light in the window" and added that opposing apartheid was "part of our 'family' history."[24]

Reforms to Canada's immigration policies introduced by the Diefenbaker government paved the way for Canada's becoming a vastly more ethnically and racially varied country. Ellen Fairclough inherited a framework for admitting immigrants that she saw as inconsistent with Canada's stated opposition to racial inequality (notably in its challenge to apartheid) in its foreign policy. She also felt that the unspoken goal of maintaining a "white-only" immigration policy was out of sync with the non-discriminatory objectives of her own government's Canadian Bill of Rights. A determined minister, she advanced her liberal views on immigration against a sometimes reluctant department and indifferent cabinet colleagues.[25]

The immigration system under the previous Liberal government, based on country of origin and family relationships, privileged certain groups and individuals at the expense of others. Its inherent bias favoured immigrants from Western Europe and the United States, who, by definition, were almost all white. J.W. Pickersgill, who admitted that his own views on immigration were "conservative," was special assistant to Mackenzie King in 1947 when King announced Canada's postwar immigration policy. Pickersgill drafted the prime minister's speech, in which he argued that Canadians did not want to "make fundamental alteration[s] in the character of our population." "Large-scale immigration from the Orient," King asserted, "would change the fundamental composition of the Canadian population."[26]

Fairclough found that position objectionable. She introduced regulations that shifted immigration criteria towards, in her own words, "individual attributes such as education, skills, and work experience," regardless of country of origin.[27] If imitation is the sincerest form of flattery, then Fairclough should have felt flattered. Within three years, the Americans implemented similar reforms, and the Australians followed suit a decade later. Subsequent Canadian governments have refined Fairclough's criteria by applying a "point system," but the important groundwork had been completed shortly before the 1962 election. The Diefenbaker government has been credited with being one of the first in the world to do away with racial criteria in its immigration policy.[28]

In addition to Diefenbaker's familiarity with the social and ethnic mix on the prairies, agricultural policies were the key to the Tories' success in the region. Credit for this goes largely to Alvin Hamilton, an archetypal "ideas man" who, as minister of northern affairs and national resources from 1957 to 1960 enthusiastically supported Diefenbaker's "Northern Vision" and the party's "Road to Resources" program. Soon after his move to the Agriculture Department in 1960, Hamilton headed a large Canadian delegation to Rome for a meeting of the United Nations Food and Agriculture Organiza- tion (FAO) charged with creating a global reserve of food products and money. Diefenbaker claimed that he had been the first to float the idea of a so-called World Food Bank in December 1957 at a meeting of NATO heads of government.[29] Whatever its origin, the plan gained great traction, and when the final negotiations got underway, it was Hamilton who represented Canada.

Seeing the twin opportunities such a program offered to help countries with food shortages as well as to promote the sale of Can- adian agricultural products, Hamilton played an important part in gaining unanimous approval for the establishment of the World Food Bank. In his words, he approached the task of getting the delegates' support "the old-fashioned way [by treating] the exercise as a political campaign – you sell each group in turn."[30] He did not mention it, but one of the groups was the Vatican, and the Pope's delegate readily signed on, which was a helpful endorsement. The World Food Bank was awarded the Nobel Peace Prize in 2020, sixty years after Hamilton attended the founding convention of the FAO initiative.

Through the Canadian Wheat Board, Hamilton also negotiated large sales of Canadian wheat and barley worth hundreds of millions of dollars. The cabinet made it clear that the sales were to be cash – no credit.[31] The sale was done against the explicit requests of the United States *not* to negotiate with the Communist Chinese regime. The move doubtless laid the groundwork for Canadian trade with China and gave Canada a head start over the United States on commercial relations with China. It opened the Chinese market to further Canadian agricultural sales (such as canola seed and livestock), some manufactured and finished goods, and natural resources. The long-term domestic political consequence of the sales was profound, for it helped to turn what had essentially been a prairie fortress of Liberal, CCF, and Social Credit support into a Conservative mainstay.

That the government saw agriculture as a vital part of the Canadian economy became even more obvious when Hamilton seized upon an initiative conceived during Harkness's tenure as agriculture minister. Early in 1961, he embarked on negotiations with the provinces that in his mind exemplified cooperative federalism at its best. Federal-provincial agreements would be aimed directly at alleviating the problems of rural poverty through the funding of projects for alternative use of low-productivity or marginal land, and – ahead of its time – developing and conserving soil and water resources in Canada.

The bill creating the program – the Agricultural Rehabilitation and Development Act (ARDA) – was approved by Parliament without a dissenting vote. It became the darling child of the Diefenbaker government in the field of agriculture and was judged, at least in the short run, to have "made a constructive and promising beginning ... to come to grips with rural poverty and regional disparities."[32] Blair Fraser, one of Canada's leading journalists and columnists, was no friend of the government. He was said to be "suspicious of the Conservatives in general and Diefenbaker in particular."[33] Nonetheless, he saw great merit in ARDA and went out of his way to praise both the government and Hamilton. To him, the program was about as "bipartisan ... a federal-provincial [agreement] as it's possible" to get, dedicated as it was to rescuing "the rural poor."[34] Under the Pearson government, the program was moved from the Agriculture to the Forestry Department, but it was preserved largely intact. ARDA has since met with a decidedly mixed fate, first as part of the Regional Economic Expansion program, and finally in a much-altered form in Agriculture Canada.

The 1958 election saw Diefenbaker campaign on his vision of national development. In advance of the election, he had charged Hamilton with designing what became a ten-point program on major infrastructure projects. Hamilton's enthusiasm for the task matched Diefenbaker's. The plan called for exploration and development of the mineral-rich territories, hydro power development of the Columbia River in British Columbia, thermal power plants in Atlantic Canada, and roads, bridges, and rail lines to the North. It was vast in scope and was premised, as Diefenbaker liked to remind his campaign audiences, on a new national purpose and national identity.

Parts of the national development program eventually fell into place. They included transportation infrastructure to the North (the Roads to Resources program, which led to the construction of 4,000 miles of roads to parts of the North previously inaccessible by land);[35] the Columbia River Treaty with the United States; the Atlantic Provinces Power Development Act; the South Saskatchewan River Dam; the advancement of geological surveys and mapping of the North; the creation of an autonomous Department of Forestry; and the establishment of the federal-provincial ARDA program.

Early in the 1958 campaign, Hamilton found Diefenbaker receptive to his idea of a federal-provincial conference on resource development. Out of that came one of the most important conferences of the period, the 1961 Resources for Tomorrow Conference in Montreal, attended by 800 delegates from across the country. It succeeded in its primary goal of creating the Canadian Council of Resource Ministers (now the Canadian Council of Ministers of the Environment). The conference was the first major gathering of its kind to highlight the importance of protecting the environment, and the ministerial council that resulted from it is now considered the "single most important body involved in federal-provincial environmental relations."[36]

Not all the promised development schemes were realized. Some northern roads and bridges did not get off the drawing board. The national energy grid that Hamilton envisaged did not receive cabinet approval as, given the state of the economy, it was felt to be an inopportune time to proceed with such a massive project. The economic downturn and growing unemployment forced the finance minister and his officials to attend to more pressing, immediate issues. Some ministers also had reservations about supporting grand development schemes rather than smaller projects with possibly greater electoral appeal in targeted areas.

The Diefenbaker government acted expeditiously to implement the principal recommendations of the Royal Commission on Broadcasting (also known as the Fowler Commission, after its chairman, Robert Fowler), a body appointed by the St. Laurent government in 1955. Speed was of the essence, for television – notably private television, which was about to challenge the monopoly of the Canadian Broadcasting Corporation – was new on the scene. Government action was needed to ensure fairness in the granting of television licences, in overseeing the content of public and private carriers, and in regulating the industry. The Conservatives accepted the Royal Commission's major recommendations. A Broadcasting Act was adopted by Parliament in 1958, and a broadly representative fifteen-member Board of Broadcast Governors (BBG) came soon after. It was to serve at arm's length from both government and industry and was charged with regulating and licensing radio and television carriers. The BBG was replaced a decade later by the Canadian Radio-Television Commission (CRTC). Its responsibilities have since been expanded to include the licensing of Internet and mobile phone providers. Not surprisingly, given its mandate, the

CRTC has become one of the more influential (and controversial) of Canada's regulatory agencies.[37]

During its six years in office, the Diefenbaker government established a number of Royal Commissions of Inquiry on a range of issues: energy, government organization, transportation, publications, taxation, and health services. Inevitably, some had a measurable impact on public policy, others very little or none. Possibly the most important agency created by the Diefenbaker government at the recommendation of one of its commissions was the National Energy Board (1959), charged with the regulation and operation of oil and natural gas pipelines across provincial and international boundaries. The Tories did not want a repeat of the 1956 pipeline fiasco in Parliament. Major recommendations contained in the three-volume report of the Royal Commission on Transportation of 1961–62 were enacted by the Pearson government in 1967.[38] The Canadian Transport Commission was established with an expanded set of responsibilities over the previous transportation body and a mandate to ensure a measure of competition and deregulation in Canada's transportation industry.[39]

The Royal Commission on Publications, chaired by Grattan O'Leary, lifelong Conservative and editor and publisher of the *Ottawa Journal*, stands as part of the continuous debate in Canada over national identity and cultural sovereignty. It was established in 1960 to examine the effect that foreign "split-run" publications, such as *Time* and *Reader's Digest*, had on Canada's magazine and periodical industry. Split-run editions of American magazines carried advertisements "directed at the Canadian market [with] content derived from the American editions."[40] American magazines enjoyed approximately 80 percent of the Canadian market and a sizable chunk of Canadian print advertising,[41] and Canadian publishers had argued for many years that they were in precarious financial shape. It was an issue tailor-made for the Diefenbaker government: American cultural dominance in one sector of the economy. Yet prolonged cabinet discussions about freedom of the press, government subsidies, tax concessions, or tariffs on foreign publications were left unresolved when the government fell. The commission's report had been issued in 1961. Its principal recommendation – to the effect that income tax deductions for advertisements carried in foreign publications would no longer be allowed for Canadian companies – was finally implemented by the Trudeau government some fifteen years later, over the objections of American-owned publications.

The *Report of the Royal Commission on Taxation* comprised six volumes that, among other things, found tax loopholes in the Canadian tax regime objectionable and urged higher tax rates for the wealthy. Pierre Trudeau's government indicated it would act on some of the commission's recommendations, but apart from a partial taxation of capital gains, it backed off from any major reforms. Critics of Canada's tax regime still point to a variety of loopholes and argue in favour of higher taxes on the wealthy. The five-volume *Report of the Royal Commission on Government Organization* led to few significant changes in either the structure or the operation of the federal government, and such changes as were implemented, particularly with respect to the Treasury Board, were said not to have worked.

Without a doubt, the Diefenbaker-appointed Royal Commission with the greatest staying power and the biggest impact on all Canadians was the seven-member Royal Commission on Health Services, chaired by Mr. Justice Emmett Hall, long-time friend of Diefenbaker since their student days at the University of Saskatchewan. The commission's two-volume report was released a little over a year after the Pearson Liberals replaced the Diefenbaker Conservatives in 1963, and it fell to the Liberals to complete what the Conservatives had begun. The Hall Commission had been charged with investigating the facilities and programs for the provision of health care in Canada and recommending ways to ensure that the best possible health care would be available for all Canadians. After reviewing a score of commissioned research studies and conducting on-site visits in other countries, the commissioners agreed unanimously to a plan that would establish "a comprehensive, universal Health Services Program for the Canadian people."[42] With the report in hand, the Pearson government ushered the necessary legislation through Parliament. Canada's Medicare system was created, although it was a good deal less radical than the Hall Report had envisioned as the Liberals considered the package of reforms too costly for the public purse. Still, it is fair to say that the implementation of the major recommendations of the Hall Commission had a profound effect on how Canadians identify and value what they regard as distinctive about their country.

The adage "all is fair in love and war – but not in politics" has a certain relevance to the implementation of the Hall Commission's report. The report remains an outstanding illustration of distinguished research and reasoned analysis. Appointed by one government, the commissioners saw many of their recommendations adopted by another. For obvious reasons, Canadians are taught that it was the Pearson government that established the Medicare system. This is entirely appropriate, but what is sometimes overlooked is that it was the Diefenbaker government that made it possible. The Liberals had staked part of their election campaign on introducing a national health insurance program if elected. A report from a commission appointed by their political adversaries, and coming so soon after they took office, made their task easier than if they had had to start from scratch with a commission of their own.

Had the Diefenbaker government survived for another few years, would it have introduced a similar Medicare system? An educated guess suggests it would have. As we have seen, early in his tenure, Diefenbaker made the national hospital insurance program accessible to all provinces that wanted to sign on. More to the point, the members of the Hall Commission were scarcely chosen at random. Their views on publicly funded medical schemes might not have been known in advance, but reasonable judgments could be made about their leanings and preferences. Emmett Hall and John Diefenbaker went back a long time, for example. They knew each other well – need one say more?[43]

What is striking about these initiatives is how varied they were and how important some of them became to Canadian society and politics: broadcasting and energy regulatory systems; northern development; liberalization of immigration and refugee standards; the Canadian Bill of Rights as a precursor to the Canadian Charter of Rights and Freedoms; a more inclusive franchise; opposition to South African apartheid; the eventual establishment of Canada's Medicare system; opening up trade with China; renewed federal-provincial constitutional negotiations; and several agricultural initiatives. A final legacy of the Diefenbaker years remains to be considered: how the political parties and the party system were altered in consequence of the 1957 and 1958 elections.

9

Turning Point for the Parties and the Party System

THE CANADIAN PARTY SYSTEM and the parties themselves underwent several major adjustments in the 1950s and 1960s. What had held during the King–St. Laurent era was swept aside as parties redefined themselves and altered their internal power structures. Most notably, leadership reviews were made mandatory under party constitutions, and what were billed as "representative and democratic" delegated leadership contests were opened to a variety of contestants who in the past would never have considered running. In earlier times, leaders were often chosen with little more than a laying of hands by the outgoing leader. This was now over. Most important was the fact that, in tandem with these intra-party changes of the 1960s, the party system was transformed as the major parties traded their respective regional power bases. The changes in the party system that began with the 1957 and 1958 elections were complete by the 1962 and 1963 elections. We are still living with their consequences.

Leadership Review

From 1919 to the 1960s, delegated conventions were used by both the Conservatives and the Liberals to select their leaders, but there were no formal institutional arrangements to deselect them. In fact, some leaders, including Mackenzie King and John Diefenbaker, were known to have beaten back challenges from cabinet colleagues by arguing that they been chosen by the party in convention and only a convention could remove them.[1]

That all changed as the Diefenbaker era ended. Internal fighting over Diefenbaker's leadership once the Tories lost office in 1963, coupled with a reform-minded group in Lester Pearson's Liberal Party, led the two major parties to adopt a "leadership review" process. The NDP soon followed suit. Two or three thousand constituency delegates would gather at annual or biennial conferences to discuss policies, adopt policy resolutions, and elect party executives. For the first time, they would be asked to vote by secret ballot on whether a leadership convention should be called. Its supporters claimed the move would "democratize" the party and make the selection (or deselection) of the leader a matter for all convention delegates to decide. The rationale had an attractive simplicity about it. It was claimed that a party in convention would be more representative of the general population than either the party's parliamentary caucus or cabinet.

As was demonstrated in Diefenbaker's case in 1967 and Joe Clark's in 1983, the new institutional arrangements "made it easier for parties to rid themselves of leaders who were no longer wanted."[2] As is often the way with institutional change, however, it had an unintended consequence, for it opened the door to bitter, often public infighting over a party's leadership in advance of a leadership review vote. This has done nothing to elevate the level of political discourse or to counter the public's often cynical view of politics and politicians. Whether the Mulroney-Clark, Chrétien-Turner, and Martin-Chrétien battles over party leadership would have taken place had there been no institutional framework for assembling scores of supporters in advance of a leadership review vote remains a moot point. If nothing else, the new process certainly had the effect of bringing internal party squabbles to the public's attention.

Be that as it may, the headline-grabbing challenges over party leadership from the early 1980s to the early twenty-first century were some remove – particularly in this day of non-stop cable news networks and social media – from the King–St. Laurent–Pearson model of party decorum and smooth leadership transition. The terms leadership "accountability," "bear-pit," and "question and answer" sessions have entered the Canadian political lexicon and become an established part of the modern Canadian party system. The adoption of a leadership review mechanism completed the circle begun in 1919 of having the leader chosen not by cabinet or the parliamentary caucus but by a delegated convention.

Post-Diefenbaker Parties and Party System

As important as leadership reviews are to individual parties, it is the transformed party system that is the most notable of the legacies of the Diefenbaker era on the political front. The twenty-two years leading up the 1957 election were characterized by one dominant party winning election after election; one formerly major party reduced to a few dozen MPs with scattered pockets of support across the country; and two new but small entrants that relied almost entirely on regional support bases. The surprise Tory win in 1957 followed by their massive victory in 1958 heralded a reversal of electoral fortunes not just for the Conservatives but for all parties.

The two smaller parties followed different paths in the wake of the 1958 election. Social Credit made a brief revival in the 1960s and 1970s, but it was on life support and disappeared completely from federal politics not long after. Following the defection of the party's federal leader, Robert Thompson, to the Progressive Conservatives in 1967, much of its Western wing was effectively subsumed by the Progressive Conservatives the following year. It was a spent force in the West. The Quebec-based Ralliement créditiste, led by Réal Caouette following his break with Thompson in 1963, survived for close to two decades, but with Caouette's death in 1976 and gradual decline in support from 26 percent in 1962 to less than 2 percent in 1980, that party too became extinct.

On the other hand, the Co-operative Commonwealth Federation (CCF) had the staying power that was predicted at its creation in the early 1930s. Its supporters were numerically small at the outset, but they comprised a broader base of interests and groups than Social Credit. As Richard Johnston has noted, the CCF appealed from the get-go to "the progressive and programmatic residue" of the earlier agrarian protest groups while at the same time bringing into its ranks labour supporters and socialist intellectuals who "came to define the party's appeal and modus operandi" in the years ahead.[3] Such a diverse base of support from 1935 to 1958 made the CCF's 1961 transition to the New Democratic Party easier to accomplish and guaranteed the new party's presence to this day.

The NDP gradually created stronger party and campaign organizations and became better financed than its predecessor. Unlike the CCF, which had always fallen well short of a full slate of candidates in federal elections, the NDP has seldom left an electoral district without a candidate since 1962. Most have had little chance of winning (the so-called token candidates), but their very presence has helped the party avoid being dismissed as a "minor" party with little more than a small regional presence. Accordingly, one of the obvious legacies of the 1957 and 1958 elections has been the reformulation of democratic socialism in Canada and the creation of a left-of-centre party that has become a permanent fixture in the Canadian party system.

The defeat in 1962 of its new leader, Tommy Douglas, in Regina signalled a dramatic shift in the fledgling NDP's support base, however. For the first time since the CCF's creation in 1935, the democratic socialists failed to win a single seat in Saskatchewan.

Their support shifted to British Columbia, where, between 1962 and 2021, over one-half (175) of the West's 302 NDP MPs were elected, versus only 15 from Saskatchewan. It is telling that following his defeat in 1962, Douglas headed West and won a seat in Parliament by way of a British Columbia by-election. He was re-elected four more times (and defeated twice), always in British Columbia, and retired from politics in 1979, forty-five years after his first election to the House of Commons as part of J.S. Woodsworth's little band of CCFers.

The NDP's poor showing on the prairies attested to several related facts, all having to do with John Diefenbaker: the prime minister's personal popularity in his home region; the marked improvement in farm income, thanks in large measure to the cash wheat sales to China and the various agricultural support programs introduced by the Tories; and the favourable reception accorded Diefenbaker's "unhyphenated Canadianism" by those of neither British nor French backgrounds. Nelson Wiseman observes that, paradoxically, the "unhyphenated Canadian" refrain did not deter those, mostly on the prairies, who identified as Ukrainian Canadians, Polish Canadians, German Canadians, and the like from voting Conservative, many for the first time. Diefenbaker appealed to their staunch anti-Soviet feelings by pledging, among other things, that "those behind the Iron Curtain would not be forgotten."[4]

Diefenbaker's leadership and activist agenda put the squeeze on the CCF in 1957 and 1958. The Tories' program and first few years in office belied the claim that the party was dominated by eastern financial interests opposed to big government. According to John Meisel, in the lead-up to the 1957 election, it "was often difficult to distinguish between CCF and Conservative criticisms of the Liberals."[5] The Conservatives' moderately left-of-centre program, coupled with their skill in positioning themselves as the obvious party to vote for to bring about the defeat the Liberals, meant there was relatively little chance that the CCF would make gains.

Both the CCF and Social Credit could trace at least part of their origin to the protest refrain of the Progressives of the 1920s. From the outset, however, how differently they operated in a first-past-the-post parliamentary electoral system was very telling. The Progressives had been sufficiently anti-institutional that they "were not sure that they even wanted to be a party."[6] Social Credit shared that "antipathy to party politics" (and so, briefly, did the CCF when it fancied itself little more than a "movement"), but Social Credit ultimately lost its raison d'être and became "indistinguishable from Conservativism."[7] The CCF/NDP, on the other hand, accepted the fundamental adversarial give-and-take of party politics and the institutional parameters imposed on parties in a parliamentary system. Like its predecessor, the NDP resisted the old ways of doing things economically and sought to change them, but it did not eschew electoral competition. If anything, having witnessed how Tommy Douglas relished election campaigning for nearly twenty years in Saskatchewan and later as federal NDP leader for a decade, the CCF/NDP engaged actively in elections and became an integral part of Canada's modern party system.

Nowhere did the turnaround in voter support in 1957 and 1958 have a more lasting effect on the Liberals than in Western Canada. Even allowing for the strength of Social Credit and the CCF in their respective provinces, the Liberals had dominated the region from 1935 to 1953, winning 45 percent of all seats in the four Western provinces. Over that period, they won close to three times as many seats in the region as the Conservatives – 167 to 61 – with the Tories placing fourth in total number of seats (Figure 9.1). No wonder Diefenbaker instructed Tory organizers in 1957 not to refer to the CCF and Social Credit in campaign literature and advertising in Western Canada as "third" or "minor" parties, for it was his own party that fit that description!

"The West," referring to the Prairie provinces and British Columbia as a unit, masked the reality of Liberal support leading up

FIGURE 9.1

Party share of total seats in the four Western provinces (Manitoba, Saskatchewan, Alberta, British Columbia), 1935–2021

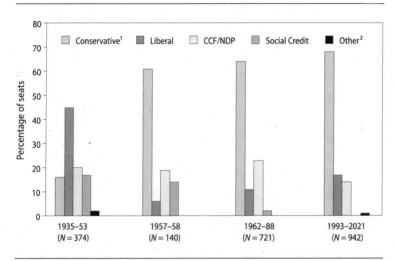

Sources: Data from Frank Feigert, *Canada Votes: 1935–1988* (Durham, NC: Duke University Press, 1989), Tables 2-4 to 2-52 for the 1935–88 elections and *Official Reports of the Chief Electoral Officer of Canada* for the 1993–2021 elections.
Notes:
1 Liberal-Conservative Party, 1935–38; National Conservative Party, 1938–42; Progressive Conservative Party of Canada, 1942–93; Reform Party of Canada, 1993–2000; Canadian Alliance 2000–03; Conservative Party of Canada, 2003–19.
2 National Government; Reconstruction; Independent; Green Party.

to the 1957 and 1958 elections. Alberta was a clear outlier. From 1935 to 1953, the Liberals won 59 of Manitoba's 81 ridings, 49 of Saskatchewan's 100, and 40 of British Columbia's 88, but they were elected in only 19 of Alberta's 85 ridings over the same period. Social Credit practically owned that province for twenty-five years.

It is true that the CCF and Social Credit gained a measure of support from former Progressive Party adherents, but it was the Liberals who had benefited most from the collapse of the Progressive Party in the 1920s and the defeat of the Bennett Conservatives in 1935. The Liberals consolidated their hold on the region in part through formidable ground-level organizations, especially in

Manitoba and Saskatchewan; in part through policy changes that catered to the agricultural sector; and in part because they were not the Conservatives! For prairie voters in the 1940s and 1950s, the mere mention of the Bennett government suggested an economically crippling drought coupled with the Great Depression. Stories were told of Liberal candidates and their campaign workers capitalizing on the fear and loathing of the Conservatives simply by mentioning Bennett's name at voters' doorsteps long after the Tory prime minister had resigned, moved to England, and died. Diefenbaker did what many thought could never be done: he made it acceptable to be a Conservative in Western Canada.

The Liberals had successfully courted the farm vote in the West for over two decades but could not match Diefenbaker's appeal to the agricultural sector by the time of the 1958 election. From the Liberals' ascendant position in the region in the pre-Diefenbaker period, their support all but disappeared in the four Western provinces. They won a mere eight seats in the region in 1957 and none in 1958. As David Smith observes in his study of the Liberals' decline on the prairies, "to have stuck with the Liberals in 1957 and 1958 would have amounted to an act of sacrifice."[8] This collapse of the Liberal vote, coupled with the disappearance of Social Credit and the shift in support base of the CCF/NDP, created a void that the Diefenbaker Conservatives filled. They, or their conservative/populist successors, have occupied it ever since.

The Liberal cause in the West was not helped by the agenda pursued by Lester Pearson and his successors. In the eyes of many in Western Canada, the Liberals were the very antithesis of their prairie populist hero. The party's platforms were seen as tailored to Central Canada, particularly those who were seen as metropolitan elites. For example, Pearson's establishment of the Royal Commission on Bilingualism and Biculturalism soon after he became prime minister was "widely perceived by Ukrainians and other central and eastern Europeans as relegating them to second-class status." The commission's reference to "two founding peoples" (which ran directly counter to what Diefenbaker constantly espoused) was seen by many Diefenbaker loyalists to be "offensive."[9]

In private, Pearson was known to be witty, but in his campaign appearances he came across as the more cerebral of the two major party leaders, somehow detached from the cut and thrust of adversarial politics. That would never be said of Diefenbaker. He thrived on the public side of politics (and the public's adulation), as was abundantly clear from his virtuoso performances in both the 1957 and 1958 campaigns. At the pinnacle of his career, he employed his powerful rhetoric in rallies and on television to capture the attention (and the votes) of Canadians. He spoke with what one might imagine as the cadence and accusatory tone of an Old Testament prophet that was perfectly suited to the Tory assaults on the St. Laurent and Pearson Liberals. In the last half of the twentieth century, except for Pierre Elliott Trudeau in 1968 at the peak of "Trudeaumania," and possibly Brian Mulroney in 1984 in his attacks on the John Turner and Pierre Trudeau Liberals, Diefenbaker in 1957 and 1958 likely had no equal in delivering spellbinding speeches. His ability to excite crowds, make headlines, and employ body language and facial expressions to his advantage paid off by engaging Canadians in the electoral process. There was no better demonstration of that than the marked jump in voter turnout levels throughout the Diefenbaker decade.

In their drive to find additional supporters in 1957, the Conservatives opened a new chapter in Canadian political history by going after the votes of the rapidly growing immigrant population in the cities and suburbs. As we saw earlier, this paid off royally for the Tories in both 1957 and 1958 in constituencies on the fringes of Toronto and Montreal and in such inner-city ridings as Toronto's Parkdale and High Park. These two constituencies were microcosms of the changes wrought by the two elections. Ironically, however, it was the Liberals who managed over the long run to capture the new immigrant vote by making ridings in the larger metropolitan areas their own and holding on to them election after election.

By the 1962, 1963, and 1965 elections on the Island of Montreal and in the city of Toronto, the Conservatives either fell back to where they had been prior to 1957 and 1958 or ended up worse off in both seats and votes. On the Island of Montreal, the Liberals, who had lost 7 seats to the Conservatives in 1958, bounced back in 1962, 1963, and 1965 by winning all but 1 of the Island's 21 seats in each of those elections. In Toronto and suburban York County, the changes were even more dramatic. The Tories went from winning 8 of the area's 18 seats in 1953, to all 18 in 1958, then being blanked out completely in 1963 and 1965. The Conservative breakthrough in Montreal and metropolitan Toronto in 1957 and 1958 proved to be but a flash in the pan.

The fate of the two largest parties in the two largest provinces speaks volumes about how fleeting the Tory success under Diefenbaker was in Central Canada. From the 1953 election, the last before Diefenbaker became the Tory leader, to the first election without Diefenbaker as leader – 1968 – both the Liberals and Tories were on roller-coaster rides in Ontario and Quebec. From electing 117 of Central Canada's 160 MPs in 1953, the Liberals dropped to 40 MPs five years later, then bounced back to 120 in 1968 under their new leader, Pierre Trudeau. The Progressive Conservatives mirrored this history, going from 37 MPs in 1953 to 117 in 1958 and falling to 21 in the face of Trudeaumania.

In the short run, the magnitude and breadth of the Tory victory in 1958 transformed the party system across the entire country, apart from Newfoundland and Labrador. At the outset, the Liberals fared badly in their Quebec bastion, and for the first time in decades the West embraced the Tories. Once the 1958 election results were final, it was clear that the Conservatives were no longer overly reliant on their traditional Toronto and rural Ontario bases. With that election, the Diefenbaker Conservatives – for that is what the party had become at that point – had been presented with a golden opportunity, unprecedented for them in the twentieth century, to reconstruct their party into a broad coalition of voters and MPs from across the country.

In the final analysis, however, Diefenbaker was unequal to the challenge of brokering a brokerage party, a party that Ken Carty and William Cross have characterized as one dedicated to "fierce *electoral pragmatism.*"[10] He was too wedded to his vision of "One Canada" to ever allow for the possibility that there were interests of "many Canadas" to reconcile: regional, linguistic, Indigenous, ethnic, religious. He proved unable to maintain a partnership between Central Canadians, notably in metropolitan Ontario and increasingly nationalistic Quebec, and Conservatives in the West. His difficulties on that front presaged the problems of successfully accommodating often seemingly irreconcilable regional interests that have haunted prime ministers of both parties from Lester Pearson to Justin Trudeau. Canadian electoral politics never returned to the pre-1957 character that had prevailed for decades.

With rare exceptions, not since Diefenbaker's time have party leaders been able to replicate the cross-national, intra-party coalition that was the distinguishing mark of the Liberals' twenty-two-year dominance under Mackenzie King and Louis St. Laurent. In other words, part of what makes the 1957 and 1958 elections turning point elections is that they marked the end of a period when one governing party brokered disparate regional, economic, and social interests and the arrival of another period in which no party has been able to successfully broker those interests for more than an election or two.

The reconfigured Conservative party that began under Diefenbaker continued, with varying degrees of electoral success, under his three immediate successors – Robert Stanfield, Joe Clark, and Brian Mulroney – all of whom had admired him at some point in their careers. Diefenbaker's statist understanding of Toryism (that governments have an obligation "to protect the weak and the less privileged"[11]) often matched their own, although gradually the Mulroney brand of conservatism incorporated a more pro-American, business-oriented conservatism that would not have been Diefenbaker's preference. Diefenbaker's strand of political ideology – labelled "Red Tory" by some and "democratic tory" by others[12] – came to an end as a serious presence on the federal scene with the spectacular defeat of Kim Campbell's Progressive Conservative government in 1993. From the ashes of what had once been the Diefenbaker Conservatives in the West rose the Reform Party, and in Quebec the Bloc Québécois. The party system had reached another turning point.

The Conservatives took the 1957 and 1958 elections with a bang in Western Canada, winning eighty-six (61 percent) of the region's ridings to the Liberals' eight (6 percent). In truth, however, the overwhelming number of Tory victories occurred in 1958, not 1957. In his account of the 1957 election, Dalton Camp pointed to a needed correction to the narrative commonly offered about that election. "For years afterwards, the illusion would persist that the West had yielded up Diefenbaker's triumph" in 1957, he wrote. The reality was otherwise. In that election, the Conservatives placed third in Saskatchewan and Alberta and won only fourteen of the forty-eight Prairie constituencies. By contrast, in the three Maritime provinces (in the two largest of which they held office), they went from five MPs 1953 to nineteen in 1957, and in Ontario the number of seats won was almost double the thirty-three in 1953.

What made the difference to the party's electoral fortunes, Camp concluded, was that the Conservatives won federally where they were "already strong" provincially.[13] He clearly implied that where there was extensive provincial organizational support of the federal Tories – backed up by the active participation of their respective provincial leaders – this proved to be the deciding factor in determining the outcome of the 1957 election. Camp's assessment drew to its logical conclusion the strategy with respect to the allocation of financial support outlined for the Conservatives by Winnipeg MP Gordon Churchill in advance of the 1957 election, namely, that campaign strategists should play to their strengths.

The flip side of Camp's argument, of course, is that where the Tories were weak provincially, they would do poorly federally. Quebec, Saskatchewan, Alberta, and British Columbia speak to that point forcefully, for in none of those provinces did the Conservatives have much (if any) provincial organization or presence. Ironically, however, despite the Conservative revival in the rest of the country in 1957–58, it was in the West where the Diefenbaker revolution went on to have its greatest lasting impact.

In the ten elections between 1962 and 1988, when the final Progressive Conservative government was re-elected under Brian Mulroney, the Tories won 466 (64 percent) of the ridings in the West – more than five times the number the Liberals won over the same period and six times what Tories had won in the four Western provinces between 1935 and 1953. The changes resulting from the 1957 and 1958 elections continued to resonate long after Diefenbaker and Mulroney had left the scene. A Western Canadian conservative party (Reform, Canadian Alliance, Conservative Party of Canada) of some sort has persisted to this day. In the post-Mulroney/Campbell period, a conservative party increased its share of the 942 Western Canadians seats to 68 percent, whereas the Liberals have come away with only 17 percent and the NDP with 14 percent. In the words of national affairs columnist Andrew Coyne, "the Conservatives have owned the West since 1958."[14] For that they can thank John Diefenbaker.

But the obvious Conservative strength in the West is only one-half of the story of the post-Diefenbaker changes in the party system. The other half is, quite simply, an increasingly wide Liberal-Conservative gap across the country along urban-rural lines. A "durable urban-rural cleavage between the major parties for the first time in Canadian history" began with Diefenbaker's years in office and has continued ever since. Over time, that cleavage has grown and has ensured that the Liberals have continued to enjoy "an enduring and substantively large urban advantage" over the Conservatives.[15] The growing urban and suburban populations have ensured that the major metropolitan centres continue to gain a disproportionately larger share of the total number of Commons' seats with each decennial seat reallocation. This, combined with Liberal dominance of the large cities, has, with few exceptions since the Diefenbaker era, benefited the Liberals and disadvantaged the Conservatives.

The economic and political upheavals of the Diefenbaker period, together with Pearson's appeal to young professionals in Toronto and Montreal as he set about rebuilding the Liberal Party during his years in opposition, can be pointed to as logical explanations of the urban-rural cleavage in party support. In addition, there is the card Diefenbaker loved to play, which in the long run did his party little good in the large cities: his prairie roots. Diefenbaker's identity as a small-town prairie lawyer, combined with his "bitter criticism of business and media elites in Canada's biggest cities," help explain why so many of the "Toronto Tory" establishment moved away from their traditional, pre-Diefenbaker loyalties.[16]

Finis

By the mid-1960s, Dalton Camp, one-time Diefenbaker supporter, strategist, and publicist, had joined the chorus of Diefenbaker critics. He soon emerged as the public face and driving force behind a move to replace Diefenbaker. At a meeting of the party's national association in 1966, he staked his bid for re-election as the party's national president on a commitment to hold a leadership convention in 1967. When it was Diefenbaker's turn to speak to those assembled at the meeting, he was booed by some in the crowd. Conservatives had reached the point where they either loved or loathed the man in almost equal measure.[17] The message was clear: the era of Diefenbaker-dominated politics had come to an end and the theme of "One Canada" no longer resonated.

Upon Camp's re-election as president, a national leadership convention attended by 2,200 voting delegates was duly held in Toronto's Maple Leaf Gardens in early September 1967, and Nova Scotia premier Robert Stanfield emerged as leader on the fifth ballot – the most ballots needed to select the leader of either of the two major parties. Ten other candidates (six of whom had been ministers in Diefenbaker's cabinet, which was an indication of how divided his party had become) had also been nominated. Diefenbaker agreed to let his name stand in order, once again, to argue the case for his vision of "One Canada" and dispute forcefully the doctrine of *deux nations*. He gave a powerful speech, reminiscent of 1957 and 1958, but it was all in vain. He placed fifth on the first ballot and withdrew after another two rounds of voting. The Diefenbaker era came to an end after eleven and a half years.

It ended much as the fifth act of a Shakespeare tragedy would conclude. By 1967, Diefenbaker had grown vastly out of touch with a different world in Quebec and a good part of urban Canada. "One Canada" was no longer a rallying cry in contemporary politics, and although the West has become more Conservative than ever, much of metropolitan Canada has become more Liberal than before.

Part of Diefenbaker's legacy remains, which is not always the case in a theatrical tragedy. A refashioned Conservative Party has remained a political player, albeit in various guises over the past several decades, not all of which Diefenbaker would have recognized or accepted. In the process, the West, notably the Prairies, has emerged as a distinctive political constituency in which successive iterations of the Conservative brand have retained a decidedly populist bent.

For his part, the former prime minister continued to serve on the opposition benches through the Pearson-Trudeau years, winning four more consecutive elections in Prince Albert, and receiving various honours and honorary degrees in Canada and abroad. His last federal election, and his thirteenth consecutive win, occurred barely months before his death at the age of eighty-three in 1979. He was buried a week later on the grounds of his beloved University of Saskatchewan, the institution from which he had graduated sixty years earlier. The Diefenbaker era had ended.

Appendix 1
List of Key Players

Balcer, Léon (1917–91): Progressive Conservative. Lawyer. Member of Parliament for Trois-Rivières, Quebec, 1949–65. Held various cabinet posts in the Diefenbaker government. Left the Conservative Party early in 1965 to sit as an Independent. Did not contest the 1965 election.

Camp, Dalton (1920–2002): Progressive Conservative. Party strategist, politician, and speechwriter. As president of the Progressive Conservative Association in the mid-1960s, was instrumental in forcing a leadership convention in 1967 to replace Diefenbaker as party leader.

Churchill, Gordon (1898–1985): Progressive Conservative. Lawyer. Member of Parliament for Winnipeg South Centre, 1951–68; Minister of Trade and Commerce, 1957–60; Minister of Veterans Affairs, 1960–63.

Coldwell, Major James William "M.J." (1888–1974): CCF. Teacher. Member of Parliament for Rosetown-Biggar, Saskatchewan, 1935–58; CCF leader, 1942–60.

Coyne, James (1910–2012): Banker and businessman. Controversial second governor of the Bank of Canada. Appointed 1955.

Resigned in 1961 after the Diefenbaker government's attempt to fire him failed.

Diefenbaker, John G. (1895–1979): Progressive Conservative. Lawyer. Member of Parliament for Lake Centre, Saskatchewan, 1940–53, and Prince Albert, Saskatchewan, 1953–79. Progressive Conservative Party leader, December 1956–September 1967. Prime Minister, June 1957–April 1963.

Douglas, T.C. "Tommy" (1904–86): CCF and NDP. Baptist minister. CCF Member of Parliament for Weyburn, Saskatchewan, 1935–44. Resigned to lead the CCF to office in Saskatchewan, where he served as premier for seventeen years. Returned to Parliament in 1962. First leader of the New Democratic Party, 1961–72; NDP Member of Parliament for Burnaby–Coquitlam, BC, 1962–68, and Nanaimo, BC, 1968–79.

Drew, George (1894–1973): Progressive Conservative. Lawyer. Premier of Ontario, 1943–48. Federal Progressive Conservative Party leader, 1948–56. Member of Parliament for Carleton, Ontario, 1948–57. High Commissioner to the United Kingdom, 1957–64.

Duplessis, Maurice (1890–1959): Lawyer. Union Nationale leader and Quebec premier, 1936–39 and 1944–59. Endorsed Diefenbaker in the 1958 election campaign.

Fairclough, Ellen (1905–2004): Progressive Conservative. Accountant. Member of Parliament for Hamilton West, Ontario, 1950–63. Canada's first female cabinet minister. Minister of various departments during the Diefenbaker government, notably Citizenship and Immigration from 1958 to 1962.

Fleming, Donald (1905–86): Progressive Conservative. Lawyer. Member of Parliament for Eglington, Toronto, 1945–63; Minister of Finance, 1957–62; Minister of Justice, 1962–63. Candidate for leadership of the Progressive Conservative Party, 1956 and 1967.

Fulton, Davie (1916–2000): Progressive Conservative. Lawyer. Member of Parliament for Kamloops, BC, 1945–63; Minister of

Justice, 1957–62; Minister of Public Works, 1962–63. Candidate for leadership of the Progressive Conservative Party, 1956 and 1967.

Gladstone, James (1887–1971): Progressive Conservative. Alberta farmer, rancher, and Indigenous rights promoter. First Status Indian appointed to the Senate, 1958.

Hamilton, Alvin (1912–2004): Progressive Conservative. Teacher. Member of Parliament for Qu'Appelle, Saskatchewan, 1957–68, and Qu'Appelle–Moose Mountain, Saskatchewan, 1972–88; Minister of Northern Affairs and National Resources, 1957–60; Minister of Agriculture, 1960–63. Candidate for leadership of the Progressive Conservative Party, 1967.

Harkness, Douglas (1903–99): Progressive Conservative. Teacher and farmer. Member of Parliament for various Calgary electoral districts, 1945–72; Minister of Northern Affairs and National Resources, 1957; Minister of Agriculture, 1957–60; Minister of National Defence, 1960–63. Resigned from the Diefenbaker government, 1963.

Hees, George (1910–96): Progressive Conservative. Businessman. Member of Parliament for various Ontario ridings: Broadview, 1950–63; Northumberland, 1965–68; Prince Edward–Hastings, 1968–79; and Northumberland, 1979–88. Minister of Transport, 1957–60; Minister of Trade and Commerce, 1960–63; Minister of Veterans Affairs, 1984–88; candidate for leadership of the Progressive Conservative Party, 1967. Resigned from the Diefenbaker government, 1963.

Howe, C.D. (1886–1960): Liberal. Engineer. Member of Parliament for Port Arthur, Ontario, 1935–57. Held various cabinet positions under Prime Ministers Mackenzie King and Louis St. Laurent: Minister of Railways and Canals, Minister of Marine, Minister of Munitions and Supply, Minister of Reconstruction, Minister of Trade and Commerce.

Knowles, Stanley (1908–97): Clergyman. CCF Member of Parliament for Winnipeg North Centre, 1942–58; New Democratic Party Member of Parliament for Winnipeg North Centre, 1962–84.

Low, Solon (1900–62): Social Credit. Teacher, farmer. Member of Parliament for Peace River, Alberta, 1945–58. Social Credit Party of Canada leader, 1944–61.

Martin, Paul, Sr. (1903–92): Liberal. Lawyer. Member of Parliament for Essex East, Ontario, 1935–68. Held various cabinet positions under Prime Ministers Mackenzie King, Louis St. Laurent, Lester Pearson, and Pierre Trudeau. Candidate for leadership of the Liberal Party, 1948, 1958, and 1968.

Pearson, Lester B. (1897–1972): Liberal. Civil servant under Prime Ministers R.B. Bennett and Mackenzie King. Canadian ambassador to the United States, 1944–46; Nobel Peace Prize recipient, 1957. Member of Parliament for Algoma East, Ontario, 1948–68. Liberal Party leader, 1958–68; Prime Minister, April 1963–April 1968.

Pickersgill, J.W. "Jack" (1905–97): Liberal. Civil servant under Prime Ministers Mackenzie King and Louis St. Laurent. Member of Parliament for Bonavista–Twillingate, Newfoundland and Labrador, 1953–67. Held various cabinet positions under Prime Ministers Louis St. Laurent and Lester Pearson: Secretary of State for Canada, Minister of Citizenship and Immigration, Government House Leader, Minister of Transport.

St. Laurent, Louis (1882–1973): Liberal. Lawyer. Member of Parliament for Quebec East, 1942–58; Minister of Justice and Secretary of State for External Affairs under Mackenzie King. Liberal Party leader, 1948–58; Prime Minister, November 1948–June 1957.

Stanfield, Robert (1914–2003): Progressive Conservative. Lawyer. Premier of Nova Scotia, 1956–67. Member of Parliament for Colchester–Hants and Halifax, 1967–79. Progressive Conservative Party leader, 1967–76.

Appendix 2
Timeline of Events

1953

August   Louis St. Laurent's government is re-elected with the Liberals' fifth consecutive majority.

1956

June   The bitterly divisive pipeline debate paralyzes the House of Commons for several days.

September   George Drew, leader of the Progressive Conservatives and leader of the opposition since he was first elected to Parliament in 1948, resigns due to poor health.

October–November   The Soviet Union suppresses an uprising in Hungary and sparks a refugee crisis.

Britain, France, and Israel attack the Suez Canal.

December   John Diefenbaker is chosen Progressive Conservative leader on the first ballot at the party's convention, winning 60 percent of the delegates' votes. He defeats fellow frontbench MPs Donald Fleming (Ontario) and Davie Fulton (British Columbia).

1957

June   Diefenbaker's Conservatives unexpectedly win more seats (112) than the governing Liberals

(105) in the general election and form a minority government.

Louis St. Laurent announces his resignation as Liberal leader.

October   Lester Pearson is awarded the Nobel Peace Prize.

1958

January   Winning 78 percent of the vote, Lester Pearson defeats fellow Ontario MP Paul Martin on the first ballot at Liberal Party convention and becomes the party's new leader.

Diefenbaker dissolves Parliament and calls an election for the end of March.

James Gladstone is appointed to the Senate, the first Status Indian to be named to that chamber.

March   Diefenbaker's Conservatives are re-elected with a massive majority, 208 seats to the Liberals' 49 and the CCF's 8.

1959

February   The Diefenbaker government cancels the Avro Arrow program.

1960

March   Status Indians gain the right to vote.

August   The Canadian Bill of Rights is approved by Parliament.

1961

June–July   The government's attempt to fire the governor of the Bank of Canada, James Coyne, backfires. Coyne immediately resigns.

August   The New Democratic Party's founding convention chooses Saskatchewan premier T.C. Douglas as its first federal leader. He defeats long-time CCF MP

Hazen Argue (Saskatchewan), winning 79 percent of the vote on the first ballot.

1962

June	The federal election results in a minority Parliament, with the Conservatives winning 116 seats, the Liberals 99, Social Credit 30, and the NDP 19.
October	The government's delay in meeting its obligations under the joint Canadian-American NORAD defence agreement during the Cuban Missile Crisis angers US president John F. Kennedy and seriously tests the bilateral relationship.

1963

January– February	Canada's unwillingness to arm the fifty-six long-range, ground-to-air missiles on its soil with nuclear warheads leads to serious division in the Diefenbaker cabinet and the resignation of three ministers.
February	The government, in disarray over defence and economic policies, is defeated in the Commons on a vote of non-confidence, forcing the second federal election in less than a year.
April	The Conservatives, reduced to 95 seats, lose the election and John Diefenbaker becomes leader of the opposition. The Liberals, with 129 seats, fall 4 short of a majority government, and Lester Pearson becomes prime minister. Social Credit wins 24 seats and the NDP 17 seats.

1965

November	Sensing a chance to win a majority, Lester Pearson calls an election. The Liberals win 131 seats but fall short of a majority once again. The Conservatives

win 97 seats, the NDP 21. Social Credit is reduced to 5 seats, while their erstwhile colleagues from Quebec, now established as Ralliement créditiste, win 9.

1966
November

Dalton Camp becomes the most outspoken of the Conservatives intent on forcing Diefenbaker out as party leader. He stakes his bid for re-election as the party's national president on a commitment to hold a leadership convention in 1967. Camp is re-elected and planning begins for a leadership convention the following year.

1967
September

Diefenbaker runs for the party's leadership, along with ten other candidates, six of whom had served in his cabinet. Winning only 12 percent of the first ballot vote, he places fifth and withdraws after two more ballots. Nova Scotia premier Robert Stanfield is elected on the fifth ballot, defeating Manitoba premier Duff Roblin by close to 200 votes.

Appendix 3
Data Tables

TABLE A1

Political parties' number of seats and vote shares by province/territory, Canadian general election, June 10, 1957

Party	BC	AB	SK	MB	ON	QC	NB	NS	PE	NL	NT + YT	Total
PC	7	3	3	8	61	9	5	10	4	2	0	112
	32.6%	27.6%	23.2%	35.9%	48.8%	31.1%	48.7%	50.4%	52.3%	37.8%	49.3%	38.8%
Liberal	2	1	4	1	21	62	5	2	0	5	2	105
	20.5%	27.9%	30.3%	26.1%	37.1%	57.6%	48.1%	45.1%	46.6%	61.9%	50.7%	40.1%
CCF	7	0	10	5	3	0	0	0	0	0	0	25
	22.3%	6.3%	36.0%	23.7%	12.1%	1.8%	0.9%	4.4%	1.0%	0.3%	0%	10.7%
Social Credit	6	13	0	0	0	0	0	0	0	0	0	19
	24.2%	37.8%	10.5%	13.2%	1.7%	0.2%	1.0%	0.1%	0%	0%	0%	6.6%
Other + Independent	0	0	0	0	0	4	0	0	0	0	0	4
	0.4%	0.3%	0.1%	1.2%	0.4%	9.3%	1.3%	0%	0%	0%	0%	2.8%
Seats	22	17	17	14	85	75	10	12	4	7	2	265

Source: Adapted from Frank Feigert, *Canada Votes: 1935–1988* (Durham, NC: Duke University Press, 1989), Table 2-19.
Note: Percentages for some jurisdictions may not sum to 100% due to rounding.

TABLE A2

Political parties' number of seats and vote shares by province/territory, Canadian general election, March 31, 1958

Party	BC	AB	SK	MB	ON	QC	NB	NS	PE	NL	NT + YT	Total
PC	18	17	16	14	67	50	7	12	4	2	1	208
	49.4%	59.9%	51.4%	56.7%	56.4%	49.6%	54.1%	57.0%	62.2%	45.2%	49.5%	53.6%
Liberal	0	0	0	0	15	25	3	0	0	5	1	49
	16.1%	13.7%	19.6%	21.6%	32.6%	45.7%	43.4%	38.4%	37.5%	54.4%	50.5%	33.6%
CCF	4	0	1	0	3	0	0	0	0	0	0	8
	24.5%	4.4%	28.4%	19.6%	10.5%	2.3%	1.8%	4.5%	0.3%	0.2%	0%	9.5%
Social Credit	0	0	0	0	0	0	0	0	0	0	0	0
	9.6%	21.6%	0.4%	1.8%	0.3%	0.6%	0.7%	0%	0%	0%	0%	2.6%
Other + Independent	0	0	0	0	0	0	0	0	0	0	0	0
	0.4%	0.4%	0.2%	0.4%	0.2%	1.9%	0%	0%	0%	0.2%	1.3%	0.7%
Seats	22	17	17	14	85	75	10	12	4	7	2	265

Source: Adapted from Frank Feigert, *Canada Votes: 1935–1988* (Durham, NC: Duke University Press, 1989), Table 2-22.

Note: Percentages for some jurisdictions may not sum to 100% due to rounding.

TABLE A3

Political parties' number of seats and vote shares by province/territory, Canadian general election, June 18, 1962

Party	BC	AB	SK	MB	ON	QC	NB	NS	PEI	NL	NT + YT	Total
PC	6	15	16	11	35	14	4	9	4	1	1	116
	27.3%	42.8%	50.4%	41.6%	39.3%	29.6%	46.5%	47.3%	51.3%	36.0%	55.0%	37.3%
Liberal	4	0	1	1	44[a]	35	6	2	0	6	1	100
	27.3%	19.4%	22.2%	31.1%	41.8%	39.2%	44.4%	42.4%	43.3%	59.0%	46.2%	37.2%
NDP	10	0	0	2	6	0	0	1	0	0	0	19
	30.9%	8.4%	22.7%	19.7%	17.0%	4.4%	5.3%	9.4%	5.2%	4.9%	0%	13.5%
Social Credit	2	2	0	0	0	26	0	0	0	0	0	30
	14.2%	29.2%	4.6%	6.8%	1.9%	26.0%	3.6%	0.9%	0.2%	0.1%	11.4%	11.9%
Other + Independent	0	0	0	0	0	0	0	0	0	0	0	0
	0.3%	0.2%	0.1%	0.8%	0.1%	0.9%	0.2%	0%	0%	0%	0%	0.4%
Seats	22	17	17	14	85	75	10	12	4	7	2	265

Source: Adapted from Frank Feigert, *Canada Votes: 1935–1988* (Durham, NC: Duke University Press, 1989), Table 2-25 (corrected).

Note: Percentages for some jurisdictions may not sum to 100% due to rounding.

a One Liberal-Labour candidate elected in Ontario is counted as Liberal.

TABLE A4

Political parties' number of seats and vote shares by province/territory, Canadian general election, April 7, 1963

Party	BC	AB	SK	MB	ON	QC	NB	NS	PEI	NL	NT + YT	Total
PC	4	14	17	10	27	8	4	5	4	0	2	95
	23.4%	45.3%	53.7%	42.7%	35.3%	19.5%	40.0%	46.9%	52.0%	30.1%	53.2%	32.8%
Liberal	7	1	0	2	52	47	6	7	0	7	0	129
	32.3%	22.1%	24.1%	33.8%	46.3%	45.6%	47.3%	46.7%	46.4%	64.5%	42.1%	41.7%
NDP	9	0	0	2	6	0	0	0	0	0	0	17
	30.3%	6.5%	18.2%	16.7%	15.9%	7.1%	3.7%	6.4%	1.6%	4.2%	3.2%	13.1%
Social Credit	2	2	0	0	0	20	0	0	0	0	0	24
	13.3%	25.8%	3.9%	7.0%	2.0%	27.3%	8.6%	0.1%	0%	0%	0%	11.9%
Other + Independent	0	0	0	0	0	0	0	0	0	0	0	0
	0.7%	0.2%	0.1%	0.2%	0.4%	0.4%	0%	0%	0%	1.3%	0%	0.4%
Seats	22	17	17	14	85	75	10	12	4	7	2	265

Source: Adapted from Frank Feigert, *Canada Votes: 1935–1988* (Durham, NC: Duke University Press, 1989), Table 2-28.

Note: Percentages for some jurisdictions may not sum to 100% due to rounding.

Notes

Chapter 1: On the Cusp of Change

1 Nelson Wiseman, *Partisan Odysseys: Canada's Political Parties* (Toronto: University of Toronto Press, 2020), 74. Two other Conservative prime ministers who held Diefenbaker in high regard were Joe Clark and Brian Mulroney (who as a teenager worked in Diefenbaker's leadership campaign).

2 Richard Sigurdson, "John Diefenbaker's One Canada and the Legacy of Unhyphenated Canadianism," in *The Diefenbaker Legacy: Canadian Politics, Law and Society since 1957,* edited by D.C. Story and R. Bruce Shephard (Regina/Saskatoon: Canadian Plains Research Center/ Diefenbaker Canada Centre, 1998), 73.

3 The definitive biography of C.D. Howe remains Robert Bothwell and William Kilbourn, *C.D. Howe* (Toronto: McClelland and Stewart, 1979).

4 "Canadian Production of War Materials," Veterans Affairs Canada, November 27, 2017, https://www.veterans.gc.ca/eng/remembrance/history/ historical-sheets/material.

5 All population data are from M.C. Urquhart and K.A.H. Buckley, eds., "Population and Migration," in *Historical Statistics of Canada* (Toronto: Macmillan of Canada, 1965), 14–29.

6 G.A. Rawlyk, "Canada's Immigration Policy, 1945–1962," *Dalhousie Review* 42, 3 (1962): 289.

7 Richard Johnston, *The Canadian Party System: An Analytic History* (Vancouver: UBC Press, 2017), 101.

8 The Liberals held office under Lester Pearson from 1963 to 1968 and under Pierre Trudeau (and briefly John Turner) from 1968 to 1984, except for the nine-month Conservative government led by Joe Clark, 1979–80.

9 The literature on Diefenbaker is vast. Good introductions to the conflicting views on his legacy can be found in D.C. Story and H. Bruce Shepard, eds., *The Diefenbaker Legacy: Canadian Politics, Law and Society since 1957* (Regina: Canadian Plains Research Center, 1998), and Janice Cavell and Ryan M. Touhey, eds., *Reassessing the Rogue Tory: Canadian Foreign Relations in the Diefenbaker Era* (Vancouver: UBC Press, 2018).

10 Details of the leadership review provisions and the lead-up to their adoption can be found in John Courtney, *The Selection of National Party Leaders in Canada* (Toronto: Macmillan of Canada, 1973), 97–104.

11 Patrick Kyba and Wendy Green-Finlay, "John Diefenbaker as Prime Minister: The Record Re-examined," in Story and Shepard, *The Diefenbaker Legacy*, 69.

Chapter 2: The Parties Heading into the 1957 Election

1 R.K. Carty, "Three Canadian Party Systems," in *Canadian Political Party Systems: A Reader*, edited by R.K. Carty (Peterborough, ON: Broadview Press, 1992), 564.

2 J.L. Granatstein, *The Politics of Survival: The Conservative Party of Canada, 1938–1945* (Toronto: University of Toronto Press, 1967), 201.

3 James Bickerton, "Parties and Regions: Representation and Resistance," in *Canadian Parties in Transition: Recent Trends and New Paths for Research*, edited by Alain-G. Gagnon and A. Brian Tanguay (Toronto: University of Toronto Press, 2017), 54.

4 The movement itself had been established the previous year by convention in Calgary. For more on Woodsworth, see Kenneth McNaught, *A Prophet in Politics: A Biography of J.S. Woodsworth* (Toronto: University of Toronto Press, 2001), with an introduction by Allen Mills.

5 Walter Young, *The Anatomy of a Party: The National CCF 1932–1961* (Toronto: University of Toronto Press, 1969), 28 and 292.

6 *Canadian Encyclopedia*, s.v. "Social Gospel," by Richard Allen, updated October 7, 2015.

7 Ivan Avakumovic, *Socialism in Canada: A Study of the CCF-NDP in Federal and Provincial Politics* (Toronto: McClelland and Stewart, 1978), 92.

8 Young, *Anatomy of a Party*, 291.

9 J. Murray Beck, *Pendulum of Power: Canada's Federal Elections* (Scarborough, ON: Prentice-Hall of Canada, 1968), 251.

10 D. Owen Carrigan, *Canadian Party Platforms: 1967–1968* (Toronto: Copp Clark Publishing, 1968), 127.

11 Leo Zakuta, *A Protest Movement Becalmed: A Study of Change in the CCF* (Toronto: University of Toronto Press, 1964), 93.

12 Beck, *Pendulum of Power,* 302. See also Zakuta, *A Protest Movement Becalmed,* 93, and John Meisel, *The Canadian General Election of 1957* (Toronto: University of Toronto Press, 1962), 201.

13 Carrigan, *Canadian Party Platforms,* 216.

14 Meisel, *The Canadian General Election of 1957,* 220.

15 Colin Campbell and William Christian, *Parties, Leaders and Ideologies in Canada* (Toronto: McGraw-Hill Ryerson, 1996), 3.

16 Campbell and Christian, *Parties, Leaders and Ideologies,* 201.

17 Labelled the "A plus B Theorem," Major Douglas's social credit theory is succinctly discussed in John A. Irving, *The Social Credit Movement in Alberta* (Toronto: University of Toronto Press, 1959), 5–7, and C.B. Macpherson, *Democracy in Alberta: The Theory and Practice of a Quasi-Party System* (Toronto: University of Toronto Press, 1953), 107–12.

18 Reginald Whitaker, *The Government Party: Organizing and Financing the Liberal Party of Canada 1930–58* (Toronto: University of Toronto Press, 1977), 5.

19 Meisel, *The Canadian General Election of 1957,* 177.

20 King Diaries, January 13, 1934, in John C. Courtney, "Prime Ministerial Character: An Examination of Mackenzie King's Character," in John English and J.O. Stubbs, eds., *Mackenzie King: Widening the Debate* (Toronto: Macmillan Company of Canada, 1978), 86.

21 Meisel, *The Canadian General Election of 1957,* 166.

22 Dale Thomson, *Louis St. Laurent: Canadian* (Toronto: Macmillan of Canada, 1967), 502. See also Meisel, *The Canadian General Election of 1957,* 165; Peter Newman, *Renegade in Power: The Diefenbaker Years* (Toronto: McClelland and Stewart, 1963), 48; Carrigan, *Canadian Party Platforms,* 213; and John English, *The Worldly Years: The Life of Lester Pearson, 1949–1972,* vol. 2 (Toronto: Alfred A. Knopf Canada, 1992), 185.

23 Howard Scarrow, *Canada Votes: A Handbook of Federal and Provincial Election Data* (New Orleans: Hauser Press, 1961), 161.

24 For a helpful, brief analysis of the Conservative Party's twentieth-century boom-and-bust cycle, see Richard Johnston, *The Canadian Party System: An Analytic History* (Vancouver: UBC Press, 2017), 83–84.

25 George C. Perlin, *The Tory Syndrome: Leadership Politics in the Progressive Conservative Party* (Montreal and Kingston: McGill-Queen's University Press, 1980), 46.

26 Dalton Camp, *Gentlemen, Players and Politicians* (Toronto: McClelland and Stewart, 1970), 133.

27 Robert Manion (1938–40), Richard Hanson (1940–41), Arthur Meighen (1941–42), John Bracken (1942–48), and George Drew (1948–56).

28 See Campbell and Christian, *Parties, Leaders and Ideologies,* especially chs. 2 and 3.

29 David McLaughlin, "The Sole Premier to Stand Up against Bill 21," *Globe and Mail,* December 2, 2019, A13.

30 Drew's wife, Fiorenza, was seen as offering some potential in Quebec. She was witty and very much at ease with people, and spoke fluent French, along with three other languages.

31 John G. Diefenbaker, *One Canada: Memoirs of the Right Honourable John G. Diefenbaker,* vol. 1, *The Crusading Years* (Toronto: Macmillan of Canada, 1975), 281.

32 Meisel, *The Canadian General Election of 1957,* 27.

33 Peter Stursberg, ed., *Diefenbaker: Leadership Gained, 1956–62* (Toronto: University of Toronto Press, 1975), 243.

34 Meisel, *The Canadian General Election of 1957,* 26.

35 Stursberg, *Leadership Gained,* 196.

36 Balcer played down the significance of the walkout. See Stursberg, *Leadership Gained,* 21.

37 Denis Smith, *Rogue Tory: The Life and Legend of John G. Diefenbaker* (Toronto: Macfarlane Walter and Ross, 1995), 205.

Chapter 3: The Players in 1957

1 R.K. Carty, "Campaigning in the Trenches: The Transformation of Constituency Politics," in *Party Democracy in Canada,* edited by G.C. Perlin (Toronto: Prentice-Hall of Canada, 1988), 84–96.

2 Dale Thomson, *Louis St. Laurent: Canadian* (Toronto: Macmillan of Canada, 1967), 274.

3 Reginald Whitaker, *The Government Party: Organizing and Financing the Liberal Party of Canada 1930–58* (Toronto: University of Toronto Press, 1977), 237.

4 F.R. Scott, "W.L.M.K.," in *The Eye of the Needle: Satire, Sorties, Sundries* (Montreal: Contact Press, 1957).

5 Thomson, *Louis St. Laurent*, 27.

6 Patrice Dutil, "Introduction: Louis St. Laurent's Leadership in History," in *The Unexpected Louis St-Laurent: Politics and Policies for a Modern Canada*, edited by Patrice Dutil (Vancouver: UBC Press, 2020), 5. St. Laurent's granddaughter provides an informal description of the prime minister in Jean Thérèse Riley, "*Grandpapa*: A Portrait of the Man and His Family," in Dutil, *The Unexpected Louis St-Laurent*, 55–71.

7 P.E. Bryden, "The Liminality of St-Laurent's Intergovernmental Relations Strategy," in Dutil, *The Unexpected Louis St-Laurent*, 156.

8 A helpful account of the national hospital insurance program is found in Malcolm Taylor, *Health Insurance and Canadian Public Policy: The Seven Decisions That Created the Canadian Health Insurance System and Their Outcomes* (Montreal and Kingston: McGill-Queen's University Press, 1987), 162–238.

9 Whitaker, *The Government Party*, 184.

10 David Smith, *Across the Aisle: Opposition in Canadian Politics* (Toronto: University of Toronto Press, 2013), 59.

11 Peter Worsley, "The Concept of Populism," In *Populism, Its Meaning and National Characteristics*, edited by Ghita Ionescu and Ernest Gellner (London: Weidenfeld and Nicolson, 1969), 245.

12 Colin Campbell and William Christian, *Parties, Leaders and Ideologies in Canada* (Toronto: McGraw-Hill Ryerson, 1996), 42.

13 Patrick Nicholson, *Vision and Indecision* (Toronto: McClelland and Stewart, 1968), 15.

14 Nicholson, *Vision and Indecision*, 17.

15 Dominion Bureau of Statistics, *Origin, Birthplace, Nationality and Language of the Canadian People: A Census Study Based on the Census of 1921 and Supplementary Data* (Ottawa: King's Printer, 1929), Table 42A.

16 Nicholson, *Vision and Indecision*, 22; John Diefenbaker, *One Canada: Memoirs of the Right Honourable John G. Diefenbaker*, vol. 1, *The Crusading Years* (Toronto: Macmillan of Canada, 1975), 99.

17 Nicholson, *Vision and Indecision,* 22.
18 George C. Perlin, *The Tory Syndrome: Leadership Politics in the Progressive Conservative Party* (Montreal and Kingston: McGill-Queen's University Press, 1980), 5.
19 Blair Fraser, "Why the Conservatives Are Swinging to Diefenbaker," *Maclean's,* November 24, 1956, 30.
20 Fraser, "Why the Conservatives," 30.
21 Denis Smith, *Rogue Tory: The Life and Legend of John G. Diefenbaker* (Toronto: Macfarlane Walter and Ross, 1995), 206.
22 Quoted in Peter Newman, *Renegade in Power: The Diefenbaker Years* (Toronto: McClelland and Stewart, 1963), 46.
23 Walter Young, *The Anatomy of a Party: The National CCF 1932–1961* (Toronto: University of Toronto Press, 1969), 73.
24 Walter Stewart, *M.J.: The Life and Times of M.J. Coldwell* (Toronto: Stoddart Publishing, 2000), 3.
25 Stewart, *M.J.,* 9.
26 Young, *Anatomy of a Party,* 239.
27 Diefenbaker, *Crusading Years,* 203.
28 Stewart, *M.J.,* 4.
29 J.W. Pickersgill, *The Mackenzie King Record: 1939–1944* (Toronto: University of Toronto Press, 1960), 601.
30 Gad Horowitz, "Conservatism, Liberalism and Socialism in Canada," In *Party Politics in Canada,* edited by Hugh G. Thorburn (Toronto: Prentice-Hall of Canada, 1967), 70.
31 Stewart, *M.J.,* 195.
32 Whitaker, *The Government Party,* 465n69.
33 R.K. Carty, "Three Canadian Party Systems," in *Canadian Political Party Systems: A Reader,* edited by R.K. Carty (Peterborough, ON: Broadview Press, 1992), 575.
34 John Meisel, *The Canadian General Election of 1957* (Toronto: University of Toronto Press, 1962), 173.
35 Meisel, *The Canadian General Election of 1957,* 173.
36 Meisel, *The Canadian General Election of 1957,* 216.
37 According to John Meisel, Social Credit followed the fundraising approach of the two older parties in the 1957 campaign and depended largely on financial contributions of business donors, in the party's case from Western Canada. Meisel, *The Canadian General Election of 1957,* 226.
38 Smith, *Rogue Tory,* 272.

Chapter 4: The Issues in 1957

1 Closure is a procedural device originally introduced in the House of Commons by the Borden government in 1913. Although it has been used sparingly, closure nonetheless greatly strengthens a cabinet's hand by enabling a minister to end legislative deliberations and force a vote on the issue that provoked the controversy.

2 Donald Creighton, *The Forked Road: Canada 1939–1957* (Toronto: McClelland and Stewart, 1976), 221.

3 Peter Newman, *Renegade in Power: The Diefenbaker Years* (Toronto: McClelland and Stewart, 1963), 36 (emphasis in original).

4 Dale Thomson, *Louis St. Laurent: Canadian* (Toronto: Macmillan of Canada, 1967), 344.

5 Newman, *Renegade in Power,* 36.

6 There is some debate about the accuracy of this quote. See John Harbron, *C.D. Howe* (Don Mills, ON: Fitzhenry and Whiteside, 1980), 51.

7 Creighton, *The Forked Road,* 264.

8 John Meisel, *The Canadian General Election of 1957* (Toronto: University of Toronto Press, 1962), 7.

9 Robert Bothwell and William Kilbourn, *C.D. Howe* (Toronto: McClelland and Stewart, 1979), 256.

10 Meisel, *The Canadian General Election of 1957,* 7.

11 See Hugh G. Thorburn, "Parliament and Policy-Making: The Case of the Trans-Canada Gas Pipeline," *Canadian Journal of Economics and Political Science* 23, 4 (1957): 527. In principle, the CCF backed the government based on its view that "the purpose of the emergency powers was to enable the minister to curb the greed of private entrepreneurs and protect the public interest if shortages of vital commodities appeared" (Bothwell and Kilbourn, *C.D. Howe,* 300). The parliamentary debates of the Defence Production Acts of 1951 and 1955 are chronicled in Bothwell and Kilbourn, *C.D. Howe,* 221–25 and 264–66.

12 Bothwell and Kilbourn, *C.D. Howe,* 301–2.

13 J.A. Corry, "Arms and the Man: Defence Powers in Parliament," *Queen's Quarterly* 62, 3 (1955): 323.

14 Reginald Whitaker, *The Government Party: Organizing and Financing the Liberal Party of Canada 1930–58* (Toronto: University of Toronto Press, 1977), 184.

15 J. Murray Beck, *Pendulum of Power: Canada's Federal Elections* (Scarborough, ON: Prentice-Hall of Canada, 1968), 291.

16 Bothwell and Kilbourn, *C.D. Howe,* 305.

17 Thomson, *Louis St. Laurent,* 420.

18 Newman, *Renegade in Power,* 42 and 43.

19 William Kilbourn, *Pipeline: TransCanada and the Great Debate: A History of Business and Politics* (Toronto: Clarke, Irwin, 1970), vii and 121.

20 Thomson, *Louis St. Laurent,* 519. John Meisel recalibrated the poll results slightly differently but came to essentially the same conclusion (Meisel, *The Canadian General Election of 1957,* 273).

21 C.E.S. Franks, *The Parliament of Canada* (Toronto: University of Toronto Press, 1987), 99; and David Smith, *Across the Aisle: Opposition in Canadian Politics* (Toronto: University of Toronto Press, 2013), 63–64.

22 Denis Smith, *Rogue Tory: The Life and Legend of John G. Diefenbaker* (Toronto: Macfarlane Walter and Ross, 1995), 217.

23 Thorburn, "Parliament and Policy-Making," 518.

24 Helpful accounts of the Suez Crisis can be found in John English, *The Worldly Years: The Life of Lester Pearson, 1949–1972,* vol. 2 (Toronto: Alfred A. Knopf, 1992), 107–46; and Thomson, *Louis St. Laurent,* 456–88.

25 Richard Johnston, *The Canadian Party System: An Analytic History* (Vancouver: UBC Press, 2017), 121.

26 Canada, *House of Commons Debates,* 22nd Parl, 4th Sess (November 26, 1956) at 28 and 33.

27 Canada, *House of Commons Debates,* 22nd Parl, 4th Sess (November 26, 1956) at 20.

28 Janice Cavell, "The Spirit of '56: The Suez Crisis, Anti-Americanism, and Diefenbaker's 1957 and 1958 Election Victories," in *Reassessing the Rogue Tory: Canadian Foreign Relations in the Diefenbaker Era,* edited by Janice Cavell and Ryan M. Touhey (Vancouver: UBC Press, 2018), 76.

29 Canada, *House of Commons Debates,* 22nd Parl, 4th Sess (November 26, 1956) at 41–42; Thomson: 487.

30 Thomson, *Louis St. Laurent,* 519.

31 J.W. Pickersgill, *My Years with St. Laurent: A Political Memoir* (Toronto: University of Toronto Press, 1975), 322.

32 Thomson, *Louis St. Laurent,* 519.

33 M.C. Urquhart and K.A.H. Buckley, eds., *Historical Statistics of Canada* (Toronto: Macmillan of Canada, 1965), Series L1–6 and Series A1–19; Statistics Canada, "Census Profile, 2016 Census," Table 32-10-0004-01, https://www12.statcan.gc.ca/census-recensement/2016/dp-pd/prof/index.

34 Winnipeg, Regina, Saskatoon, Calgary, and Edmonton.

35 Bothwell and Kilbourn, *C.D. Howe,* 323.

Chapter 5: The 1957 Campaign

1 John English, *The Worldly Years: The Life of Lester Pearson, 1949–1972,* vol. 2 (Toronto: Alfred A. Knopf Canada, 1992), 185.

2 J. Murray Beck, *Pendulum of Power: Canada's Federal Elections* (Scarborough, ON: Prentice-Hall of Canada, 1968), 307.

3 Dale Thomson, *Louis St. Laurent: Canadian* (Toronto: Macmillan of Canada, 1967), 502.

4 Peter Stursberg, ed., *Diefenbaker: Leadership Gained, 1956–62* (Toronto: University of Toronto Press, 1975), 58.

5 Stursberg, *Diefenbaker: Leadership Gained,* 58.

6 John Meisel, *The Canadian General Election of 1957* (Toronto: University of Toronto Press, 1962), 11.

7 Cara Spittal, *The Diefenbaker Moment* (PhD diss., University of Toronto, 2011), 78.

8 Meisel, *The Canadian General Election of 1957,* 179.

9 Quoted in Meisel, *The Canadian General Election of 1957,* 179.

10 Meisel, *The Canadian General Election of 1957,* 184 and 185.

11 Meisel, *The Canadian General Election of 1957,* 74.

12 Dalton Camp, *Gentlemen, Players and Politicians* (Toronto: McClelland and Stewart, 1970), 280–81.

13 Patrick Kyba, *Alvin: A Biography of the Honourable Alvin Hamilton* (Regina: Canadian Plains Research Center, 1989), 102.

14 Denis Smith, *Rogue Tory: The Life and Legend of John G. Diefenbaker* (Toronto: Macfarlane Walter and Ross, 1995), 226.

15 Camp, *Gentlemen, Players and Politicians,* 333–34.

16 Max Weber, *The Theory of Social and Economic Organization* (Toronto: Collier-Macmillan Canada, 1964), ch. 3; Robert C. Tucker, "The Theory of Charismatic Leadership," *Daedalus* 97, 3 (1968): 742–43.

17 Gordon Churchill, "Conservative Strategy for the Next Election," *Queen's Quarterly* 77, 4 (1970): 509 and 510. Once Churchill's recommendation became public knowledge, it was criticized in some circles as being "anti-French and anti-Quebec." This missed the simple empirical fact central to Churchill's argument, namely, that the history of Tory election upsets showed that Quebec was not "decisive" in determining the outcomes. See also Churchill's explanation of the memo's contents: Gordon Churchill, "Recollection and Comments," *Queen's Quarterly* 77, 4 (1970): 499–506.

18 Meisel, *The Canadian General Election of 1957*, 247.
19 Meisel, *The Canadian General Election of 1957*, 247–48.
20 Howard Palmer, *Ethnicity and Politics in Canada since Confederation* (pamphlet) (Ottawa: Canadian Historical Association, 1991), 20.
21 Thirstan Falconer, "Andrew Thompson, Liberal Party Reforms and the Engagement of Ethnocultural Communities, 1957 to 1961," *Canadian Ethnic Studies* 50, 3 (2018): 116.
22 Falconer, "Andrew Thompson, Liberal Party Reforms," 116–18.
23 Meisel, *The Canadian General Election of 1957*, 56 and 180.
24 Meisel, *The Canadian General Election of 1957*, 163.
25 Diefenbaker's television performances were not universally lauded. One of his harshest critics among Liberal cabinet ministers, J.W. Pickersgill, claimed not to understand Diefenbaker's television appeal: "He never says anything. People say he is a great performer, but you know, I have always preferred opera to rock!" (Stursberg, *Diefenbaker: Leadership Gained*, 53). This was quite likely the only time Diefenbaker was compared to a rock musician.
26 Dean E. McHenry, "The Impact of the C.C.F. on Canadian Parties and Groups," *Journal of Politics* 11, 2 (May 1949): 380.

Chapter 6: A New Parliament, a New Leader, and Another Election

1 Howe lost his Port Arthur seat to a CCF candidate, librarian and school-teacher Douglas Fisher.
2 The others were in 1896, 1926, 1962, 1979, 2019, and 2021. In the 1925 general election, Mackenzie King's Liberals won fewer seats *and* fewer votes than the Conservatives but retained office for a few months with the support of the Progressives: Liberals, 40.4 percent of the vote and 99 seats; Conservatives, 47.3 percent of the vote and 116 seats; and Progressives, 9.8 percent of the vote and 24 seats.
3 Dale Thomson, *Louis St. Laurent: Canadian* (Toronto: Macmillan of Canada, 1967), 519.
4 John Meisel, *The Canadian General Election of 1957* (Toronto: University of Toronto Press, 1962), 249.
5 J. Murray Beck, *Pendulum of Power: Canada's Federal Elections* (Scarborough, ON: Prentice-Hall of Canada, 1968), 294. For their part, the Liberals in the three elections with St. Laurent as leader placed great emphasis on him in their posters and advertisements, as had the Tories with George Drew in 1949 and 1953. Drew was never a match for

Diefenbaker on the campaign trail, however, and the edge that the Liberals had enjoyed with St. Laurent in his first two elections as leader was gone by 1957.

6 C.E.S. Franks, *The Parliament of Canada* (Toronto: University of Toronto Press, 1987), 74. See also one of the classic analyses of membership turnover in the US Congress: Nelson Polsby, "The Institutionalization of the House of Representatives," *American Political Science Review* 62, 1 (1968): 144–68.

7 Carlyle Allison, "Notes on the Election of the Diefenbaker Government," 1957, 6, University of Saskatchewan Archives and Special Collections, Carlyle Allison Fonds, MG 543.

8 Allison, "Notes on the Election of the Diefenbaker Government," 4.

9 In addition to Ellen Fairclough, author and columnist Margaret Aitken (niece of Max Aitken, the first Lord Beaverbrook), first elected in 1953, was re-elected in both 1957 and 1958.

10 Beck, *Pendulum of Power,* 306.

11 Beck, *Pendulum of Power,* 313.

12 Michael Hart, as quoted in Francine McKenzie, "A New Vision for the Commonwealth: Diefenbaker's Commonwealth Visit of 1958," in *Reassessing the Rogue Tory: Canadian Foreign Relations in the Diefenbaker Era,* edited by Janice Cavell and Ryan M. Touhey (Vancouver: UBC Press, 2018), 34.

13 Diefenbaker's ultimately unsuccessful attempt to stem the drift towards North American continentalism is explored in George Grant's *Lament for a Nation: The Defeat of Canadian Nationalism* (Toronto: McClelland and Stewart, 1965).

14 Patrick Kyba and Wendy Green-Finlay, "John Diefenbaker as Prime Minister: The Record Re-examined," in *The Diefenbaker Legacy: Canadian Politics, Law and Society since 1957,* edited by D.C. Story and R. Bruce Shephard (Regina/Saskatoon: Canadian Plains Research Center/Diefenbaker Canada Centre, 1998), 63.

15 Robert Malcolm Campbell, "The Diefenbaker Years Revisited: The Demise of the Keynesian Strategy in Canada," *Journal of Canadian Studies* 18, 2 (1983): 106–31.

16 John English, *The Worldly Years: The Life of Lester Pearson, 1949–1972,* vol. 2 (Toronto: Alfred A. Knopf Canada, 1992), 208.

17 Lester Pearson, *Mike: The Memoirs of the Right Honourable Lester B. Pearson 1957–1958,* vol. 3, edited by John A. Munro and Alex I. Inglis (Toronto: University of Toronto Press, 1975), 12.

18 Denis Smith, *Rogue Tory: The Life and Legend of John G. Diefenbaker* (Toronto: Macfarlane Walter and Ross, 1995), 275.

19 Peter Stursberg, ed., *Diefenbaker: Leadership Gained, 1956-62* (Toronto: University of Toronto Press, 1975), 88.

20 Jack Pickersgill, *Seeing Canada Whole: A Memoir* (Markham, ON: Fitzhenry and Whiteside, 1994), 484.

21 The ranking was as follows: Lester Pearson (1963–68); Brian Mulroney (1984–93); Pierre Elliott Trudeau (1968–79 and 1980–84); Louis St. Laurent (1948–57); Jean Chrétien (1993–2002); and John Diefenbaker (1957–63). L. Ian MacDonald, "The Best Prime Minister of the Last 50 Years – Pearson, by a Landslide," *Policy Options*, June 1, 2003, https://policyoptions. irpp.org/magazines/the-best-pms-in-the-past-50-years/the-best-prime -minister-of-the-last-50-years-pearson-by-a-landslide/.

22 "Labour Force and Employment Trends in Canada, 1950–60," *Monthly Labour Review*, June 1962, 669.

23 Beck, *Pendulum of Power*, 312.

24 Jack Pickersgill, *The Road Back: By a Liberal in Opposition* (Toronto: University of Toronto Press, 1986), 19.

25 Peter Stursberg, ed., *Diefenbaker: Leadership Lost, 1962–67* (Toronto: University of Toronto Press, 1976), 94.

26 Beck, *Pendulum of Power*, 316.

27 Stursberg, *Diefenbaker: Leadership Lost*, 95.

28 Beck, *Pendulum of Power*, 313.

29 Peter Regenstreif, "The Canadian General Election of 1958," *Western Political Quarterly* 13, 2 (June 1960): 358.

30 Reginald Whitaker, *The Government Party: Organizing and Financing the Liberal Party of Canada 1930–58* (Toronto: University of Toronto Press, 1977), 208.

31 Stursberg, *Diefenbaker: Leadership Gained*, 95. Douglas's observation was borne out in a voting study of a pair of federal and provincial elections in Saskatchewan. See John C. Courtney and David E. Smith, "Voting in a Provincial Election and a Federal By-Election: A Constituency Study of Saskatoon City," *Canadian Journal of Economics and Political Science* 33, 3 (1966): 338–53.

32 Walter Stewart, *M.J.: The Life and Times of M.J. Coldwell* (Toronto: Stoddart Publishing, 2000), 200.

33 D. Owen Carrigan, *Canadian Party Platforms: 1967–1968* (Toronto: Copp Clark Publishing, 1968), 235.

34 The Gallup Poll asked: "If a federal election were being held today, which party's candidate do you think you would favour?" There were 1,112 usable responses.

35 In only two other federal elections since 1921 has any party matched this feat: Mackenzie King's Liberals in 1940 and Brian Mulroney's Progressive Conservatives in 1984.

36 The strength of the Liberal vote in Newfoundland and Labrador outside St. John's reflected the dominance of the Liberal Party provincially and the popularity of the province's premier, Joey Smallwood.

37 Regenstreif, "The Canadian General Election of 1958," 69 and 71.

38 Diefenbaker rued the day he appointed McCutcheon, describing the decision in his memoir as "the error to end all errors." The prime minister found him "charming in a blustering sort of way," but "possessed of Machiavellian cunning": John G. Diefenbaker, *One Canada: Memoirs of the Right Honourable John G. Diefenbaker*, vol. 3, *The Tumultuous Years* (Toronto: Macmillan of Canada, 1977), 146.

39 Janice Cavell, "Introduction," in Cavell and Touhey, *Reassessing the Rogue Tory*, 13.

Chapter 7: Challenges, Failures, Defeat, and Regrouping

1 Denis Smith, *Rogue Tory: The Life and Legend of John G. Diefenbaker* (Toronto: Macfarlane Walter and Ross, 1995), 368.

2 D.C. Story and R.S. Isinger offer one of many accounts of the cancellation of the Arrow program in "The Plane Truth: The Avro Canada CF-105 Arrow Program," in *The Diefenbaker Legacy: Canadian Politics, Law and Society since 1957*, edited by D.C. Story and R. Bruce Shephard (Regina/Saskatoon: Canadian Plains Research Center/Diefenbaker Canada Centre, 1998), 43–55.

3 Smith, *Rogue Tory*, 325.

4 John G. Diefenbaker, *One Canada: Memoirs of the Right Honourable John G. Diefenbaker*, vol. 2, *The Years of Achievement* (Toronto: Macmillan of Canada, 1976), 274.

5 Peter J. Stursberg, ed., *Diefenbaker: Leadership Lost, 1962–67* (Toronto: University of Toronto Press, 1976), 232.

6 Smith, *Rogue Tory*, 409; James Powell, "The Coyne Affair," *Today in Ottawa's History* (blog), November 29, 2014, https://todayinottawashistory.wordpress.com/2014/11/29/the-coyne-affair/.

7 Smith, *Rogue Tory*, 408.

8 Powell, "The Coyne Affair," 6.

9 Peter Newman, *Renegade in Power: The Diefenbaker Years* (Toronto: McClelland and Stewart, 1963), 295.

10 Knowlton Nash, *Kennedy and Diefenbaker: Fear and Loathing across the Undefended Border* (Toronto: McClelland and Stewart, 1990), 56.

11 Smith, *Rogue Tory,* 382.

12 Janice Cavell, "Introduction," in *Reassessing the Rogue Tory: Canadian Foreign Relations in the Diefenbaker Era,* edited by Janice Cavell and Ryan M. Touhey (Vancouver: UBC Press, 2018), 13.

13 Stephen Azzi notes an often-overlooked fact about the Cuban Missile Crisis: Canada was not alone in resenting the secretive manner in which the White House handled the issue in advance of the blockade. Several NATO countries, including West Germany and Italy, were similarly treated. Stephen Azzi, "The Problem Child: Diefenbaker and Canada in the Language of the Kennedy Administration," in Cavell and Touhey, *Reassessing the Rogue Tory,* 109.

14 Azzi, "The Problem Child," 113.

15 Michael D. Stevenson provides a useful corrective to the standard, somewhat negative account of Green's time as external affairs minister (1959–63). During his years as a senior member of the government and a devoted supporter of Diefenbaker, Green was at the centre of several controversies with the Americans that played a big part in the government's ultimate demise. See Michael D. Stevenson, "Sidney Smith, Howard Green, and the Conduct of Canadian Foreign Policy during the Diefenbaker Government, 1957–1963," in Cavell and Touhey, *Reassessing the Rogue Tory,* 249–68.

16 Thirstan Falconer, "Andrew Thompson, Liberal Party Reforms and the Engagement of Ethnocultural Communities, 1957 to 1961," *Canadian Ethnic Studies* 50, 3 (2018): 111–29.

17 John English, *The Worldly Years: The Life of Lester Pearson, 1949–1972,* vol. 2 (Toronto: Alfred A. Knopf Canada, 1992), 218.

18 David Armstrong, Jack Lucas, and Zack Taylor, "The Urban-Rural Divide in Canadian Federal Elections, 1896–2019," *Canadian Journal of Political Science* 55, 1 (2022): 84–106.

19 Lester Pearson, *Mike: The Memoirs of the Right Honourable Lester B. Pearson 1957–1958,* vol. 3, edited by John A. Munro and Alex I. Inglis (Toronto: University of Toronto Press, 1975), 52.

Chapter 8: Legacies

1 Ellen Louks Fairclough, *Saturday's Child: Memoirs of Canada's First Female Cabinet Minister* (Toronto: University of Toronto Press, 1995), 131.

2 J. Murray Beck, *Pendulum of Power: Canada's Federal Elections* (Scarborough, ON: Prentice-Hall of Canada, 1968), 367. An excellent summary of the decline of the post-1963 Conservative Party and Diefenbaker's ultimate removal as leader in 1967 can be found in George C. Perlin, *The Tory Syndrome: Leadership Politics in the Progressive Conservative Party* (Montreal and Kingston: McGill-Queen's University Press, 1980), especially chs. 4 and 5. Several brief but valuable accounts by former cabinet ministers, party officials, and Tory backbenchers of the events leading up to Diefenbaker's removal can be found in Peter Stursberg, ed., *Diefenbaker: Leadership Lost, 1962–67* (Toronto: University of Toronto Press, 1976), chs. 3–11.

3 Beck, *Pendulum of Power,* 381.

4 Denis Smith, *Rogue Tory: The Life and Legend of John G. Diefenbaker* (Toronto: Macfarlane Walter and Ross, 1995), 458.

5 Robert Campbell situates the debates and controversy over the government's economic policies of the late 1950s within an analysis of "the futility of a Keynesian approach in Canada." New economic strategies were adopted that "would be more ambitious than Keynesian ones (hence, more liable to error and failure) and more interventionist (hence, more open to political scrutiny and controversy)": "The Diefenbaker Years Revisited: The Demise of the Keynesian Strategy in Canada," *Journal of Canadian Studies* 18, 2 (1983): 106.

6 Fairclough, *Saturday's Child,* 123.

7 Gladstone's remarkable life is recounted in Hugh A. Dempsey, *The Gentle Persuader: A Biography of James Gladstone, Indian Senator* (Saskatoon: Western Producer Prairie Books, 1986).

8 John F. Leslie, *Assimilation, Integration or Termination? The Development of Canadian Indian Policy, 1943–1963* (PhD diss., Carleton University, 1999), 394–95.

9 Smith, *Rogue Tory,* 191.

10 P.E. Bryden, "Money and Politics: Relations between Ontario and Ottawa in the Diefenbaker Years," in *The Diefenbaker Legacy: Canadian Politics, Law and Society since 1957,* edited by D.C. Story and R. Bruce Shephard (Regina/Saskatoon: Canadian Plains Research Center/Diefenbaker Canada Centre, 1998), 129 and 135.

11 Stursberg, *Diefenbaker: Leadership Lost*, 226–27.

12 Bryden, "Money and Politics," 133.

13 See Agar Adamson, "The Fulton-Favreau Formula: A Study of Its Development, 1960–1966," *Journal of Canadian Studies* 6, 1 (1971): 45–55.

14 Christopher MacLennan, "The Diefenbaker Bill of Rights and the Question of a Constitutionally Entrenched Charter, 1960–1971," in Story and Shephard, *The Diefenbaker Legacy*, 120.

15 Smith, *Rogue Tory*, 346.

16 The Union Nationale government of Maurice Duplessis "served as a brake on any discussions of an entrenched rights guarantee": MacLennan, "The Diefenbaker Bill of Rights," 115.

17 *Canadian Encyclopedia*, s.v. "Canadian Bill of Rights," by W.H. McConnell and Jon Tattrie, updated September 9, 2020, https://www.thecanadian encyclopedia.ca/en/article/canadian-bill-of-rights.

18 MacLennan, "The Diefenbaker Bill of Rights," 120.

19 See Norman Hillmer, "Different Leaders, Different Paths: Diefenbaker and the British, 1957–63," in *Reassessing the Rogue Tory: Canadian Foreign Relations in the Diefenbaker Era*, edited by Janice Cavell and Ryan M. Touhey (Vancouver: UBC Press, 2018), 53.

20 Kevin A. Spooner, "The Diefenbaker Government and Foreign Policy in Africa," in Cavell and Touhey, *Reassessing the Rogue Tory*, 205.

21 Spooner, "The Diefenbaker Government and Foreign Policy in Africa," 190.

22 "Address by Nelson Mandela to the Parliament of Canada," June 18, 1990, quoted in Fen Osler Hampson, *Master of Persuasion: Brian Mulroney's Global Legacy* (Toronto: Signal/McClelland and Stewart, 2018), 74–75.

23 Paul Burrows, "Nelson Mandela, Brian Mulroney and Canada's Anti-Apartheid Record," *The Media Co-op*, December 16, 2013, http://www.mediacoop.ca/blog/burrows/20445#_edn37.

24 Hampson, *Master of Persuasion*, 60. Diefenbaker became a hero to Mulroney and Clark. Even Stephen Harper had a fondness for him, claiming that "no other prime minister of any stripe did more for the cause of fairness and equality and inclusion" than Diefenbaker. Nelson Wiseman, *Partisan Odysseys: Canada's Political Parties* (Toronto: University of Toronto Press, 2020), 74.

25 Robert Vineberg, "The Winds of Change: Ellen Fairclough and the Removal of Discriminatory Immigration Barriers," in Cavell and Touhey, *Reassessing the Rogue Tory*, 227–46.

26 Jack Pickersgill, *Seeing Canada Whole: A Memoir* (Markham, ON: Fitzhenry and Whiteside, 1994), 293.

27 Fairclough, *Saturday's Child,* 110–11.

28 Richard Sigurdson, "John Diefenbaker's One Canada and the Legacy of Unhyphenated Canadianism," in Story and Shephard, *The Diefenbaker Legacy,* 75. Fairclough's handling of the immigration file was not without incident. Some in the Italian community who had supported the Conservatives in 1958 turned away from the party when they thought that the government's tightening of the sponsorship system was aimed at them. The crackdown on illegal Chinese immigration may have led to the defeat in 1962 of two or three Conservatives in ridings with large Chinese populations: Howard Palmer, *Ethnicity and Politics in Canada since Confederation* (Ottawa: Canadian Historical Association, 1991), 21. Fairclough was of the opinion that Diefenbaker moved her from Citizenship and Immigration to Postmaster General as a result of the loss of those ridings.

29 John Diefenbaker, *One Canada: Memoirs of the Right Honourable John G. Diefenbaker,* vol. 2, *The Years of Achievement* (Toronto: Macmillan of Canada, 1976), 140–42.

30 Patrick Kyba, *Alvin: A Biography of the Honourable Alvin Hamilton* (Regina: Canadian Plains Research Center, 1989), 180.

31 To the initial sale of $60 million in late 1960 was added another sale, worth $362 million, a year later. Kyba, *Alvin,* 164 and 167.

32 J.N. McCrorie, *ARDA: An Experiment in Development Planning* (Ottawa: Canadian Council on Rural Development, 1969), 112.

33 Patrick H. Brennan, "Diefenbaker and the Press: A Case Study of *Maclean's,* 1958–63," in Story and Shephard, *The Diefenbaker Legacy,* 139.

34 Blair Fraser, "Backstage in Ottawa," *Maclean's,* September 19, 1964, 2.

35 On the campaign trail, Liberal leader Lester Pearson dismissed the Roads to Resources program as a construction scheme "from igloo to igloo." Diefenbaker seized upon this as another example of Liberal condescension. Smith, *Rogue Tory,* 281.

36 Patrick Kyba and Wendy Green-Finlay, "John Diefenbaker as Prime Minister: The Record Re-examined," in Story and Shepard, *The Diefenbaker Legacy,* 65.

37 As a reflection of its added responsibilities, the CRTC has again been renamed the Canadian Radio-television and Telecommunications Commission. An excellent account of the rapid growth of television (both public and private) and the push for the establishment a regulatory and licensing

authority is found in Frank H. Peers, *The Public Eye: Television and the Politics of Canadian Broadcasting, 1952–1968* (Toronto: University of Toronto Press, 1979).

38 The Royal Commission on Transportation was chaired by M.A. Mac-Pherson of Regina. A ten-year veteran of the Saskatchewan legislature and one-time attorney general of the province, MacPherson ran twice for the leadership of the federal Conservatives, in 1938 and 1942, placing second both times.

39 The National Energy Board has been supplanted by the Canadian Energy Regulator and the Impact Assessment Agency of Canada. The Canadian Transport Commission is now the Canadian Transportation Agency.

40 Stephen Azzi, "Magazines and the Canadian Dream: The Struggle to Protect Canadian Periodicals, 1955–1965," *International Journal* 54, 3 (1999): 503.

41 Isaiah Litvak and Christopher Maule, *Cultural Sovereignty: The Time and Reader's Digest Case in Canada* (New York: Praeger, 1974), 30.

42 Malcolm G. Taylor, *Insuring National Health Care: The Canadian Experience* (Chapel Hill: University of North Carolina Press, 1990), 135. The report was signed by six of the original seven members. Wallace McCutcheon, the seventh, resigned when he was appointed to the Diefenbaker cabinet in 1962.

43 Dr. David Baltzan was another member of the Royal Commission from Saskatchewan. A distinguished member of the medical profession, he had attended high school in Saskatoon with Diefenbaker, and the two remained close for the rest of their lives. Dr. Baltzan had the distinction of having defeated John Diefenbaker in a Grade 12 school debate in Saskatoon.

Chapter 9: Turning Point for the Parties and the Party System

1 John Courtney, *The Selection of National Party Leaders in Canada* (Toronto: Macmillan of Canada, 1973), 128–29.

2 David Stewart, "Factions, Review, and Reformers: Diefenbaker's Legacy to the Progressive Conservative Party," in *The Diefenbaker Legacy: Canadian Politics, Law and Society since 1957,* edited by D.C. Story and R. Bruce Shephard (Regina/Saskatoon: Canadian Plains Research Center/Diefenbaker Canada Centre, 1998), 97.

3 Richard Johnston, *The Canadian Party System: An Analytic History* (Vancouver: UBC Press, 2017), 244.

4 Nelson Wiseman, *Partisan Odysseys: Canada's Political Parties* (Toronto: University of Toronto Press, 2020), 72. Richard Sigurdson's account of this

aspect of Diefenbaker's appeal is particularly apt: "John Diefenbaker's One Canada and the Legacy of Unhyphenated Canadianism," in Story and Shephard, *The Diefenbaker Legacy,* 71–86.

5 John Meisel, *The Canadian General Election of 1957* (Toronto: University of Toronto Press, 1962), 271.

6 Johnston, *The Canadian Party System,* 248.

7 Johnston, *The Canadian Party System,* 248.

8 David E. Smith, *The Regional Decline of a National Party: Liberals on the Prairies* (Toronto: University of Toronto Press, 1989), 51.

9 Howard Palmer, *Ethnicity and Politics in Canada since Confederation* (Ottawa: Canadian Historical Association, 1991), 21.

10 R. Kenneth Carty and William Cross, "Political Parties and the Practice of Brokerage Politics," in *The Oxford Handbook of Canadian Politics,* edited by John C. Courtney and David E. Smith (New York: Oxford University Press, 2010), 193 (emphasis in original).

11 John G. Diefenbaker, *One Canada: Memoirs of the Right Honourable John G. Diefenbaker,* vol. 1, *The Crusading Years* (Toronto: Macmillan of Canada, 1975), 266.

12 See Colin Campbell and William Christian, *Parties, Leaders and Ideologies in Canada* (Toronto: McGraw-Hill Ryerson, 1996), 40–41; and Wiseman, *Partisan Odysseys,* 73–74.

13 Dalton Camp, *Gentlemen, Players and Politicians* (Toronto: McClelland and Stewart, 1970), 339.

14 Andrew Coyne, "It All Comes Down to Ontario," *Saskatoon StarPhoenix,* October 3, 2019, NP6.

15 David Armstrong, Jack Lucas, and Zack Taylor, "The Urban-Rural Divide in Canadian Federal Elections, 1896–2019," *Canadian Journal of Political Science* 55, 1 (2022): 86 and 96. This study is profoundly important. It establishes a new theoretical framework for studying an oft-neglected aspect of electoral studies: the divide between urban and rural voters and the effect it has on the party system. For an examination of the policy implications of the divergent preferences of urban and rural voters, see Peter Loewen, Sean Speer, and Stephanie Bertolo, *Fault Lines and Common Ground: Understanding the State of Canada's Rural-Urban Divide* (Ottawa: Public Policy Forum, 2021), https://ppforum.ca/publications/fault-lines-and-common-ground/.

16 Armstrong, Lucas, and Taylor, "The Urban-Rural Divide," 100.

17 Wiseman, *Partisan Odysseys,* 73.

Suggestions
for Further Reading

"Suggestions for Further Reading" should perhaps be labelled "the author's preferences for further reading," for that more accurately captures the subjective nature of the exercise. The following are among my favourites for the period covered by this book.

Elections and Parties

The best place to gain an appreciation of the first of our two elections is John Meisel's classic *The Canadian General Election of 1957* (Toronto: University of Toronto Press, 1962). The first of its kind in Canada, the book has stood the test of time. It is a balanced and informative analysis of the parties, their leaders and candidates, the issues, the media, and Canadian society in the mid-1950s.

Meisel's first book was soon followed by his *Papers on the 1962 Election* (Toronto: University of Toronto Press, 1964), an edited volume of fifteen essays by various scholars centred on Diefenbaker's penultimate election as Tory prime minister. A decade later, Meisel included a major critique of the Liberal Party in his post-1972 election book, *Working Papers on Canadian Politics* (Montreal and Kingston: McGill-Queen's University Press, 1975), titled "Howe, Hubris and '72: An Essay on Political Elitism." It stands as a reminder of how long-term governing parties, such as the Liberals, can become (as they were, going into the 1957 election) overly self-assured and arrogant.

There is no finer study of what Richard Johnston terms the "disjointed character" (p. 239) of Canada's party system than *The Canadian Party System:*

An Analytical History (Vancouver: UBC Press, 2017). The work combines Johnston's skillful use of survey datasets (notably those of the Canadian Election Studies) with his remarkable understanding of Canadian history – not simply party history or political history but *Canadian* history.

One study of Canada's party system that has stood the test of time is R.K. Carty's "Three Canadian Party Systems" in Carty's edited volume *Canadian Party Systems: A Reader* (Peterborough: Broadview Press, 1992). It provides a helpful tripartite analysis of the changing internal dynamics of Canada's parties, from patronage- and caucus-focused (1867–1917), through brokerage- and ministerialist-dominated (1921–57), to what Carty describes as "electronic politics and personal parties" since the early 1960s. The Diefenbaker/Pearson rivalry played out on the cusp of the transition from the second to the third phase.

Murray Beck's review of 100 years of elections – from 1867 to 1968 – includes helpful descriptions of the five elections in which Diefenbaker led the Progressive Conservatives: 1957, 1958, 1962, 1963, and 1965. Drawn largely from newspaper and magazine accounts of individual elections, *Pendulum of Power: Canada's Federal Elections* (Scarborough, ON: Prentice-Hall of Canada, 1968) is a handy reference work on Canada's first century of elections. It also includes a useful short table of election results for each of the elections discussed.

On that note, two reference books of election data are of great value to anyone studying Canadian elections. Both were compiled from available sources, principally the *Official Reports of the Chief Electoral Officer of Canada,* and provide detailed data on federal, provincial, and riding election results. Howard Scarrow's *Canada Votes: A Handbook of Federal and Provincial Election Data* (New Orleans: Hauser Press, 1961) covers the period from 1878 to 1958, and Frank Feigert's *Canada Votes, 1935–1988* (Durham, NC: Duke University Press, 1989) completes the record up to and including the 1988 "Free Trade" election.

The Progressive Conservatives

George Perlin's examination of the frequent upheavals over the leadership in the Progressive Conservative Party from 1956 to 1976 is a notable contribution to the literature on Canadian parties and leaders: *The Tory Syndrome: Leadership Politics in the Progressive Conservative Party* (Montreal and Kingston: McGill-Queen's University Press, 1980). Relying on survey data, the book's principal focus is the 1967 Tory convention, which led to Robert Stanfield's selection as Diefenbaker's replacement.

Peter Regenstreif's *The Diefenbaker Interlude: Parties and Voting in Canada, an Interpretation* (Toronto: Longmans Canada, 1965) combines data available from Elections Canada and Gallup Polls together with the author's admittedly "subjective" interviews with party notables and activists. The result is a short, informative account of the Conservative Party, its supporters, and Canadian electoral behaviour from 1957 to 1963.

A valuable addition to the literature on the Diefenbaker years comes from an unconventional but important source – Peter Stursberg's edited two-volume set of recorded interviews with party notables and opinion leaders in the principal parties at the federal level and in some of the provinces: *Diefenbaker: Leadership Gained, 1956–62* (Toronto: University of Toronto Press, 1975), and *Diefenbaker: Leadership Lost, 1962–67* (Toronto: University of Toronto Press, 1976). It adds immeasurably to our understanding of the politics of the time by presenting pointed recollections (both favourable and critical) of Diefenbaker and his leadership.

The Liberals

Reginald Whitaker's *The Government Party: Organizing and Financing the Liberal Party of Canada 1930–58* (Toronto: University of Toronto Press, 1977) is far and away the best account of the Liberal Party's electoral and financial machine during the Mackenzie King and Louis St. Laurent eras. This fine book paints a picture of a party increasingly certain of its place as "Canada's natural governing party" and its close links with business. The party's reliance on regional and provincial organizations dominated by strong cabinet ministers during the St. Laurent period (an organizational system that came back to haunt them once they lost power in 1957) is one of the important contributions of this well-researched book.

Two studies shed light on the Liberal Party's organization after its disastrous showing in 1958. The first is David Smith's account of the failure of the party to remain a relevant player on the prairies in the wake of the Diefenbaker period: *The Reginal Decline of a National Party: Liberals on the Prairies* (Toronto: University of Toronto Press, 1981).

The second complements Smith's work to the extent that it explains the shift in the direction of the Liberal Party from one that had made its mark by constructing a broad, pan-Canadian electoral support base to one that espoused a more left-of-centre, reformist, and nationalist agenda that held little appeal for prairie voters. In "Andrew Thompson, Liberal Party Reforms and the Engagement of Ethnocultural Communities, 1957 to 1961," *Canadian Ethnic*

Studies 50, 3 (2018): 111–29, Thirstan Falconer examines one of the Liberals' reforms aimed at attracting non-British, non-French "new Canadian" supporters to the party, notably in the rapidly growing metropolitan centres. The transformation of the party during Lester Pearson's early years as leader proved to be a fundamental component of its return to office in 1963.

With time, the policy and personnel changes that began under Pearson transformed the party into a more urban, moderately left-of-centre organization than it had been under St. Laurent. For their part, the Conservatives in the post-Diefenbaker/post-Mulroney period moved in the opposite direction by drawing an increasingly larger share of their support from rural – notably prairie – voters who responded favourably to the party's populist messaging. Two recent studies should be consulted on the growing urban-rural divide in Canadian party politics: David Armstrong, Jack Lucas, and Zack Taylor, "The Urban-Rural Divide in Canadian Federal Elections, 1896–2019," *Canadian Journal of Political Science* 55, 1 (2022): 84–106, and Peter Loewen, Sean Speer, and Stephanie Bertolo, *Fault Lines and Common Ground: Understanding the State of Canada's Rural-Urban Divide* (Ottawa: Public Policy Forum, 2021), https://ppforum.ca/publications/fault-lines-and-common-ground/.

The Co-operative Commonwealth Federation and the New Democratic Party

Walter D. Young's book on the thirty-year life of the CCF is a comprehensive piece of research: *The Anatomy of a Party: The National CCF 1932–61* (Toronto: University of Toronto Press, 1969). It can be paired with Stanley Knowles's brief account of the period immediately before the creation in 1961 of the yet unnamed New Democratic Party: *The New Party* (Toronto: McClelland and Stewart, 1961). Keith Archer and Alan Whitehorn's *Political Activists: The NDP in Convention* (Toronto: Oxford University Press, 1997) is a sound, survey-based piece of research focusing on the changing attitudes of NDP activists over the party's early years of competing in federal elections.

Party Insiders

Party operatives and news reporters on intimate terms with politicians often provide good, gossipy accounts of cabinet decisions and those who made them. Such books are generally welcomed by political junkies. Armed with their own opinions on pretty well everything that relates to their time in the political arena, these insiders give admittedly one-sided accounts – so, reader beware. Dalton Camp, speechwriter, strategist, and eventual nemesis of

John Diefenbaker, and Patrick Nicholson, Ottawa journalist and staunch Diefenbaker loyalist, offer their versions of "The Chief." Camp's *Gentlemen, Players and Politicians* (Toronto: McClelland and Stewart, 1970) covers the decade of Conservative politics leading up to the 1957 upset, while Nicholson's *Vision and Indecision* (Toronto: Longmans, 1968) offers an unapologetically favourable version of Diefenbaker's time in office and his eventual removal from the leadership in 1967.

One would be hard-pressed to point to a party insider more "inside" from the mid-1940s to the mid-1960s than the Liberals' J.W. Pickersgill. Following the Second World War, Mackenzie King put Pickersgill in charge of the Prime Minister's Office. Jack, as he was known to everyone in Ottawa, followed that with a short stint as Clerk of the Privy Council (the senior civil servant at the federal level) before entering St. Laurent's cabinet in 1953. He continued to serve as an MP, strategist, speechwriter, and party confidant to Prime Ministers St. Laurent and Pearson until he stepped down from politics in 1967. When the Liberals were in office, he held senior cabinet positions. Three of his books (he also co-edited Mackenzie King's diaries in a four-volume set) covering his time with King, St. Laurent, and Pearson give a good glimpse of the Liberals in government and opposition, along with his unfavourable opinion of John Diefenbaker: *My Years with St. Laurent: A Political Memoir* (Toronto: University of Toronto Press, 1975); *The Road Back: By a Liberal in Opposition* (Toronto: University of Toronto Press, 1986); and *Seeing Canada Whole: A Memoir* (Markham, ON: Fitzhenry and Whiteside, 1994).

Biographies and Memoirs

Canadians have been well served by biographies of prime ministers and political leaders. Among the best for the period covered by this book are Denis Smith's *Rogue Tory: The Life and Legend of John G. Diefenbaker* (Toronto: Macfarlane Walter and Ross, 1995); Dale Thomson's *Louis St. Laurent: Canadian* (Toronto: Macmillan of Canada, 1967); John English's two-volume study of Lester Pearson: *Shadow of Heaven: The Life of Lester Pearson, 1897–1948* (Toronto: Lester and Orpen Dennys, 1989) and *The Worldly Years: The Life of Lester Pearson, 1949–1972* (Toronto: Alfred A. Knopf Canada, 1992); and Walter Stewart's studies of CCF leader M.J. Coldwell, in *M.J.: The Life and Times of M.J. Coldwell* (Toronto: Stoddart Publishing, 2000), and of the first federal NDP leader, T.C. Douglas, in *The Life and Political Times of Tommy Douglas* (Toronto: McArthur, 2003). In addition to providing a biographical narrative, each of these books adds to our understanding of leadership, party organization, policy formulation, insider intrigue, and all the ingredients that go into a good read about parties, leaders, and elections.

Two welcome additions to the prime ministerial *oeuvre* have been published recently by UBC Press. Janice Cavell and Ryan M. Touhey's edited *Reassessing the Rogue Tory: Canadian Foreign Relations in the Diefenbaker Era* (2018) wrestles with the question of whether the Diefenbaker government's failure on the international front stemmed from the prime minister's indecisiveness and distinctive personality or from shifts in global affairs. The book covers Canada and the Commonwealth and the developing world, Canadian-American relations, and the nuclear weapons issue that strained Canada's relationship with the United States. Patrice Dutil's edited collection *The Unexpected Louis St-Laurent: Politics and Policies for a Modern Canada* (2020) sheds new light on Canada's twelfth prime minister and makes the case that on several domestic and international matters of substance, St. Laurent ushered Canada into the modern era.

D.C. Story and R. Bruce Shephard edited a series of papers delivered to a University of Saskatchewan conference on the fortieth anniversary of the election of the Diefenbaker government in 1957: *The Diefenbaker Legacy: Canadian Law, Politics and Society since 1957* (Regina/Saskatoon: Canadian Plains Research Center/Diefenbaker Canada Centre, 1998). It provides a helpful assessment of the lasting impact on Canadian politics, law, and society of the Diefenbaker period.

There are, of course, the inevitable memoirs by prime ministers and party leaders that warrant mention. Canada had few of these in its first hundred years, Robert Borden and Charles Tupper being the exceptions among the prime ministers. From Diefenbaker onward, however, the penstocks have opened for politicians of all stripes and of any importance to tell their story. Of the leaders who played a major role in the period covered by this book, neither St. Laurent nor Coldwell wrote memoirs, but Diefenbaker and Pearson more than made up for that. Both felt they needed three volumes to set forth their own interpretation of their lives in and out of politics. That is open to question.

Memoirs are to be taken at little more than face value, for politicians are not short of ego and selective memories. In the words of University of Toronto historian Robert Bothwell, a memoir amounts to "a recognized form of special pleading, its author's literary tombstone" ("The Art of the Memoir," *Acadiensis* 6, 1 [1976]: 134). Approach the recollections of early life, formative events, political leadership, colleagues, policy formulation, scandals, intra-party intrigue and rivalries, and election campaigns of Diefenbaker and Pearson with a watchful eye:

John G. Diefenbaker, *One Canada: Memoirs of the Right Honourable John G. Diefenbaker,* vol. 1, *The Crusading Years* (Toronto: Macmillan of Canada, 1975); *One Canada: Memoirs of the Right Honourable John G. Diefenbaker,* vol. 2, *The Years of Achievement* (Toronto: Macmillan of Canada, 1976); *One Canada: Memoirs of the Right Honourable John G. Diefenbaker,* vol. 3, *The Tumultuous Years* (Toronto: Macmillan of Canada, 1977).

Lester B. Pearson, *Mike: The Memoirs of the Right Honourable Lester B. Pearson 1897–1948,* vol. 1 (Toronto: University of Toronto Press, 1972); *Mike: The Memoirs of the Right Honourable Lester B. Pearson 1948–1957,* vol. 2, edited by John A. Munro and Alex I. Inglis (Toronto: University of Toronto Press, 1973); and *Mike: The Memoirs of the Right Honourable Lester B. Pearson 1957–1958,* vol. 3, edited by John A. Munro and Alex. I. Inglis (Toronto: University of Toronto Press, 1975).

Index

Printed and bound in Canada by Friesens

Set in Zurich Condensed and Minion by Artegraphica Design Co.

Copy editor: Francis Chow

Proofreader: Kristy Lynn Hankewitz

Indexer: Judy Dunlop

Cartographer: Eric Leinberger

Cover designer: Will Brown

Cover image: University of Saskatchewan Archives and Special
Collections, JGD/3573/XB